I shall pass through
this world but once.
Any good therefore
that I can do or any
kindness that I can
show to any human
being, let me do it now.
Let me not defer or
neglect it for I shall
not pass this way
again.

EX LIBRIS

$12.50

"TOM McCALL: MAVERICK" is one of the most illuminating books ever written about American politics. It is, at the same time, a significant contribution to the history of the Pacific Northwest. Here is the complete McCall story, based on his private papers and personal recollections. The momentous years of the McCall Administration are described with candor, wit, and self-criticism. McCall tells how Oregon became a national showcase for its environmental and energy programs. He also discloses what happened behind the scenes during such crises as the Nerve Gas battle; the Vortex I rock festival; and his losing campaigns for tax reform. The evolution of McCall's "Visit Oregon, but Don't Stay Doctrine" is recounted as is the development of the landmark "Bottle Bill."

McCall's autobiography is full of anecdotes about Presidents from Dwight Eisenhower to Jimmy Carter. McCall pulls no punches in this often salty narrative. He discusses his views of Wayne Morse, Richard Neuberger, Mark Hatfield and Bob Packwood. For the first time, McCall offers an intimate analysis about why he declined three opportunities to become a U.S. Senator.

Here also are the colorful figures of the McCall family—two legendary grandfathers and a remarkable childhood on the "Ranch Under the Rimrock." McCall writes about his years as a journalist, his political education as an aide to Governor Douglas McKay, and his ill-fated race for Congress against Edith Green. McCall brings to light his triumphs, setbacks and compromises. He presents a history of the magnetic "Third Force" and his decision not to run for the presidency in 1976.

The autobiography, like the man, is entertaining and provocative. McCall is, as the University of Oregon put it in a citation, "still the complete newsman, gifted with the reporter's curiosity and the writer's wit who continues that restless search for the truth that makes men free."

TOM McCALL: MAVERICK

Merry Christmas, 1977,
to Tom
from another:

Tom
McCall

Gerry Lewin

TOM McCALL

TOM M^cCALL: MAVERICK

an autobiography with Steve Neal

 Binford & Mort

Thomas Binford, Publisher

2536 S.E. Eleventh • Portland, Oregon 97202

Tom McCall: Maverick

Printed in the United States of America
Library of Congress Catalog Number: 77-85394
ISBN: 0-8323-0288-0 (hardcover); 0-8323-0289-9 (softcover)
First Edition 1977

For Audrey McCall

CONTENTS

ACKNOWLEDGMENTS

Unhappily, it is not possible to include the names of all those who aided in the preparation of this volume. Looking over its pages, I note a lack of credits to some people who deserve special attention.

My wife, Audrey, has been of invaluable assistance. In her public utterances, she is characteristically short on verbiage and long on good sense. Her patience and tolerance have been remarkable over the 38 years of our marriage.

I am also indebted to my collaborator, Steve Neal. We worked together for nearly four years in the research, writing and editing. During this time, we taped more than thirty hours of interviews. With his voluminous files and mine, we produced the book. Steve, a special projects writer for *The Philadelphia Inquirer*, is a native of Oregon and his professional work honors the state.

Ron Schmidt, my former administrative assistant, made his papers and files available to me. I am also indebted to Susan Neal for her able and scholarly research and to secretaries Mary Ann Lauer and Judy Belonia for typing various stages of the manuscript.

Gerry Lewin of the Salem *Capital Journal*, one of the world's greatest photographers, kindly allowed us to publish prints from his personal archives. Bill Sanderson, the most gifted editorial cartoonist to come out of the Northwest since Homer Davenport, made some of his McCall illustrations available to us. David Milne of *The Philadelphia Inquirer* designed the cover and provided technical advice. Pete Falchetta, also of *The Inquirer*, was of invaluable assistance in preparing prints for publication.

Our thanks also to an understanding publisher, Tom Binford, and our skillful editor, Laura Phillips, who has now edited three books by members of the McCall clan.

INTRODUCTION

When I closed my hyper-active period as Governor of Oregon, there were twinges of regret that I didn't get some things completed, but none because I missed trying any reasonably essential improvement. For better or for worse, I wanted to write an autobiography about the forces that shaped my life and times.

I became governor through rather unusual byroads. In the first place, there was none of that fervent ambition that causes some politicians to tramp up and down on their grandmothers to get higher in the pecking order.

Since childhood, I had wanted to be a newspaperman. That's the course that absorbed me—and that absorption helped compensate for an inferiority complex. Every once in a while I would look around to check where I was in relation to the rest of the scenery. What I saw wasn't always encouraging. In Idaho in 1941, I perceived I was going backward, starting to stagnate—and my 1954 congressional defeat broke my morale. Still, whether reporting as a newspaperman or radio-television commentator, longshoring, or representing President Johnson in Vietnam, or fencing with the Legislature, there was one invariable plus: people and I got along. Not because there was a feeling that we had to but because we liked to. It was a buoying constant in a career that developed and matured. Some of the rest follows.

CHAPTER 1

Early Memories

Our family was quite a bit like the Kennedys in its orientation to public affairs. We were devoted readers and listeners and Mother would spend hours reading Dickens, Thackeray and Tolstoy out loud to us. And we were followers of the public scene, had lively discussions, put out our own newspaper at the ranch, and had our own orchestra. I think this all came from parents who had tremendously dynamic parents, my two grandfathers— Governor Samuel Walker McCall of Massachusetts and Thomas W. Lawson, the "Copper King."

There were five of us young ones on the ranch—all conceived in Oregon and born in Massachusetts where both grandfathers held sway. My brother, Harry, was born in 1912, I was born in 1913, and my sister, Dorothy, in 1914. Sam and Jean were twins who arrived July 1, 1919—the day prohibition went into effect.

Although the family fortune gave out on the eastern end, we lived on, and still hold, the last green patch of the financier's empire, down between frowning rimrocks on the Crooked River in Central Oregon. We had the biggest ranch house anywhere, with long shelves of books, saddles, rifles, fireplaces, old statuettes and gently gleaming Tiffany crystal and silver, and rooms and rooms, seemingly without end.

There, outnumbering our neighbors by varying margins of up to eight-to-one, we preserved a definitely unindigenous accent. Uncle Doug, out from Boston, audited the sounds of the children and allowed as how we sounded "like a cross between Calvin Coolidge and a Texas ranger."

We milked the cows, shocked the hay—and, occasionally, the neighbors—and argued the relative merits of our *remudas*. I never won at anything—except gameplaying and storyweaving for the much younger twins, Sam and Jean. But my column in the *Westernwold World,* our engaging spoof of a weekly newspaper, was the most professional part of that teenage inspiration. It was titled, "Butches Sports Meat."

I was the worst athlete in Crook County. My brother, Harry, was well-coordinated and was a good football player at Prineville High School. I came along a couple of years later and tried out for football at Prineville. I soon learned, somewhat painfully, that just because my brother "did it well" was no guarantee that I was going to be any good. I was an uncoordinated, clumsy, fast-growing mess, possessing the ruggedness of a Stradivarius in my 6-foot, 4-inch, 130-pound round-shouldered frame. My football career came to an end in a dusty early-season scrimmage. The first time they high-lowed me, I lost one kneecap. The second time, I lost the other one. Everything hurt. Everything was scary. When I went back, years later, I told some friends that it was very nostalgic returning to the area where your heart lay—and both your kneecaps.

It was a funny thing. I couldn't go into a room where there were two people without being violently embarrassed. No one ever saw such an inferiority complex. Mother went to Principal John Johnson of Prineville High School and said, "What are we ever going to do, Mr. Johnson, with Tommy? He's just sinking into his shell. He's timid and not grasping the challenges of life at all."

The graying Johnson patted her knee and reassured her, "You just wait till Harry graduates, Tom will blossom."

Much to everyone's astonishment, the prediction came true. I transferred to Redmond Union High School, 19 miles to the west, and before graduating, played in the band, took a lead part in the senior class play, coached and played on the varsity baseball team and was elected president of the student body.

Despite having earned letters in baseball and tennis, the physical awkwardness of growing too fast persisted. I tried to play basketball to take advantage of my great height. The Latin class, of which I was a member, challenged the faculty in a preliminary game one night. We lost, 9-7, with the deciding field goal coming on a basket I sank for the other team.

Later on, when I filled out and developed, had been to college and had some successes, I was fairly respectable as a lineman in some Central Oregon town team football games. We had some really tough football players, including an All Coast tackle from Washington State named Rollo Weigand. And I was able to hold my own.

I was, however, much better writing about sports than playing, and so part of my earliest ambition was to become a sports writer. With a father a great athlete at Harvard and a brother a fine athlete, I became a keen follower of athletics. While gaining insight into sports from the inside, I developed a profound respect for the participant and the grinding work he put into excellence, even if he were gifted to begin with. I was sports editor of the *Daily Emerald* at the University of Oregon and later wrote a sports column and put out a sports page for a daily newspaper.

By 1931, when I went to the University as a freshman, I was a gregarious soul, always very friendly and over the inferiority complex except when it came to making speeches. On the campus, I was a great fun guy and always liked to be with the boys. We used to have a few beers and go sing—we loved to serenade the sorority houses. I was generally involved and often led the singing. I used to have some darling girls I associated with innocently.

I wasn't much of a student, graduating at the bottom of my class with an even "C" average. It was the lowest average you could have to graduate. But I did a lot of things in terms of campus activities. I was president of my fraternity, Phi Delta Theta, president of the Inter-Fraternity Council, and associate editor and sports editor of the *Daily Emerald*. Robert Clark, former president of the University of Oregon, has said that my academic record was based "on a belief that the classroom ought not to interfere too much with college life."

I was a member of the campus Establishment. Dick Neuberger was a student at the same time and was already selling articles to national magazines. He was rather a thorn in the side of the university Establishment. Although I was a member of that Establishment, I still thought there were good points to some of the arguments that Neuberger and his sidekick, Steve Kahn, had. They were the flaming liberals of the campus. They were ahead of their age. For example, they objected to the extraction of monies from student fees to support athletics. Whenever there was a major issue to be debated, there they were, zapping The Establishment.

My relationship with Neuberger in those days was one of an admiring fellow writer, a beginner in a sense. I wanted to be a professional journalist and respected Dick as probably the most consummate writer who had been a student at the University of Oregon in a decade. I didn't always agree with his ripping The Establishment. But he was the stinger that kept The Establishment quivering and kept it from becoming too apathetic and stodgy. Years later, when I was a newsman, and he was starting out in the State Senate, our paths came together again. I then found myself considerably more sympathetic to his ideas because I'd seen more of life and I was not in my sheltered campus habitat with a Dick Neuberger trying to knock it down.

The first contact I can remember with Wayne Morse came in April of 1935. On April 24, the day before the campus elections, a fellow journalism student named Velma MacIntyre called and said, "Why don't you run for Senior Class President?" I said, "Velma, you're out of your mind. The election is tomorrow morning."

She said, "Well, I've got some friends, and we'll get on the telephone." I told her to go ahead, figuring I might get 10 votes. A fellow named Grant Eade, from Portland, was running. He was on the ballot, unopposed.

I'll be darned if I didn't win on Velma's last-minute write-in campaign. I defeated Eade by some 20 votes. Someone, not Eade, protested that the write-in was not proper. The matter came to Wayne Morse, who was dean of the law school and chairman of the ASUO judiciary committee, which decided such things. The question was that even though the ASUO constitution provided for an Australian ballot, which inherently provides for a write-in space, they forgot to put the write-in space on the ballot. Clearly, the students had written in on the margin so that no one could really mistake their intentions. But Morse held, in one of the few instances, I think, where he was on a very unsound legal ground, that I was not elected. "After reading the constitution in its entirety the committee decided it was not the intention of the framers to permit write-in elections," Morse announced after the hearing. I accepted his verdict because it was a bauble that was not really mine anyhow. This was my first encounter with Morse, later to become the feared "Tiger of the U.S. Senate."

There were no jobs when I graduated from Oregon, with a journalism degree, in June of 1936. The market for newspaper people or anybody else was gone because of the Great Depression. But Mother was a long-time friend of Judge Bob Sawyer, publisher of the *Bend Bulletin.* My parents and I went to see Sawyer, who said, "We're having the same trouble with the depression everybody else is. But if Tom will help us out over the 4th of July, there will be at least three days that he could work on the *Bulletin.* Get his feet wet on a real newspaper."

I stayed at the *Bulletin* for about three months and covered City Hall and the County Courthouse. I also did the sports. I tried to sharpen my poker game at the Pastime pool hall which was just around the corner from the *Bulletin.* I was a terrible poker player. There was a dealer at the Pastime named Blackie. I'd go over there and play in the afternoons. It was the kind of game where there were people gently drinking a lot of cheap white wine. They'd store their bottles in the back of the toilet in the water to keep the wine cold. And they'd keep swigging away. I kept losing. And finally, Blackie told me, "Don't play a stud hand unless you have the Ace of Spades in the hole." He took the Ace of Spades out of the deck to teach me patience. It never showed up. I used to look on the poker as sort of a vehicle of conviviality and had a little gambling trouble in those days. When I moved on to Moscow, Idaho, I fell in love with the slot machines in the Elks Club, which was right next to my apartment.

The move to Idaho came about after I read in the alumni bulletin that Bob Moore, a classmate of mine, was the advertising director of the Moscow *News-Review*. I called him and asked, "Any opening over there?" It just happened that it was a new paper and they were staffing it. So I went there at $22.50 a week. I was making $15 a week on the *Bulletin*. I went over in February in sub-zero temperatures with a dime in my pocket. In an un-Horatio Alger turn of events I left five years later, $1,200 in debt. Most of those people who arrived with a dime usually boast that they became millionaires.

I was rail-thin then and took after the movie scoops—hat tipped forward over a protruding cigarette and exuding a faint essence of Old Crow. Part of my life in Moscow included covering events that our advertisers put on. So they assigned me in 1939 to go down to the Grange Hall. City Editor Porter Ward thought it would be a nice gesture to Washington Water Power if I covered its cooking school and did a story on it for the *News-Review*. When I walked in, there was this darling blonde girl seating old ladies and cooking roasts, steaks and cakes all over the place. She was Audrey Owen, the local home-service girl for Washington Water Power. And I was completely enthralled by her. She was absolutely so polite and sweet to everyone and so competent. Three months later, on May 20, 1939, we were married at the First Christian Church. We were religious, God-fearing people. But we weren't formal members of a church. We didn't become formal members until 1951 when I was with Governor McKay in Salem and we were confirmed in the Episcopal Church.

Everybody in Moscow wanted to see me marry Audrey. But the marriage had to be kept secret because during the depression both husband and wife couldn't hold jobs. Our marriage more than doubled my income; even though Publisher Bill Marineau had given me a raise to $25 a week, Audrey was making more than I. The news about our marriage wasn't secret for long. So when J.D. Lewis of Washington Water Power learned about it, he broke the bad news to us—gently but firmly.

Marineau was responsive and sympathetic. He raised my pay another $2.50 a week. I don't believe he added to my duties since I was already something of a one-man gang.

During my five years in Moscow, I got involved in conservation and environmental issues. I suppose, having lived on the ranch, I had always been involved in them. As kids, we were never allowed to shoot deer. We were allowed to trap and fish. The out-of-doors was our life. I think, therefore, I always had a respect for the land. It would nurture one not only in the physiological sense but also in the matter of spirit.

It was in Moscow that the Latah County Wildlife Federation asked me to become its publicity chairman. I helped publicize the activities of the Federation, which is strongly conservation-minded —but also believed in hunting and fishing and the joys of the outdoors.

I enjoyed fishing the reaches of the North Clearwater—beautiful wild country—and the St. Joe River, now under attack by mining interests in North Idaho. I remember I wrote a column after fishing on the Clearwater about an eagle with a nest in a nearby snag. I was really absorbed by the activities around that nest and the beauty and the symbolism. What an eagle in that kind of surrounding can do for your spirit is something.

I first participated in non-campus politics in Moscow. An insurance man from Pennsylvania, Dave Evans, appliance salesman Bill Brown and I started a Young Republican club. It was a kind of clandestine organization—it had to be considering the power and popularity of Franklin Delano Roosevelt. We sort of went underground, holding biweekly meetings in a small conference room of the Moscow Hotel. Perhaps 10 or 12 would attend—and that was a flourishing number considering that the program generally consisted of Tom McCall reading aloud the recent columns of David Lawrence.

Later, in 1940, Mayor Bill Anderson, who owned a clothing store, got me in a room with several other civic dignitaries and urged me to run for mayor. Bill was a reliable mayor. He was just getting tired of the job—and of chewing those putrid cigars through those long night meetings.

I was both honored and excited. So much so that I forgot to mention I'd been caught early the same morning playing poker in a crummy bistro when Heap Jordan of the sheriff's office raided the place after-hours.

It made no difference how I'd felt because my editor Louis Boaz vetoed the idea. Louis and I had a small office together and I could tell when he thought I wasn't working hard enough or was otherwise displeased with me—because he would tap his right foot and jiggle his right knee. Sometimes it was to let me know he hadn't liked something I had written, especially when my sports columns got sort of fanciful. On some occasions, the air in our tiny joint cubicle reflected my partiality the night before toward a pint of gin. Then, indeed, the foot and knee would go into indignant motion. The ritual was accompanied by words the morning I brought up the proposition about running for mayor.

"How in the name of God," Louis asked, "can you cover City Hall fairly, impartially and objectively, when you're sitting there as mayor?"

I suppose if I had been a wealthy person I might have taken a whirl at City Hall and forgotten the working part of life. The compelling logic of his question made me go back to Bill Anderson and his people and say, "Thank you. But it's impossible." Louis never mentioned the subject again—in our office or in the building.

He was the fastest typist I have ever seen—before or since. We used to get Associated Press news from Spokane twice a morning. It would be telephoned in to the office—it was called the AP pony —and Louis would take it down so fast that his typewriter wouldn't clatter—it would make a swishing sound. Taking the pony required a great deal of concentration. Louis wouldn't be bothered by anything. So the first time he got a telephone call during transmission, I coined a temporarily celebrated gaffe by explaining to a demanding woman who called insisting on talking to Louis, "He can't come to the telephone, he's taking AP!" A

Tom McCall, class of 1936, University of Oregon. McCall was associate editor of the *Daily Emerald* and president of the Interfraternity Council. He was later elected president of the senior class by a write-in vote, then disqualified by Wayne Morse, Dean of the Law School.

Seaman Tom McCall, U.S. Navy. McCall enlisted and became a Navy war correspondent in the South Pacific.

snort of dismay and the sound of a telephone banged into its
cradle came from the other end of the line.

Perhaps my most humiliating experience there was an appearance before the Moscow Chamber of Commerce. It was mid-
autumn of 1941 and I was supposed to speak about the University
of Idaho's football game with Oregon State. The Vandals had
been undefeated going into the game. But the Beavers ground
them to a pulp, something on the order of 52-7. And I hit the
panic pedal even trying to tell my friendly neighbors about it. It
was bad enough losing the game and the unbeaten season but
what was worse was to find when I stood up to tell my mournful
story I was scared speechless. I fumbled and sweated along for a
couple of minutes; then sank into my chair, beet red and trembling, the account of the game barely out of the first period. I
went from beet-red to ashen and was still so pallid and shaky I
had to go home even before the noon meeting ended.

Audrey looked up, and became pale herself, when I wobbled
through the door and cried out, "Honey, what's the matter?" In
those days, she was the speaker of the family.

I got hung up in some really rough university politics during my
last days in Moscow. I was disillusioned by a fight over the
coaching staff. Beloved veteran Cap Horton was removed as Idaho's athletic director and replaced by Gale Mix. The next step in
the upheaval was the firing of Forrest Twogood as head basketball
coach. Then head football coach Ted Bank and line coach Bob
Tessier also got the gate. They still had some time to run on their
contracts and stayed around town. I got increasingly hot under
the collar about what had happened to them. In effect, I sort of
walked the plank when they did. My column reflected my bitterness to the point that Marineau called me in one morning and suggested I might be ready for a bigger newspaper:

"Take your time. . .no hurry, mind you," he said. "Pick and
choose until you find what you want."

At any rate, I left Moscow ahead of the coaching staff I had de-
fended so furiously. I took a bus south to Portland to look for a
job. Audrey stayed behind in Moscow as a sort of hostage to my

creditors, clerking at David's and sharing her meager pittance with those we owed. Helpful friends, the Wes Jonases, let Audrey sleep in their basement, free of charge. The only drawback was that a Jonas daughter used the area where Audrey's bed was as living space for her experimental white mice.

I was trying to get a job at the *Oregonian*. But I went back and forth between the *Oregonian* and the *Oregon Journal*, talking with Palmer Hoyt, Bob Notson, and Jalmar Johnson. Donald Sterling, managing editor of the *Journal*, never would see me. After about 15 days of this, I was still trying to see Sterling.

His secretary, Jean Yount, who is *Journal* Sports Editor George Pasero's wife now, was on my side. Finally, Jean said happily, "Mr. Sterling will see you now." But I had just gotten a job on the *Oregonian* an hour before, and I said, "You tell Mr. Sterling that I hope I never have to look at him."

When I signed up with the *Oregonian*, they gave me senior status, which entitled me to $75 a week. They generously declared that I was an experienced reporter, even though they usually required that top-scale reporters have experience on larger newspapers than the *Bulletin* and *News-Review*.

We had sort of a good guys/bad guys situation at the *Oregonian*. The Guild was then fighting to gain a foothold. The good guys, in effect, were some of my friends—Don McLeod, Night City Editor Holly Goodrich, and Phyllis Loritz, with whom I had gone to college. We were sort of the socialites of the *Oregonian* in a caste system. We thought we were superior because we felt we could get by on skill and didn't have to organize. Ep Hoyt let the feeling get around that he'd take care of us. It was a lot better as professionals not to be organized, to go on your own merit. Hoyt wasn't making an open argument. But the feeling was that your promotion and your pay ought to be judged on your doing a good job without the third party—the Union—getting in between.

After a few months in Portland, things began to stabilize. I was a reporter, covering the night police beat, with sports and the Federal beat to follow later. The Moscow debts were being scaled down. Audrey and I were reunited and found a stunning new Portland Heights apartment for $25 a month.

The tragic death of Ben Titus, the news director of the *Oregonian's* two radio stations, KEX, the red network of NBC, and KGW, the blue network of NBC, propelled me into that job. I began preparing those long half-hour two-voice World War II radio newscasts for on-duty announcers.

I got the job on the recommendation of Bill Moyes, Yale-educated radio columnist of the *Oregonian.* As a reporter, I had been paid five dollars to be a voice on a KGW public-service program concerning how a service station operator would get more help in the war. I had about a five-line part. And KGW wanted Moyes to hear a recording of this program. When he heard my voice, Moyes said, "Stop the record! There is the most interesting voice in radio." Then they told him, "Bill, that is Tom McCall who has had his desk next to yours for the last two years!" And he wouldn't believe it. I got recommended for the radio job on that basis.

When they popped me into this new assignment, I was still spooked by public speaking. Even though I had done a little broadcasting on sports down at the University of Oregon, I found the idea of going on as a newsman such a nightmare that they didn't even put me on for three weeks. Arden X. Pangborn, the station manager, said, "I just won't tell you when you're going to go on because you won't sleep between now and then." He finally let me know the day I was going to start. "You'll be on the noon news today with Mel Baldwin," Pangborn said.

I got all the copy ready. And at 11:45, Mel Baldwin began literally to carry me to the second floor news studio. We got halfway up the stairs when we were joined by another announcer, Mel Bailey. "It's just a precaution," he said. "Pang thought we ought to have another newscaster in the studio when you collapsed." It wasn't "if" I collapsed but "when." But I got through it, high stomach, palpitations and all, probably roaring along in the neighborhood of 250 words a minute.

There was a call for me when I got back in the newsroom. It was from Howard Manson, a friend from Moscow. "Congratulations, Tom," he said. "You're making it in the big time." Then, he chuckled, "If you get a chance you might send me an English translation."

Another Idaho friend, Mike Sullivan, came to visit us. He was a lieutenant in the Navy. He had been spot-promoted during combat action on Guadalcanal. He'd been through Hell. Every time a car going by his hotel window would backfire, he'd dive under the bed. Most people of my age group, unless they had gone very early of their own volition, were at the stage where the last draft-call had passed them by. I had a major dilemma. I had the great job on the *Oregonian*, was going into radio, and we had a cozy little red house out on Custer Street, a lovely little garden and a new baby.

"I don't know what to do on this," I told Mike.

He said, "You know, Tom, as one of your oldest friends, I'd feel better if you went."

Here I was, scot-free, at an age when it would have been appropriate not to have gone. But I went down and volunteered. I remember a friend of mine, Tom Klosterman, saw me the day after it was announced that our age group was no longer subject to call into the Armed Service. "God, isn't it great!" he said.

I looked at him sorrowfully and said, "I'm going."

Within a few days I was back in Idaho, at Camp Farragut. I was a source of serious embarrassment to the Navy because there were all these calisthenics to go through and I was really too tall to be in the Navy and was plagued again by the lack of coordination for this quite extreme physical exercise. I was a mortal liability at camp as the only one out of all the tens of thousands who passed through there who couldn't chin himself. This went all the way up to the Bureau of Naval Affairs in Washington. How does a man get out of boot camp who can't chin himself? Somehow my muscles were so distributed around this nearly six-foot, six-inch frame that, sweat and strain as hard as I could, I couldn't produce a single chin-up. But finally, they let me do a "running chin-up."

After 90 days of boot camp, I was admitted to the Control Tower Operators School in Atlanta. I was known as "Pop." At 31, I was the oldest man in the company. It was a miserable life. We couldn't, naturally, divine when the war was going to end. But all of a sudden, the Navy came up with an enlisted combat correspondents program, which the other services had already begun. They sent down orders to look through all the rosters to find out who had a background of journalism. Thus, a couple of weeks before I was to go to Atlanta, orders came through to report to San Francisco. I didn't have the foggiest notion where I was going from there. But I was heading someplace as an enlisted combat correspondent, Seaman First Class.

It was with some trepidation that I arrived in San Francisco. Without orders to our destination, we were herded around like cattle. You couldn't correspond to let anybody know where you were consigned or where you were. One night our ship took out under the Golden Gate Bridge. It was a troop transport. And it was not only rolling, it was pitching. I never saw so much throwing up in my life.

We went to Pearl Harbor. It was like paradise. That's where they gathered us for indoctrination into being enlisted correspondents. Most of us already knew how to write. The officer in charge of the program was the celebrated Captain Fitzhugh Lee. He was a towering figure in the Navy, a great advancer of public communications. I was the third to go out to a forward area. The first one out was blasted to death on an aircraft carrier that was stricken off Japan. We were right there. We saw her go up in the morning light. They finally got her back to the United States. She became a great symbol. The kamikaze buzzards tried to finish her off as she made it back to the rear area. Another correspondent, from Oregon, was Gene Jewett from Lakeview, who drew an old battleship, the *USS Nevada*. He got ulcers and had to come home.

I drew a light cruiser called the *St. Louis*. She was fairly modern. She had been known as the "mystery cruiser" because she had a lot of electronic and radar gear. I was only on overseas status for a year—my total service was only 16 months—yet I did a lot of good. I put out a news broadcast that I prepared every day on the ship. I helped with the entertainment. They were all waiting for me aboard the *St. Louis* because they had read in my background that I played the saxophone. They wanted me in the ship's band. But I couldn't remember any songs and my fingers were no longer accustomed to playing the sax. All I could remember was a few bars of "Dancing with Tears in My Eyes."

Since I was older and had been a newspaperman, I was often asked to help guys with their "Dear John" letters. I wrote a history of the *St. Louis.*

The Lucky Lou—so named because of her survival record in kamikaze attacks—led the bombardment of Okinawa for more than three months. It was claimed she spent more consecutive days firing than any ship in that war, propelling more than 27,000 shells against Okinawan targets.

Near the end of the marathon shelling, the *St. Louis* drew a new executive officer, a sort of a truculent maverick named Andrew Jackson Smith. He was quite a drinker—a fact we didn't know until we had been ordered to a rest area, Subic Bay in the Philippines. The new exec came back to the ship from the beach—passed out on the cowl of his small boat.

We didn't see him for a couple of days afterward; then he summoned me, Seaman First Class McCall, to his cabin.

"McCall," he said, "you're a newspaperman, you understand these problems. Why don't you kind of reacquaint me with the crew?"

I helped all I could and suddenly found myself advanced to Specialist X 3rd class—a rating that embraced a hodgepodge of miscellaneous activities including writing news for the Navy.

As a correspondent, I sent my stories to the Navy's hometown news center in Chicago for processing. Most of the stories wouldn't have made the wires, but they were of interest to the subject's local paper and radio station.

When the war ended, orders came aboard the *St. Louis* for me to go ashore as soon as convenient and await more specific orders. I debarked at Subic Bay, landing squarely in the middle of the maddening congestion of the homeward bound. The brass had no way to move masses of uniformed men back to the States. They gave you hope, though, by moving you by landing barge every once in a while—but, as it turned out, only a few miles down the coast.

Maybe, the new stop was worse than the old one. Nowhere was there enough food. There were torrential rains. I used to sleep under stacks of boards, soaking. Never had a nickel in my pocket —but at least the war was over!

My final orders never caught up with me. But when I limped into Pearl Harbor weeks later and saw them, I turned inside out. If I'd been a little more patient—stayed on the *St. Louis* a few days longer—I would have been *flown* to Tokyo Harbor to become correspondent on the new cruiser *USS Chicago*. She got in on the surrender and the whole thing.

Back at Pearl Harbor, the Navy informed us that it wanted to keep some of us correspondents. The brass felt that the hometown formula would work well in peacetime, too.

"What would induce you to stay in, McCall?" asked young Ensign Walsh who had graduated in journalism from Northwestern.

Specialist X Third Class McCall answered without hesitation, "Full Commander."

"Why," the taken-aback Walsh blurted, "I am only an ensign."

I asked, "But have you ever worked on a newspaper?"

"No," came the reply, "but I hope to."

I didn't stay, but I am glad I went, mainly because I performed a useful service but also because my father hadn't been able to get into the Army in World War I. It always bothered him that he didn't go. So he would get off the sidewalk for some big windbag Legionnaire who might have spent 90 days in the Armed Forces billeted at Seattle. It was a cross he bore all of his adult life.

The American Legion had been a powerful political lobby in Oregon. It's not as strong now but still important. I suspect that Mike Sullivan, in counseling me to join the Navy, sensed I had a political future. He was hinting, I guess, it would have been aborted if I hadn't gone. Besides, my big brother, Harry, was already out there as a naval aerial gunnery officer.

Some people said my decision was stupid—to abandon a happy existence, security, growing job success and a lovely wife and baby. But it's just the way I had to do things.

The family got together in Portland after my discharge in Seattle in January, 1946. Audrey and little Tad had been staying with her mother, Grace Sweeney, in Spokane. We resumed our Oregon residency in the Congress Hotel.

Waiting there for us was an invitation and ticket to the annual Junior League Ball. I put on my dress blues, bars and stars and walked across the street to scout out things at the dance, then getting underway at the Portland Hotel. When I presented my ticket, they said, "You can't get in, it's formal." I said, indicating my dress blues, "This *is* formal." The blockheads wouldn't budge, even though clucking friends interceded. You'd think that after all the years of war, they would have had more sensitivity and savvy.

Shortly after that I rejoined KEX and one of my assignments was a weekly commentary, "Talk of the Town." The fact that my mother and a scad of aunts had been Junior League members in Boston couldn't save the Portland snobs from a scourging in my first KEX offering.

KEX was a Westinghouse station then. I liked my work there, particularly the "Talk of the Town." After about six months, I had a fateful encounter with E.B. MacNaughton. He was president of First National Bank and chairman of the board of the *Oregonian*. It was generally known that he was going to step down at First National. So I just sort of made a rumor story out of it. His lawyer promptly summoned me to talk to MacNaughton. My sponsor was Sandy's Camera Shop. MacNaughton's bank had a hefty mortgage on Sandy's. When I saw him, I said, "Mr. MacNaughton, hasn't it already been in the paper? Isn't it a known fact that you are going to step down, and that you are of an age when you should retire as president?" He said, "Yes, of course. But I don't like to hear it on radio."

I was dropped. Sandy was scared out. So I began doing the 10 o'clock evening news. I had Portland Auto Dealer Joe Fisher as a sponsor. KOIN (CBS) and Jim Wyatt were my chief competition. The Richfield report on NBC had made the 10 p.m. news supreme. Since nearly everybody listened to the 10 o'clock news, you were always trying to crack Jim Wyatt who was top dog at that hour.

During this period I did some work with the Young Republicans. Among the promising articulate, progressive Republicans who were becoming involved at the same time were Robert Elliott, Clay Myers, Shirley Field, and William Lambert, who later won a Pulitzer Prize as an investigative reporter on the *Oregonian.*

I still dreaded public speaking. Nevertheless, when the Republican Club of Oregon asked me to give a luncheon speech at a meeting to be attended by Governor Douglas McKay, I screwed up my courage and accepted.

In the 1940s, McCall became active in Portland's Young Republican group. He briefed San Francisco newspaper publisher, Paul Smith, who was in Portland to address a Republican meeting.

CHAPTER 2

A Political Education

This, really, was the first formal address of my life. I knew that with more than four years of radio experience, I could read all right. Still and all, this was one of the toughest assignments I had ever undertaken because I wanted to impress this influential group with eye-contact as well as words and thoughts. I didn't have the confidence to wing it. So I tried to memorize my speech on "The Future of the Party."

Somehow, shakes and all, I made it all the way through. I urged the Republican Club of Oregon to become "forward looking" and not to "get embraced by the past." It drew a delighted reception with a rousing round of applause at the end. What I didn't know until later was that, midway through my presentation, the grande dame of Oregon Republicanism, Betty Patterson, had leaned close to Governor McKay's ear and whispered, "Why, there, Douglas, is the young man you've been looking for to be your executive secretary."

Her suggestion resulted in McKay calling me down to Salem. He had gotten the job of Executive Secretary stepped up to the magnificent sum of $6,000. McKay wanted to make it a high-powered job. Previous assistants to the governor—Pinky Joslin to Governor Martin and Sig Unander to Governor Sprague—had been little more than office boys. I had reservations about taking the job. I was making $7,200 a year. This was $6,000. I didn't have any cushion at all. It was terribly hard, for that reason, to accept.

I went down because if a governor asks you to do something important, to be a number-one man in his office, you should have the courtesy to talk to him about it and turn him down face-to-face. You don't just handle it by telephone or mail. So I appeared in the Governor's Office. McKay was a tremendously feisty guy and was swearing a lot. I kind of liked his combativeness. But I thought: could we really work together? After a lengthy conversation, I decided we could. On July 1, 1949, I was sworn in at the Capitol.

McKay was a dynamic salesman type. He had run a highly successful Chevrolet dealership in Salem for many years. Although he had been gravely wounded in World War I, he had also served in World War II. He was honest and never afraid to take a position. He was really quite concerned about Oregon. His family had lived in the Pacific Northwest before Oregon was even a U.S. territory. One of his ancestors, Malcolm McKay, had been a storekeeper for the Hudson's Bay Company.

Governor McKay had an interesting cabinet. Even though I was the only other man in the office, I was really the junior member. Ralph Emmons, a Salem public relations man, was the power behind the throne. Emmons had been Governor Earl Snell's close advisor and confidant. He directed McKay's successful 1948 primary campaign against Governor John Hall. Emmons wrote many of McKay's speeches and was a marvelous writer. It might be considered rhetoric now. But he made, I thought, a great use of words. He was very unpopular with state employees. He had been head of some state board and something he had done had turned the public employees against him. Emmons would slip in the back door to see McKay.

George Flagg, who was public utility commissioner and had been assistant secretary of state under Governor Snell, was another member of McKay's inner circle. Flagg had a great feel for Oregon politics, except where Flagg himself was concerned. He was running for Secretary of State in 1948, predicting he was going to win by a landslide. Earl Newbry just slaughtered him. I never had seen anyone so confident with so little reason.

The third member of the troika behind McKay was Harry Dorman, the state budget director. He was a very key figure. Dorman was an old World War I buddy of McKay's. He was a businessman from Portland, a smooth, soothing type.

My duties under the title of executive secretary were in later administrations split out into a number of positions including executive assistant to the governor, administrative assistant, press secretary and general liaison between the governor and scores of agencies and institutions. Shortly after I started this job, State Senator Angus Gibson of Junction City paid a visit to McKay's office. He took one look at me, towering there—almost a foot taller than the governor—and said: "Did you hire him as an assistant or as a bodyguard?"

I took a goodly part of the load off McKay's shoulders by meeting with many constituents who would come to visit him. If they had a problem, I would do my best to find a solution. The hours were considerably longer than they had been in my radio and newspaper work. I didn't mind because McKay worked long hours, too.

Many of the issues back then loomed as mountains that were almost unclimbable. McKay often used me as a troubleshooter. Less than three months into my service with McKay came the longshoremen's strike riots at The Dalles. When several men began unloading a barge of Hawaiian pineapple, they were roughed up by some angry longshoremen. McKay sent state police in to keep order. "I am not a labor arbiter," McKay said, "but I will move in whenever violence occurs, whether the violence is caused by unions or someone else. My oath of office requires this." The longshoremen asked that future "hot" cargoes of pineapples be refused admittance to Oregon ports.

Since I had been a longshoreman in World War II and knew their leaders, McKay utilized me in this labor crisis. The union leaders, Fred Kamahoahoa from Hawaii, and Matt Meehan of Portland, trusted me. Instead of dealing with them at arm's length, we were able to discuss intimately the complications of the dispute. We reached a workable compromise and there was no further violence.

Another strike I helped mediate was at the Oregon State Penitentiary. I went out and met with the inmate negotiating committee. There were eight convicted murderers on the committee. I walked into the room by myself—with no guns over me. I asked, "How do you settle something like this?" One fellow began reciting all the prisons he'd been in. He said, "Well, when I was in West Texas, we did it this way. And when we were in Joliet. . . ." I told them, "You've got to stop this strike before any of these grievances can be met." They were, for the most part, simple grievances—basic things that prisoners should have, mostly concerned with mail and visitation matters. The warden was old-fashioned and the state had been neglectful.

So they said, "If we do stop, who is going to guarantee then that the grievances will be taken up?" I said, "Governor McKay." They said, "He's a politician." I said, "Earl Newbry." They said, "He's another." I added, "Walter Pearson and he's a Democrat."

"But what do *you* say, Mac?" they said.

"You stop this, and I'll guarantee you that these grievances will be given a fair hearing by the Board of Control—but not with a pistol in their face."

They said, "That's good enough for us."

I got on the telephone and spoke over their public address system. A great, coarse shout of joy just rang out over this huge compound. And the strike was over.

Later, Newbry argued that there was a conflict because I was "attacking" the Board of Control while working for the Board of Control. But others thanked God that there was somebody with that relationship. I was president of the Oregon Prison Association. That's what really settled a strike which might have become quite ugly.

McKay put together a committee in 1950 to draft the first pure-air law in the nation. I was the secretary and worked with two deans from Oregon State College, spending a year drafting it. It provided a framework for pollution control. It was really a pre-amble—a statement of policy that air quality and the health of the people and Oregon's climate would be maintained. It also required monitoring to see that air quality standards—to be set later —would be implemented.

It was one of the first bills to come up for hearing in the 1951 legislature. Senator Jack Lynch, a Portland Republican, was chairman of the Senate Health Committee. When they gave the bill a hearing, billions of dollars worth of industry marched right in and fought it; aluminum companies, the power companies, and all these big business allies made an intensive lobbying effort. So it was laid on the table, this year of work, after 90 minutes of hearings. We were absolutely furious about it. Nowadays industry wouldn't be so heavy-handed, but this was how calloused they were then about such matters that now are determined to be of primary importance to the quality of life.

McKay was sympathetic. He said, "Do anything you can, within reason, to try to get it resurrected." So we called all these lobbyists into the Ceremonial Office. I remember Alan Hart of Reynolds Metal and all those glib lawyers representing billions of dollars worth of business, coming into the office where Elmer McClure and I were standing. McClure was Master of the State Grange, which was a powerful organization in Oregon then. He said, "Boys, if you think that's a tough bill, wait till you see the one the Grange is going to initiate on air quality to put on the ballot in this state." Suddenly the lobbyists said, "Just a minute, Elmer, please." And the bill came off the table and we passed it.

Another controversial issue concerned the United World Federalists. It was an idealistic organization committed to world government and a sense of community among nations. Senator Phil Hitchcock of Klamath Falls had been a leading advocate for it and his resolution supporting its goals went through the 1949 legislature. The American Legion later decided that the World Federalists were somehow un-American.

There was a ripper of a fight in the 1951 legislature to rescind recognition. The Legion had gotten on McKay and Harry Dorman, who were strong Legionnaires. I can remember a stirring debate between the National Commander of the American Legion from Seattle, a huge man and flag-waving orator, and Chief Justice James T. Brand of the Oregon Supreme Court, a strong internationalist and civil libertarian who fought for retention of the resolution. It's to the discredit of the Oregon legislature that it failed to survive.

I also can remember, during the 1951 session, a discussion in the Senate about some Air Force general. Dick Neuberger made a disparaging remark about him. I was standing in the back of the chamber and told Dick, "I agree with you." State Senator Warren Gill of Lebanon, a Republican who had been a much decorated war hero, overheard my conversation with Neuberger. The next thing I knew, Gill was bolting into McKay's office to report my defection and my lack of patriotism. McKay didn't attempt to muzzle me. But he did have an explosive temper. I once saw the governor pick Cecil Posey up by the seat of his pants and scruff of his neck in climaxing some discussion of school matters. Posey was the executive secretary of the Oregon Education Association, and considered quite a liberal. Voices rose in McKay's office, which was next to mine, and there was McKay hustling him out and saying, "I'll be damned if you'll impugn my honesty."

If McKay was feisty, he was also self-deprecating. I wrote a speech for his appearance before a Seaside meeting. He put aside my text as he was about to speak, saying, "This is the speech Tom McCall wants me to give. But I thought I'd just talk." He was such a genuine person that he recognized that we spoke a different language.

He also did not like to read speeches. And he had more confidence in Ralph Emmons' writing than mine. If he had given my speech, he felt that people would say, "Look at McKay, he's gone intellectual on us." Intellectualism wasn't his appeal—and he knew it. He thought the speech would be out of character. That's how really genuine he was about it.

McKay did, however, like me to give speeches as his representative. For every speech he accepted, he had to turn down ten. I helped him reduce that ratio by making many appearances. This gave me quite a bit of visibility. On one occasion, I went before the Lebanon Chamber of Commerce to speak against the Brannan farm plan which, in retrospect, might have been an answer to the farm problem. It was the proposal of Charles F. Brannan,

President Truman's Secretary of Agriculture. Under it, you would let the market seek its own natural level and then the Federal government would pay the farmer the difference—between what he had received in the natural market and what he had to have to turn a reasonable profit. As it was, the taxpayer paid the farm subsidy to hold the prices up, and then got it in the neck both ways—through taxation to hold the prices up, and by paying higher prices when he went to the market to buy produce. Senator Robert A. Taft said it would cost $30 billion or so, and this was one of those articles of faith that Republicans lived by.

I didn't go for too many of them. Indeed sometimes I would criticize Republican demagoguery. In August of 1951, Senator Joseph McCarthy of Wisconsin attended a state GOP picnic. I denounced McCarthy as a "character assassin" and said inviting him to speak in Oregon "was anything but smart public relations on the part of the Republican party."

One of the most volatile issues of the McKay years was President Truman's proposal for a Columbia Valley Authority. Senator Morse came out against it, which was a tremendous stroke for the Republicans. Morse was mercurial but always an all-out fighter for what he supported. Morse's opposition to CVA had a profound effect. The battle to model the handling of our power development and distribution after the Tennessee Valley Authority was coming to a climax. Liberal Democrats generally favored it. After Morse came out against it, so did other liberal Republicans. In a speech at Ashland, I described CVA as "creeping socialism." I later suggested creating a regional corporation so we could independently finance the construction we needed on the river.

I soon learned that I wasn't a very good debater. I was very diffident about debates because if my opponent made up something, I took it as the gospel. I wouldn't think he was capable of being devious, or would try any shenanigans. Jim Collins, a young attorney who was president of the Young Republicans, asked me to join him at a debate at Reed College, on the CVA, facing Norman Stoll, a liberal attorney, and Monroe Sweetland. Both were the darlings of the liberal student body and faculty. In

Senator Richard L. Neuberger and McCall shared a professional bond as politically active journalists. McCall hailed Neuberger as the finest Pacific Northwest writer of his generation and Oregon's most effective U.S. Senator.

Oregon Governor Paul Patterson and the McCalls were on hand to greet House Speaker Joseph W. Martin during the Massachusetts Republican's 1954 visit to Oregon. Barnstormer Martin was of dubious value to McCall's congressional campaign, urging voters to elect "Douglas" McCall.

those surroundings, our winning was out of the question. I told Collins that it would be impossible to make any converts. No matter what you said, you weren't going to get off the ground. So I said, "Jim, no, I've got more sense than to get into that."

Collins pulled something of an end run by going directly to McKay. The governor instructed me, "You'd better do it."

It was the worst slaughter you ever saw. I would get some fairly good points together. Then I would be completely deflated when Stoll and Sweetland would dismiss my arguments as less genuine and pertinent than their arguments.

I was getting lower and lower in the water, booed, and knowing I should never have been there in the first place. It was a miserable experience. Finally, Collins, who had been taking notes, just ripped them to pieces, calling them liars and dissemblers. My faith in human nature was shaken. I suppose it was in the bounds of proper debate to use their tactics but it was quite a shock.

During my two races for governor with Bob Straub, we had many joint appearances. Generally, we agreed and when we didn't, it was more a quibble than a Lincoln-Douglas-type bell-ringer. But the Reed College debate was a nasty experience which hammered me back into my lair.

Again though, I was in demand as a speaker and McKay liked me to go out. This is where I developed an advocacy for a lieutenant governorship. They would invariably call up for the Governor to make an appearance. Then I would be offered as an alternative. Well, being his executive secretary was not a very suitable title. If there had been a lieutenant governor, he could have filled ceremonial roles without inherent inferiorities that come from a lesser title. To most people, a secretary is somebody who runs a typewriter. Thus, I repeatedly advocated a strong lieutenant governorship to take some of the ceremonial load off the governor. I advocated that the two run on the same ticket. The State Grange, Democrats and I favored this proposal. Republicans didn't.

When I was in Governor McKay's office, the progressive wing of the Republican party was promoting some of the most advanced civil rights legislation of the time. Phil Hitchcock, Bob Elliott and I worked on bills guaranteeing equal employment opportunities and other basic rights.

There was a seesaw battle to change the Real Estate Code to eliminate mention of restrictive covenants. Language in the code said it was unethical to permit the entry into a neighborhood of a prospective resident who would be incompatible or tend to lower property values. Of course, I had been secretary of the board of the Urban League of Portland, and had long been working to eliminate this language. But the Real Estate Commissioner, Claude Murphy, called me into the Governor's Office and said, "I think we've got a way to get around these guys on the removal of this language."

I responded bluntly, "Mr. Commissioner, I happen to be one of those guys."

It was a jarring awakening for me: the realization that civil rights hypocrisy dwelt so close to the governor's office. Candidates had made appearances with the token Negro on the campaign trail. And that was almost all anybody thought about it. So this was a conflict between the old and the new—a modern political thinker and the old way of doing business.

Some time later, when blacks were banned from the swimming pool and dance hall at Jantzen Beach Park, I spoke out against this injustice. A Republican luncheon had been scheduled for Jantzen Beach and I suggested moving it "to beautiful Washington Park, where the air is free and the turf and flowers are complete strangers to the sordid meaning of the word prejudice."

The years working in the Governor's Office were challenging and rewarding, but the Tom McCalls were getting awfully lean financially. McKay finally got $600 more a year for me. He said that was the best he could do. H. Quenton Cox, the station manager of KGW radio, called me late in 1951. He offered me $7,500 to do a job I had outlined while I was serving on the *USS St. Louis.* Cox still had my letter on his desk.

"Why," I had written then, "if stations pay millions of dollars to pipe Gabriel Heatter, Drew Pearson, Elmer Davis and other

national commentators out of Washington, shouldn't local stations pay a few thousand to have an analyst sounding off from a
state capitol?"

The immediate reply was soothing and noncommittal. But,
after I had been with McKay nearly two and a half years, Cox
called and said, "You weren't ready to be a commentator. With
this background as the lieutenant governor of the State of Oregon, you now have the depth and the grasp of the issues that
would indeed qualify you."

KGW's new owners, Crown Stations of Seattle, were in a hot
battle to get Portland's Channel 8. They needed a record showing
they were innovative enough to employ a commentator of standing. This was supposed to impress the Federal Communications
Commission. I had finally ripened, I guess, because I was signed
on as the region's pre-eminent radio commentator. The worst and
most indifferent, too, because there was no other with that full-
time status in all the vast Northwest.

In late January, 1952, KGW Radio turned Tom Lawson McCall
loose on a 15-minute nightly news analysis dealing largely with
state-local government and politics. In fact, I was soon known as
the official bore of the medium because it was the first time that
radio news dwelt on such tedious items as school, city and state
budgets, tax rates and Bancroft bonds. It was written out, typed
out, thought out by me. Sometimes we had interviews and sound
cuts when they were appropriate.

I committed something of a *faux pas* that spring. It happened as
the deadline for filing in the Oregon presidential primary approached. I was down in the capitol waiting, as the whole state
was, to see if Bob Taft was going to enter against Eisenhower in
Oregon's 1952 Presidential Primary. There was a long line there.
And I had to make a broadcast deadline. I didn't have enough
material because nothing much materialized. Taft was going to be
the big story of the day. So I went by the desk of Paul Harvey,
the Associated Press man, and here in his typewriter, was the
bulletin, "Ex-Governor Walter M. Pierce died today at the age of
80." Of course we were a client of A.P., so I was entitled to use

the material. Not knowing it was "ready copy"—copy prepared in advance—I went on the air embroidering, and said, "The usual merriment in the halls was muted by the death of former Governor Walter Pierce." I really had to fill 15 minutes, talking about how "This giant oak had fallen."

Somebody called me about midnight at my Southwest Portland house. The caller asked, "Where did you get the story about Governor Pierce? He's still alive!"

Lord, that was an awful shock.

I was among the first radio newsmen in the Northwest to give localized on-the-scene coverage of the national political conventions. Both the 1952 Republican and Democratic conventions were held in Chicago. Oregon's Democrats were just beginning to come into power. They were still disorganized and not used to authority. Senator Estes Kefauver of Tennessee had won the Oregon primary—and the delegation was committed to him. Kefauver led in the first two ballots but fell short of a majority. Adlai Stevenson was nominated on the third ballot. There was a deep rift between the liberals and the conservatives in the Oregon delegation. Monroe Sweetland and C. Girard "Jebby" Davidson personified the liberals. State Senator Tom Mahoney, a conservative, took a swing at Davidson. That's how strong the acrimony was. Mahoney missed and cartwheeled over a line of chairs onto the floor. I was standing right there and nearly got hit.

There was a great deal of action at the Republican Convention. The contest between Eisenhower and Taft was the most bitterly fought in more than 40 years. As a commentator, I had noted that Eisenhower was clearly the popular choice. And, if the convention rejected him, I suggested that he lead a political third force. Ralph H. Cake, Oregon's Republican national committeeman, helped Eisenhower win the nomination. It was Cake who devised the "Fair Play" amendment strategy which enabled the Eisenhower forces to win a critical vote involving 68 delegates from Georgia, Louisiana and Texas. Cake's stroke gave Eisenhower the momentum he needed. Cake also had a hand in the selection of Senator Richard M. Nixon of California as Eisenhower's running-mate.

I was sitting next to Senator Morse, on the convention floor, when it was announced that Nixon was Eisenhower's choice. Morse clutched my knee and said, "Tom, how could they do it? This Jew baiter, this labor baiter. How could they try to foist him upon the American people? Why couldn't it have been a progressive Republican like Leverett Saltonstall?"

Since Morse had been the first senator to endorse Eisenhower— and had himself been mentioned as a vice-presidential candidate, I rushed him up to a wing of the International Amphitheater where I had my recording equipment.

He was gray, ashen and shaken. I turned on the equipment and asked, "Senator, what is your reaction to the ticket?"

Astonishingly, Morse literally crowed, "The Republicans have nominated the greatest ticket in the history of America: the soldier-patriot, beloved across the world, and a new generation of progressive politician, expert in government, to run with him."

Morse was unpredictable. But this incident reflected the turmoil going on inside him. It began with the chicanery in Salem that summer when the Oregon Republican delegation held its organizational meeting. The Arlington Club smarties, led by Cake, upset the tacit understanding that McKay and Morse had— namely, that McKay would be chairman of the delegation and Morse would serve on the platform committee. They staged this great coup; instead of producing a place for Morse on the committee, they came up with a 29-year-old State Representative named Mark Hatfield. Morse was stunned. This jolt came right out of the blue. It was the kind of smart-aleck trickery that debases politicians—and, in this case, put the Democratic Party on its way to dominance in Oregon.

These were the convolutions that Morse went through in turning on Eisenhower, becoming an Independent and then moving into the Democratic Party. I think the suffering, the humiliation and the agonizing crystalized in him the day Nixon was nominated for vice president. It was a myth that Morse expected the nomination himself. As he saw it, his party had fallen into the clutches of the conservatives, and there was no longer any room for him. He campaigned for Stevenson, knowing that Eisenhower would win in a landslide. But it was an act of conscience.

In the meantime, Governor McKay was emerging as a leader in the Eisenhower campaign. Along with Governor Sherman Adams of New Hampshire and Governor Thomas E. Dewey of New York, McKay had sponsored the resolution which brought Eisenhower the dramatic pre-convention endorsement of the Republican Governors' Conference. McKay worked extensively for Eisenhower in western states. By election night, I predicted McKay would be appointed Secretary of the Interior. I repeated this prediction in several subsequent broadcasts.

When Eisenhower named McKay, the governor was surprised. "Tom, you were the only person who predicted the appointment," he told me. "And when I heard you, I didn't believe it."

I chuckled when a national wire service reporter wrote that McKay "had never been mentioned as a likely choice for a cabinet post." I felt some professional pride having a beat on Oregon's first Cabinet appointment in 80 years.

After McKay's appointment, he met with "Jebby" Davidson, who had been an assistant secretary of the Interior in the Truman administration. Davidson recommended that McKay take me back with him. "You are going into a den of lions," he warned. "You've got to have a guy who is absolutely loyal to you—and who has a little savoir-faire at the same time." Of course, Republicans were so suspicious of Davidson, a liberal Democrat, that McKay turned down the idea. I'm sure it was the counsel of Emmons and Dorman that he take someone else as his assistant— even though I was the kind who would have laid down my life for him. I wouldn't have let the vultures in close to him to work him over so badly.

What happened was, I had been at a disadvantage because McKay had a great friend, Larry Smyth, who was political editor of the *Oregon Journal*. He used to ride around with McKay in the governor's limousine. Here I was in charge of press relations and I would pick up the *Journal* and read where McKay had just made an important appointment. Naturally, the left-out press jumped on me. Larry was reassuring and hearty and bluff, a good cigar chomper. He was a pleasant fellow and good companion. But Larry just didn't have the sensitivity. He just let McKay charge into all the thickets from which no politician can emerge alive. All the power companies gathered around the table at the Interior, gleefully shouting, "Smorgasbord."

McKay spoke to the Portland Chamber of Commerce on his first trip back to the Northwest in 1953. He threw his script away and said, "I know I'm not supposed to have a position on the licensing of dams on the Snake River by the Federal Power Commission." This was the most bitter and controversial public power/private power fight in history. McKay said, "I want you to know I stand up for free enterprise on this issue."

As I walked out of the luncheon, with Monroe Sweetland, I said, "Wasn't it refreshing to see a member of the Cabinet throw away his script and tell you without a note what he really thinks about these great issues?"

"It's great," Sweetland said. "But you wait and see. He'll never survive."

My Democratic friend was prophetic. It was on that speech that they got up and hanged McKay. McKay's political opponents said he didn't care about natural resources, the people or anything else. They nicknamed him "Giveaway McKay" and "No-Dam Doug."

I had an interview with Morse during this period. Near the end of the broadcast, I said, "We have 25 seconds. I won't ask you the question. But would you tell me what opponent you prefer for the Senate?"

Morse leaned down and said, "Bring on McKay, that vendor of the public's rights." He delivered a slashing attack in 22 seconds. Morse was the master of the vituperative epithet, as I would painfully discover in my congressional campaign.

I took my ill-fated political excursion in 1954. Homer D. Angell, the Republican congressman, was 79. There was an Eisenhower wing of Republicans, including some businessmen at the

Arlington Club, who thought it was time for Angell to step down. They thought I might be a suitable person to run against him.

Before an interview with Angell that winter, for radio, he said, "If you are thinking about running, why don't you let me have two more years so I can complete the four full years with my president, President Eisenhower?"

I told him, "I can't tell you for sure. It might be possible. This thing is just too sudden. It's germinating now."

He said, "All right, I'll announce immediately for re-election." So I put him on my program and had the scoop on his decision to run for re-election.

Shortly afterward, State Senator John Merrifield called me. "I just heard you and Homer," John said. "By the way, did Homer happen to promise you that he would support you for his seat in Congress in '56?"

I confirmed Angell's proposition. "He made me the same promise yesterday," John said.

So this was when I concluded that a politician never quits unless he is hauled off to the bone yard—this would have gone on and on. Angell, though, probably would have been a good congressman until he was 90. He was a very vigorous man.

Thus, I ran on the basis that certainly Angell had been an admirable public servant. Sometimes, though, the party would lose a congressional seat when voters decided a man had served too long. We were just trying to find out if Republicans wanted Angell to go on—or have some new blood. It was a very gentle campaign.

Angell was seeking a ninth term. He was undefeated since his election in 1938. Angell was 65 when he came to Washington in January of 1939. Ben Selling, a prominent Portlander, bought him two suits and a straw suitcase.

Angell had a tremendous relationship with organized labor. He nearly always won the endorsement of all the unions. This enabled him to persevere in one of the strongest union and Democratic districts in the West. He also had support from senior citizens. Angell always was a Dr. Francis Townsend backer, and advocated a fixed income for the elderly. It wasn't just lip service. He felt it. He rose to a position of influence in Congress. By 1954, he was the second-ranking Republican on the Interior Committee.

Yet we sensed that his political strengths in the Third District were crumbling. Mrs. George Gerlinger, Oregon's Republican national committeewoman for many years, was against me. When anybody disagreed with her, she'd give a speech and talk about that "dreadful person." Once you made her dreadful-person list, you never got off. So she wired Homer to come back and campaign or this dreadful radical might take his place.

Most of the "Citizens for Eisenhower" people, who had been active in the 1952 presidential campaign, were backing me. Ralph Cake, Gordon Orputt and Ray Vester persuaded me to run. There were problems finding a campaign chairman. Sid Woodbury, who had been Portland's "First Citizen," indicated he would take the chairmanship. When I went to his house, I said, "Of course, we are going to have a tough time with Hell's Canyon."

He said, "Tom, that's way up there in Idaho. That's not going to be an issue in Multnomah County for Congress."

I told him, "It's going to be the issue." And he quit, right there, as my campaign chairman. He had thought it would just be a bland, friendly campaign. Finally, they got another Arlington Club member, Joseph W. Smith, as chairman.

Dams and power development were the dominant issues. I strongly pushed a plan for regional corporations, which would give us independence in our power development and multi-purpose dam development in the Northwest. This was a compromise between the CVA and the status quo. The power companies didn't like it. I can remember a campaign buffet in Pete Snedecor's basement. Pete later became a vice president of Portland General Electric and was then their chief lobbyist. "That was a fine presentation," he said. "But do you always have to talk about the same damned thing?"

For years, power was the main bone of contention that tended to divide people in Oregon. Secretary McKay had taken a position for private development at Hell's Canyon. I was bound by friendship, and I suppose a sense of party loyalty, to a position that didn't slap him in the face.

Congressman Angell put out a regular questionnaire and one of the questions was, "How should Hell's Canyon be developed?" A Republican precinct committeewoman wrote a letter to the editor, published in the *Oregonian*, which said, "Why can't we hear from Mr. Angell and Mr. McCall on this questionnaire?"

This is when he came out for federal development, a high dam built by the federal government instead of "pygmy dams" built by a private corporation in the Hell's Canyon of the Snake River. That issue was so volatile that if you didn't take the traditional Republican position in the primary, you couldn't get nominated. And if you took the Republican position in the primary, you probably couldn't win in November because the Democratic position and the Republican position were diametrically opposed. Angell was taking the Democratic position.

I took the classic stance of Governor Patterson and most of the party leaders. The position was that you let the matter rest with the Federal Power Commission, which had to issue the licenses that would result in the building of the dam. It was something of a cop-out because the FPC was Republican. And the general feeling was that they would authorize private development—which was exactly what happened.

An *Oregonian* editorial on Hell's Canyon said, "McCall lives in the political reality of the time and knows that federal appropriations just aren't going to come."

I defeated Angell by 13,884 votes in the May primary. Associated Press noted that it was the closest thing to a major political upset that spring. McKay was absolutely infatuated and electrified by the fact that I had beaten Congressman Angell. McKay never really quite understood me. He and other Republican politicians had considered Angell unbeatable.

After the primary, I went back to Washington, D.C., and met President Eisenhower. The Republican Congressional Committee had a whole bunch of congressional candidates there, and they were herding them through like cattle. I had a brief visit with the

President. He was very affable. He gave me a small lecture to the effect that even though a congressman might come from a small county, such as his Dickinson County in Kansas, the congressman had to rise above the parochialism of local issues. He had to take care of his constituencies. But as a citizen of the United States, looking out for the domestic and international interests of the country was the obligation of a congressman.

Eisenhower was a great man for the season. Some sneered at him because he wasn't a politician, seemed naive, or played too much golf. I just thought this nation really needed somebody it could look up to. If they wanted to get the computer operator to do the details, let them have a computer operator. But having that image—the father image, the patriot image, the soldier image— was important. He managed to end the Korean War quickly and went on to keep Americans from fighting elsewhere.

I remember Eisenhower had a position on reinsurance for health insurance. It was a private plan—but if there were catastrophic or very extensive medical obligations, the government would extend itself and take care of them. The president of the Multnomah County Medical Society came to me and said, "We can't support you if you go along with this."

I said, "Nobody's going to win in this district going to the right of General Eisenhower."

Edith Green, who had been a lobbyist for the Oregon Education Association, and had made a good run for Secretary of State in 1952, was my Democratic opponent. Traditional labor allies of Angell began drifting into her camp. Segments of labor were putting on a tremendous campaign for her. They really used some unfair things on me, charging that I was the most un-union beast that ever ran for public office. How could I have been anti-union when I was the only active union member in the race? My own union, of which I had been president, AFTRA, had endorsed me. Yet I couldn't get through to the rank-and-file troops. It was a maddening thing. The Teamster magazine and the Labor Press absolutely ripped me day and night. In later years, they were great friends.

President Dwight D. Eisenhower hosted McCall at the White House after his primary upset over Portland Congressman Homer Angell. McCall had campaigned as an "Eisenhower Republican." In 1952 he had suggested that Eisenhower lead an Independent Third Force in the event Republicans denied him the nomination. "It was clear that the people wanted him," said McCall.

Left: Senator Joseph R. McCarthy of Wisconsin delivered a speech to Oregon's Young Republicans in 1951. McCall denounced McCarthy as a "character assassin." Right: Governor Douglas McKay brought McCall into state government as his executive secretary.

Senator Morse linked me with the private power trusts. He coined the phrase, "McKee, McKay and McCall." Paul B. McKee was the president of Pacific Power and Light Company and McKay had tremendous power company leanings. Morse just tucked me in with them with devastating effect. Because I had worked for McKay, Morse knew I was loyal enough not to turn on McKay. The Democrats adopted the alliterative epithet as their battle cry. It was a hairy, thorny situation.

I was really pictured as a black conservative, and I couldn't get through with my views. Another handicap was having Senator Guy Cordon as my running-mate. He was probably the most conservative member of the Senate: a pro-McCarthyite, an isolationist—and as bad on race as there was. The *Oregon Journal* was very perceptive. The editor of its editorial page, Tom Humphrey, said, "We can't let you carry this millstone. The difference between you and Cordon is like day and night. Can't you turn on him, and we'll cover it? Can't you speak out?"

I was shrouded by these affiliations through a sense of loyalty to the Republican Party. I could have made distinctions ad nauseum as the opposition was throwing Cordon and McKay at me all the time, along with McKee. It was particularly frustrating because I was a professional communicator and reasonably articulate. Yet I wasn't getting across. I really wouldn't have minded the loss of Republicans if I had exercised some independence in enunciating positions that were contrary to party dogma. But I would have really minded hurting Secretary McKay. So, Morse recognized me as a good fellow and drove it home.

This campaign bruised me. I remember six U.S. senators came out to help Cordon. Edith and I were having a debate in the YMCA that same night. Somehow a rumor was started that Cordon was going to be gutted at Reed College, so all my supporters and the six senators were out at Reed helping Cordon.

The YMCA debate just did violence to my psyche. My whole family was there. Judge Lowell Mundorff was going to moderate it, but we immediately got into an argument about whether it should be recorded or not. The other side fought it all the way. A woman swung on me with a purse amid the uproar. It was a lynching party-type meeting—completely stacked and engineered by a labor leader, Roy Renoud, who was Edith's faithful shadow.

Her other chief tacticians were Ken Rinke, then the county Democratic chairman and a lobbyist, generally regarded as reasonably ruthless; and even-more-ruthless Howard Morgan, the state chairman. They groomed Edith carefully, moving her around and giving her lots of exposure. They shrewdly exploited our joint appearances—the little woman against the big man. When we would have one of these appearances, she would be down visiting her mother or sister in San Francisco. They were "sick" more that fall than was credible. So, there in her place would be Morgan or Rinke. At the Benson Hotel, Morgan just took off without any relationship to the issues to rip me on natural resources. It was just a bunch of scurrility—but still, a well-calculated, vitriolic attack. So they would work me over. And when Mrs. Green and I would finally get together, I'd be about ready to explode. Here was the big man being discourteous to the little woman.

My name became a burning issue. Rinke said I was flying under false colors because I was calling myself Tom Lawson McCall. I had been a broadcaster under the name of Lawson McCall. He was accusing me, then, of trying to be a man of the people in dry-gulching this very formal name.

When I first went on the air at KGW, they wanted a distinctive name in contrast to all the Jimmy and Bobby, and Mel and Lynn newscasters. Arden X. Pangborn said, "Don't you have a middle name? We'd like to give you a more dignified name."

I said, "Well, here are my names—Thomas William Lawson McCall."

"Lawson McCall, that's fine," Pang said.

He was excited about it. I never really cared for it too much. You could date my friends before and after 1944, by the ones who called me Tom and the ones who called me Lawson. I got back to Tom Lawson as soon as I could.

Mervin Shoemaker, the political editor of the *Oregonian*, de-flated Rinke's issue by publishing my commission from Governor McKay, dated July 1, 1949. It said, "Having faith in you, I hereby appoint Tom Lawson McCall."

During the campaign, House Speaker Joseph W. Martin flew to Oregon to give me a supposed boost. I winced when, in his major speech in Portland, he urged us to be fair to our Indian brethren. And, at a fund-raising breakfast the next morning, I tried to look grateful when he said, "Congress needs him. The Republicans need him in Washington. Please send us Douglas McCall." He later introduced Cordon as "My good friend, Cy Gordon."

There was a poll three weeks before the election, showing I couldn't possibly win. I had to go through all the motions, any-way.

Hal Short's advertising firm was handling our account. They put together the raunchiest speech I'd ever read, which was ab-solutely out of character for me—about "labor bosses pulling the strings that made this little lady dance and flip." We had this meeting in the Congress Hotel to decide whether to use the speech on radio. I shouted, "I wouldn't touch one word of that crap!" I thew it out the window, into the well of the Congress Hotel.

Joe Smith, my chairman, was sitting on the bed and seemed to be having a heart attack. He said, "I'm going to ask you one thing. It may be my last request. Give that speech."

"All right, I said, knowing he had a history of heart trouble. "Go get it," I said to somebody. "Bring it back up. Clean it up and I'll consider it."

Suddenly, Joe sprang to his feet perfectly well.

They were mistaken thinking I could win by going to the gutter. And I did go to the gutter. It was the most shameful thing I ever did. People said it cost me the election, but I had already been down too many points.

I hit my peak when I beat Angell. Everybody was completely surprised and said, "Look at this new powerhouse." The real truth was that Edith had the horses. Helen Stoll, a Democratic activist from a Portland Republican enclave, organized the best telephone campaign Portland had ever had.

We had more people ringing doorbells than had ever done so in the district. I would jog along and the station wagon would be running down the street, and I would trot beside it. There would be five or six of my people in the block and they would say, "The candidate is in the neighborhood if you would like to talk to him." So I was there, just as if I was ringing every doorbell.

In an October 26 editorial, the *Oregon Journal* endorsed me as "an ardent fighter against waste and corruption in government. . . an internationalist in the Eisenhower tradition, a true liberal in the fields of civil rights and social welfare." They were trying to show that I was genuinely different from Cordon and McKay.

On election night, we had a rousing reception at the Congress Hotel. Just before midnight, I was 2,700 votes ahead. Bill Hedlund, a lobbyist whose father had been appointed postmaster by Franklin D. Roosevelt, said, "Tom, you don't have enough of a lead to survive the wave of votes from the north end." The north end was solidly Democratic.

The *Oregonian* came and said, "You're ahead. Why don't you and Audrey give each other a congratulatory clutch so we can get a beautiful picture." We obliged them even though we doubted if I'd survive when the counting began the next morning.

When they started counting the north end, the truth became evident. Edith defeated me by about 9,500 votes out of nearly 200,000. A small group of friends began consoling each other. Shirley Field and Marion Hughes gathered Audrey and me in, and we went over to Jim Hart's. He was a professor at Portland State, a great friend and a liberal Democrat who had come out for me in the campaign. We just sort of drowned our sorrows. I remember roaring up Canyon Road in Marion's red jeep, all of us singing in the gloomy belly of defeat.

The only consolation in the returns was that I had run some 4,000 votes ahead of Cordon in Multnomah County.

I scrawled out this concession statement:

"My warmest congratulations to Edith Green on her solid victory in the third congressional district. I wish her every success in her great assignment in the nation's capital. It was my wish to save the district for President Eisenhower that drew me into the race in the first place. I sincerely trust that Mrs. Green will put the good of America above narrow partisan considerations and give the President the backing he deserves in all matters that manifestly stand for a stronger, more prosperous, more peaceful America.

"Good luck, Edith."

Some editors and reporters wanted to get the two candidates together to discuss our evaluation of the campaign. I asked, "Will she be at the *Oregonian*? I'll come downtown." The newsroom stopped and everybody withdrew when I came in. Edith and I walked back and forth in an open circle. The *Oregonian* people were deferential to our privacy. It was sort of tearful. I had my arm around her. I wasn't completely stoned. I had only had a few drinks. "All I ask, Edith, is that you be fair with President Eisenhower."

I'm not sure if Mrs. Green could have defeated Angell nose to nose in 1954. She certainly would have the next time. In those days, she was perceived as the liberal. Later, when she shifted to the right, I stayed where I had always been—in the middle of the political spectrum.

We became good friends in later years. She had a pretty good political antennae and sensed that I could be elected governor. In 1963 she told me that she'd give speeches all over the state for me, if I would change parties, become a Democrat, and run for governor.

We moved from a position of wariness, dislike and distrust to a mutual trust and friendship. When I was chairman of the Education Commission of the States, I introduced her as the "First Lady of American Education." I offered to appoint her Superintendent of Public Instruction when she retired from Congress in 1974. She was among the trustees at Linfield College, who invited me to become president.

I damned near went broke as a result of my 1954 defeat. Nobody wanted to sponsor me on radio. I was Mr. Republican.

John Higgins, a Portland lawyer and Republican power broker, who had once been the Wall Street law partner of John Foster Dulles, gave me just enough money to eat in exchange for helping some Republican legislators with their press work. It was a very low level of existence. I didn't even have enough to starve on properly.

Edith Green defeated McCall in the 1954 congressional race. She later urged McCall to run for governor.

CHAPTER 3

Prime Time

It was difficult trying to find a sponsor so that I could resume doing the news. An advertising executive bluntly explained that I was "Mr. Republican" and said, "Our bank has just as many Democratic depositors as Republican. We can't inject partisanship into this thing."

For a brief period, I went into the public relations business, full time. I had written some releases before, helping out my old night city editor on the *Oregonian,* Holly Goodrich. His fledgling firm had consisted of him and his sister, Mary Goodrich. Whenever he needed me, I was available. I didn't get into politics or any con- troversy—just straight, commercial, grist-of-the-mill publicity.

After my defeat, Holly and I organized the public relations firm of Goodrich, McCall and Snyder with a good friend of mine, Ed Snyder. We held forth in the Terminal Sales Building on Port- land's West Side. One of our first accounts was the Masonry Association, the people who do brickwork. We won a bid to handle the Oregon Trucking Association account. We started con- tests about "driver of the year" and "truckeramas" and things like that to produce a better image. I think we got $150 a month from the Truckers' Association.

These were the days when publicity was a strange and alien word. To get your foot in the door, you had to take what would now be incredibly low compensation so you could expose them to what you hoped publicity would do. Public relations was very much on a trial basis with most businesses. Now, it is in-house in any organization of any size. Our business was low-key and apolitical. We didn't do any lobbying.

Goodrich and Snyder are still associated. And we remain friends. But I missed doing the news when I was in the firm.

Public relations struck me as drudgery. It wasn't as inspiring as the news. You weren't engaging with a commodity that had all the spontaneity of a breaking news story. It was all right. But you were just hacking and whacking the stuff out. In broadcasting, you not only found the news and wrote it, you also delivered it. That integration was much more challenging.

By June of 1955, the "Mr. Republican" stigma had worn off. I got into television as a newscaster and commentator for KPTV. Ivan Smith was the news director and we worked very well together.

Unhappily, there were some outcries about my work. People read different meanings into things I was saying and writing. I was a great admirer of Adlai Stevenson. But Oregon's Democratic Central Committee claimed I was "unduly partisan." This sort of thing wouldn't even have been thought of if I hadn't run for office, so it was very difficult to get re-established.

Political and government reporting was my specialty. There was an attitude of wariness about broadcasters in the State Capitol. I know when there was a fight, in 1953, over broadcasting a legislative hearing by radio, the *Oregonian* took the position that "the radio microphone had no place in the hearing room." Their thinking was that it would cause a lot of posing by politicians and witnesses and the session would be prolonged by legislators trying to make history. But former Governor Charles Sprague, publisher of the *Oregon Statesman*, took just the opposite view.

I had permission from the leadership, I thought, to broadcast what was expected to be a volatile welfare hearing. There was a certain uneasiness in the committee because Senator Warren Gill, a Republican from Lebanon, felt that at least one broadcaster had been bootlegging material with hidden microphones and then excerpting the material in such a way that in his case he felt violently misquoted. Anyhow, Henry Semon, an ultra-conservative Democratic leader from Klamath Falls, was one of the people who rescinded the permission. Gill was a member of the Senate Establishment and had a lot of sympathy among his colleagues.

It was my protest and Governor Sprague's that caused the Senate and House to call emergency caucuses. They lifted the ban and the broadcast went on. I told them, "We'll show you that you can excerpt, you can reduce a two- or three-hour hearing to 30 minutes. An objective selector of the material can do that." So this was one of the most careful cutting jobs in the history of radio. I put on a 30-minute version later. I think it did a lot to allay the suspicions of the Legislature and open up its proceedings.

It was a marked departure from the long-held prejudices against broadcast journalism. Instead of covering hearings and public matters with a pen and pencil, reporters could now use a microphone and tape. It was a landmark in open government, a step forward for journalism and freedom of the press.

At KPTV, the major political story of the year was the upcoming race for the U.S. Senate. Governor Paul Patterson, perhaps the most popular public figure in the state, was urged by the White House and Attorney General Herbert Brownell to run against Senator Morse in 1956. Patterson, who had easily won the governorship in 1954, while Cordon and I went down to defeat, would have been a formidable candidate.

Patterson launched his campaign on January 28, 1956. Three days later, he met with his advisors John Higgins and Ted Gamble at the Arlington Club. They were to map out his strategy against Morse, but Patterson suddenly was stricken. A doctor was quickly called. Patterson died, minutes later, from the heart attack.

His death at the Arlington Club gave Democrats an unspoken issue. The club, where Oregon's power brokers held court, had always been a whipping boy in campaigns. Most of the time Democrats used it against Republicans, yet when McKay ran for re-election against Austin Flegel, in 1950, he effectively campaigned against "the Arlington Club liberal." Flegel was a member and a wealthy businessman. In his campaign brochures, he posed in a lumberman's shirt. On this, McKay really nailed him.

So when Patterson died there, it did not go unnoticed. Howard Morgan, the most brutally caustic man I've ever known, said,

"The Democrats would have been smarter. They would have wrapped the body in a rug or carpet and carried it across the park blocks and dumped it in front of the Roosevelt Hotel" (a strong union house).

I covered the state funeral for Governor Patterson at the State Capitol. Secretary McKay attended. After the services, when I was in the outer offices of the Governor's Office, Secretary McKay grabbed me by the arm and we went into the Ceremonial Office. We sat down around the corner, in two chairs where nobody could see us. He said, "I have to know what you think about my chances to beat Wayne Morse." Since my victory over Angell, McKay had quite a bit of respect for me as a political seer.

"They don't exist," I told him. "You wouldn't have a chance of a snowball in Hell. You can blame your friends out here for not upholding you or supporting you—or the Republicans for not being enthusiastic enough. But this happens to be a fact of life. Your popularity has been destroyed in Oregon." I tried to be gentle and not put the blame on him.

Visibly shaken, he said, "If you feel that is the case, I've got to hurry back and get with President Eisenhower before Herb Brownell, Len Hall and Sherman Adams get to him. They are going to advise him to urge me to run for the Senate against Morse."

It struck a chilly note. I think he believed me. Everybody had been pounding him on the back and not telling him the truth. That's the trouble with politics. Politicians hardly ever get the truth. They move in an aura of friendship—some of it highly fabricated. I suppose anybody who wants to be really frank with them says, "But why should I take the risk of ruining this beautiful relationship?" Kings of old expressed their gratitude to lieutenants from the front lines who reported that the battle was going badly by slaying them.

The politician doesn't hear enough criticism. So he resents it. He thinks it is negative and counterproductive, but in this instance, Mrs. McKay was adamant against his running. "Why give up being one among ten Cabinet members for one among 96 senators?" she said then. Finally, as a good trouper, she went along with the idea when President Eisenhower asked Secretary McKay to run.

Eisenhower was anxious to have Morse, his most outspoken detractor, defeated. A poll financed by John Higgins and sent to Thomas E. Dewey showed McKay leading Morse in Oregon. The poll was shown to McKay by Adams, Brownell and Hall. They apparently convinced McKay that it was his duty to resign and run against Morse. So when Eisenhower gave his blessing to the idea, McKay went along like a good soldier.

I didn't know about it until the last minute. Nobody in Oregon had been notified. Governor Elmo Smith and State Republican Chairman Wendell Wyatt heard rumors and tried, without success, to find out what was going on. McKay's closest friend, William Phillips, a Salem Ford automobile dealer, had been left out of the decision-making process.

On March 8, McKay flew to Oregon, using a pseudonym on the airplane and at the Multnomah Hotel. Late that night, he called former State Senator Philip Hitchcock and Lamar Tooze, a Portland lawyer, the two announced candidates for the Republican Senate nomination. He invited them to breakfast the next morning.

I met him in his hotel suite, shortly after his meeting with the two candidates. Tooze was elated that McKay was going to run, but Hitchcock would not get out of the race. McKay was very distressed, for Sherman Adams had told him that there would be no primary opposition. Apparently nobody had bothered to check with Hitchcock. McKay told me he didn't know what to do. He checked back with the White House and was told that a press release was about to be distributed announcing his resignation. So he went to Salem and, at the last minute, filed for the Senate.

There was much resentment that McKay had been pushed into the race by the White House. Governor Sprague, an old friend of McKay's, wrote a scathing editorial against White House interference in state politics. Hitchcock, who had a brilliant record in the Legislature, had a strong appeal to younger voters. He received 99,296 votes to McKay's 123,281 in the May primary. I suspect Hitchcock, who had none of McKay's Washington, D.C. liabilities, would have given Morse a good run.

But the Morse-McKay campaign was an exciting one to cover. The two men had run together in 1950, yet they were bitter adversaries within two years. President Eisenhower came to Portland on McKay's behalf—against the advice of his brother Edgar Eisenhower, a Tacoma, Washington lawyer.

Perhaps the most dramatic confrontation of the campaign was their debate in the Crystal Room of the Benson Hotel. It was before a Republican audience, which applauded McKay's opening attack on Morse. But the senator pulled a telegram from his pocket and, his voice ringing with indignation, disclosed that McKay had asked him to abstain from voting on a tidelands oil bill if he couldn't support it.

"When my opponent sent me that wire he disqualified himself for all time from holding political office," Morse said. "It means he advised me to walk out on my convictions, to walk out on my intellectual honesty. That I have never done and will never do."

It was tremendously dramatic. But McKay was such a believer in free enterprise that it did not shock him. He just believed that the preservation of the free enterprise system was one of the justifications of his serving in public life. He was simply not the type who took money under the table. He had principles that were as rigid and unbending as Morse's. In this age of environmental consciousness, the candidate who sent that telegram would have dropped through the floor and never shown his face again. But McKay surged back and forth, taking the fight to Morse that day.

The morning after McKay's defeat, I went to see him in a dumpy little campaign headquarters on the West Side of Portland. He was very philosophical. "You know, it's the first time I ever lost," he said. "And I think it's an experience that would benefit everyone." It had been a bitter, raucous campaign, and still he came out a pretty normal citizen.

In mid-November, 1956, not long after that campaign, I was unceremoniously fired by KPTV. The *Oregonian's* "Behind the Mike" column described it this way:

"KPTV is minus its two top newscasters—Tom McCall and Ivan Smith—as the result of a blowup just before the News Central program was to take the air the other afternoon.

"The fuss was over a banner and some cans of merchandise that were to have been used as a background during the program. Since the sponsor had bought only a spot and not the entire program, Smith refused to go on with the advertising material showing all the time. He quit before the show.

"Studio executives then asked McCall to take over Smith's part of the program in addition to his own. McCall refused, saying he didn't want to be a quisling. McCall expects to stay in the TV business a long time, must get along with others in it, so felt he shouldn't be asked to take over work others have declined to do. McCall thereupon was fired."

What really happened was that a studio executive turned to me and offered to double my income. "All right, Tom, you take over tonight and you're the news director," he said.

"I have to live with my friends," I answered. "Whether we live in a piano box down on the mud flat on the Willamette, I'm going to stay with my friends."

I put on my old felt hat and walked out with Ivan.

There were several missed paychecks. But Crown Stations, Inc., of Seattle, had finally won approval for KGW-TV. They were interviewing people. Tom Dargan was the program director. He was somewhat wary of Ivan and me because of what happened at KPTV. Dargan thought we might be troublemakers. We had to live that down to get hired. But he signed both of us on his news team.

So on December 16, 1956, I went on the air as KGW's news analyst. I stayed there for eight years, doing commentaries, documentaries and talk shows. The other members of the news staff— Dick Ross, Ivan Smith, Jack Cappell and Doug LaMear—stayed as a unit for 11 more years. That kind of stability is unusual in such a pressure business where egos are no less sensitive than prima donnas of the opera. I was to become the first defector.

The official KGW announcement said:

"Walter E. Wagstaff, KGW-TV Station Manager and John H. Eichhorn, KGW Radio Station Manager, have announced that Tom McCall has joined the station as news commentator and analyst of local, regional, national and international events.

"McCall will continue his evening editorial on KGW radio, and assume his new duties in the 6:30 news show on KGW-TV."

It was at Channel 8 that I began dealing with issues at length in documentaries. These were programs I would do in a week in grainy black and white, with a director and a cameraman. Perhaps the most significant of these early broadcasts was "Crisis in the Klamath Basin," which we filmed at the Klamath Reservation in the midst of swirling controversy. The great issue was the Indians' million-acre yellow pine forest.

The crisis began when the McKay administration urged Congress to terminate federal trusteeship over the Klamath Indians. A bill, sponsored by Senator Arthur Watkins of Utah and Congressman Sam Coon of Oregon, passed in 1954. Under the Watkins-Coon bill, the Klamaths were given a choice of organizing a private corporation to manage tribal properties; designating a trustee to replace the government as supervisor of the properties; or liquidating the assets, then valued at $100 million, at auction.

At the Menominee Indian Reservation in Wisconsin, which was terminated in this same period, the reservation was consolidated into a county and the tribal council chartered a corporation to manage their timber properties and other interests.

A vocal segment of the Klamaths wanted to sell in anticipation of the $43,500 per person settlement. "Boom and bust" land speculators and lumber interests plotted to control the Klamath Basin.

I warned that the finest stand of yellow pine in North America would have to be clear-cut unless the government intervened. If a company had bought it for $100 million, they would have had to level the whole forest to turn a profit. They couldn't operate under sustained yield management, paying $5 million a year interest. We showed how such action would destroy the economy

McCall interviewing Robert F. Kennedy, then chief counsel of the Senate Rackets Committee. In a commentary, McCall criticized Kennedy's "foul ball" tactics in his questioning of Portland Mayor Terry Schrunk. In later years, McCall praised Kennedy's commitment to civil rights.

McCall interviewed Nobel Peace Prize laureate and United Nations Under-secretary-General Ralph Bunche. "I have a deep-seated bias against hate and intolerance," Bunche told McCall.

of the entire Klamath region. The Isaac Walton League of Oregon gave me their "Golden Beaver" award for this production.

Senator Dick Neuberger showed "Crisis" to the House and Senate Interior committee staffs in Washington. The documentary really sort of caused the issue to come alive. Neuberger made a magnificent thrust with his bill for the Winema National Forest. I believe it was one of the greatest, most striking legislative coups in history. The age of Sputnik had just dawned and public opinion and Congress were bent on catching up with the Soviets. It was into education that we were putting all our dollars. And here was a tribe of Indians, way out in Southern Oregon, that Neuberger managed to get $120 million for. Neuberger was able to use the documentary as an instrument which, combined with his marvelous engineering of the legislative process, produced the funds for the Indians. I don't think Neuberger ever received proper credit for his leadership in preserving the Klamath Basin. If anyone earned the title of "Mr. Conservation," it was Dick Neuberger. Oregon will never have a better senator.

Oddly enough, when Neuberger was first elected, he went back there and made a spectacle of himself. His wife Maurine was still in the Legislature and served that session. During those first few months, he got into some terribly shallow publicity-seeking efforts. For example, he attacked Eisenhower for trying to remove squirrels from the White House lawn. Dick and Maurine were a remarkable team. As soon as she got back there and they were reunited, one drew strength and direction from the other. This resulted in a whole new approach of working with the members and not trying to harass people into doing things, not doing the grandstand play—which was very un-Neuberger like.

I had a friendly relationship with Neuberger. When I was with McKay and Dick was in the Legislature, I had enough of a sense of history to know that he was going to lift the Democratic Party from invisibility and impotence in Republican Oregon if anybody could. I knew what he meant to Oregon, to good government, to conservation and public power.

For all his early rhetoric and publicity seeking, he understood human nature. This knowledge was more important in the U.S. Senate than a lot of speeches and a lot of posing, in getting legislation passed. He was an avid athlete in the sense of doing calisthenics. A lot of companionship, friendship and discussion took place in the Senate Gymnasium. Morse became terribly jealous because Neuberger established a relationship with other senators that Morse hadn't been able to achieve. I am not condemning Morse, for he had chosen to be the outspoken, liberal maverick. Neuberger was remarkably perceptive in picking up the real approach to legislation on Capitol Hill. Morse became dedicated to Neuberger's destruction. He was the hardest hater I've ever known.

Neuberger and I had worked together on civil rights issues during the time we were both in Salem. And we shared similar views. He paid me the high tribute of nominating me for the executive directorship of President Eisenhower's Civil Rights Commission. He made a speech on my behalf from the Senate floor and sent a letter to Attorney General Brownell. He wrote:

"Let me begin by telling you that Mr. McCall is a Republican and therefore not of my political party. . . . In 1954 Mr. McCall was a candidate for Congress from the 3rd Oregon congressional district when I actively supported his victorious Democratic opponent, Mrs. Edith S. Green.

"However, the position as executive director of the civil rights commission should be beyond partisan considerations. . . . I am confident that Mr. McCall is fully qualified, from the standpoint of philosophy and ability, to serve as executive director of the civil rights commission."

It came as no surprise that the Republican White House did not heed the recommendation of Oregon's liberal Democratic senator. But I was appreciative of Neuberger's generous gesture.

What seemed a more promising opportunity to return to public service came on election night in 1958. Secretary of State Mark O. Hatfield had defeated Governor Robert D. Holmes for the governorship. Mark had a very interesting administrative assistant named Travis Cross. Travis and I worked tremendously well together. I had asked him to be my administrative assistant in Congress back in 1954. He had his house on the market. At the time, he was assistant to the Chancellor of Higher Education. Travis was with Hatfield on election night as the governor-elect came through the KGW studio for some election-night interviews.

"I'm going to have a tough decision as to whether I am going to stay on the first floor with you or go to the second floor with Mark as governor," Travis told me.

It was a semi-subtle way of letting me know that Mark was considering me for Secretary of State—more than considering me, I felt. So, a few days later, I went down to Salem to have an audience with Mark that Travis had arranged. We talked for nearly two hours. Our conversation was general. We talked about state government, the Secretary of State's office, the governorship and the national Democratic landslide.

I never heard a word from Mark until I wrote him about six weeks later and said I felt I was owed the courtesy of some kind of response. I don't know what happened. Maybe I wasn't properly deferential. I thought I had been fairly cooperative.

During our meeting, Mark had some private papers on his desk. Among them was a receipt for a car payment. I looked at the receipt—just glancing at it. Perhaps he had it there simply to see if I was nosey. I never could tell. I was never able to figure out what I had done not even to rate the courtesy of being told, "Thanks for coming down. I think I might go some other way. I hope you'll help me in my administration." Or, simply, "I'd like to see you continue your fine career as a journalist."

My relationship with Hatfield has always been kind of prickly. He finally chose Howell Appling, Jr., a tall, conservative Portland businessman—and transplanted Texan—who had been Multnomah County chairman of Hatfield's campaign. Holmes and Hatfield became embroiled in a controversy over which would name a Secretary of State. Holmes contended that Hatfield must present a formal resignation as Secretary of State before he could be sworn in as governor. Holmes appointed David O'Hara, longtime head of the Elections Division of the Secretary of State's office, as Hatfield's successor. The Oregon Supreme Court upheld Hatfield's position and Appling took office with the new governor.

As a newsman, I covered Hatfield pretty well. I remember one day when the Legislature was cutting out Civic Defense and he called a news conference. I said, "Governor, naturally you're concerned about civil defense. But you're an educator. Don't I hear any outcry at all about what is happening to the budgets for education?"

Hatfield rose to the bait, lambasting the Ways and Means Committee for being penurious toward education. This was where he talked about the "Meat Axe" Ways and Means Committee. To this day, every one of those legislators on that committee wears a gold meat axe symbol on his lapel.

Another incident I remember involved the question of whether to have a special session of the Legislature. It was a very hot issue. Hatfield and Senate President Ben Musa already were feuding over something else: the squawk box Mark had in his office, so he could listen to the Legislature's floor debates. Musa saw it there and just exploded. He said Hatfield was eavesdropping on the Legislature. So Hatfield pulled it up by the roots and said, "Here, take it!" (When I became governor, I put the squawk box back in. I told legislative leaders, "You ought to be delighted. The governor can't go in and listen to the debate. But you don't mind if I listen, do you? I want to know what you're doing. I want to be informed.")

When Hatfield, Musa and House Speaker Clarence Barton finally got together to make a decision about the special session, I was standing in the outer office along with most of the Capitol press corps. Hatfield, Musa and Barton walked into the Ceremonial Office and locked the double doors—right in our faces. Here they were about to make a most important decision—and the press was rudely brushed aside.

I did a blistering commentary that night on secrecy and the lack of openness in state government. I helped expose how this decision of great vitality to our state was made behind closed doors. "Why couldn't the press have been in on this decision?" I asked. When I showed up at the Capitol the next morning, I was hailed by Ken Rinke, who reported that Hatfield was furious.

I used to have periods of indignation. They were fairly rare—you can't just run on indignation as a routine. But I didn't like it when Mayor Terry Schrunk was gaffed by Bobby Kennedy in that foul-ball rackets hearing in Washington, D.C. I became indignant at Hatfield's closed administration—when, as in the case of the special session meeting, a major question was being decided.

My attitude probably didn't endear me to Hatfield. He did, however, appoint me to his Blue Ribbon Committee on Reorganization. It was a prestigious committee, with former governors Sprague and Holmes presiding on it.

Hatfield was something of an enigma to those of us who tried to analyze him. Sometimes he would use phrases that if there were five people hearing him, they would get five different interpretations of it. He gave a stirring Keynote Address at the 1964 Republican National Convention in which he condemned right-wing extremism. But then he turned around and loaned Travis Cross to Barry Goldwater. Hatfield, almost alone among leading Republican moderates, campaigned for Goldwater. Perhaps it was the upward-mobility factor. He was always looking ahead for potholes in the road or flowers at the roadside.

The most ambitious effort in my years at KGW-TV was "Pollution in Paradise," a documentary which described the Willamette River as "an open sewer." It was the idea of Tom Dargan, our program director and now my boss again, at KATU-TV in Portland. Dargan is a crusader and a great devotee of public service programming. I had sort of been hinting, in some of my commentaries, that perhaps Oregon had symptoms of malaise—environmental malaise—that had attacked the Potomac, the Cuyahoga and a lot of other streams and areas man had laid waste to. So Dargan suggested that we ought to get on the back of the State Sanitary Authority because of the deterioration of the Willamette. Our plan was to ring an alarm for the people of Oregon, to say,

"You think pollution is something that is happening someplace else. But here are the symptoms of these afflictions right here in Oregon. Let's get working on them."

We started filming way up with the cleanest water and the smallest rivulet contributing to the Willamette River system. Then, we showed what happened to this water as it went down, showing how it had become one of the most polluted rivers in the West. It was unfit for swimming. Indeed, it was so filled with wastes during the fall that salmon could not move upstream. The oxygen level of water at the mouth of the river was nearly zero.

Air pollution was another horror story. We filmed the flow of the atmospheric effluent from the Crown Zellerbach plants up in Camas. It was just a direct flow into Portland. I can remember reading a Harvey Plant press release claiming that their incoming plant at The Dalles would be non-polluting and free of emissions. As I read the press release, we showed their smoke stack with everything coming out of it except poison gas.

I went on location when the shooting was being done. We got trunkloads of materials, especially when we got into water pollution and the pulp and paper industry. After nearly a year of work, I really became stultified with the thing. I couldn't face it anymore. It was virtually done—though it was a bit too long. So Bob McBride, who had been with the Portland *Reporter*, came over to KGW and finished it up. I had done most of the writing and then narrated the film.

We tried to put over such points as cleaning up pollution should be looked at as a cost of doing business. Shortly after the story was broadcast, we got a citation from the Salem City Council. They credited "Pollution in Paradise" with passing a huge bond issue for sewage facilities. Later, KGW-TV received a national Sigma Delta Chi award for the outstanding documentary film of 1962.

"Pollution" represented quite an effort for a local station. I think we put about $18,000 into it. It was a pioneering effort and was the first really dramatic message of that kind that local television had tried as far as we can tell. KGW made copies of it and

"Pollution" has been shown all over Oregon and across the United States. It is sort of crude when you look at it now. But it still holds up pretty well. I was proud of the constant direction we took in behalf of the environment in our news analyses and editorials as well, and in commentaries on both radio and television.

I continued doing documentaries and my commentaries until the spring of 1964. Secretary of State Appling, then regarded as the heir apparent for the governorship, suddenly announced he would not run for re-election. Hatfield called me and suggested that I run. He and Appling wheedled me for several weeks to fill the vacuum by running for Secretary of State and, if I made it, to seek the governorship two years later. I wavered back and forth.

"I know how hard it is," Appling told me. "I didn't want to do it. I thought of turning down Mark's offer in 1958. I just pondered."

It was tough for me to decide so relatively soon after the congressional debacle of 1954. Memories of lost paychecks, dead-horse political debts and a nasty campaign still wrenched.

Hal Lesser

Television news analyst McCall covered the opening of the 1957 Oregon Legislature. He later won a national award for his documentary, "Pollution in Paradise."

CHAPTER 4

Road to the Governorship

It was a dilemma. I was willing to make another try at politics. But I didn't know if I could afford to do it. The turning point for me came when I happened to be getting a Coke at the same time as Tom Dargan. There was a red Coke machine in this dimly lit corridor right outside the newsroom.

"Dammit, Tom," I said, "I could only be governor if you'd let me."

He said, "I think it would be great. How do I stand in your way?"

I discussed my conversations with Hatfield and Appling and how Federal Communications Commission regulations would make it impossible for me to keep appearing on the air while campaigning. Dargan knew that I would have no security, no way of making a living if I became a candidate. He urged me to run and devised a plan to keep me on salary. "We're going to be doing a documentary on cybernetics and you'd go into a research phase there. While you wouldn't be on the air, you would still be the writer and researcher."

So because of that chance meeting at the Coke machine, I was able to file as a candidate for Secretary of State in March of 1964.

Shortly afterward, I had a luncheon appointment with Ed Westerdahl and Ron Schmidt at the Aladdin Restaurant, to begin planning the campaign. Despite their youth—both were 28—they seemed confident and self-assured about political matters. I told them my concern about not going into debt. They convinced me that raising campaign money would be no problem. When the waiter brought the check, I was stiffed with the bill.

Schmidt immediately began cultivating the movers and shakers of Portland. One of the first people he called was John Higgins, the crusty old patron of Oregon Republicanism. Higgins almost always contributed $1,000 or more to the party's statewide candidates. So Ron called Higgins to ask for help.

"Yes, I'll have something for Tom McCall," Higgins said. Ron put on a conservative suit and went to the old man's apartment, which was next to the University Club. A male secretary gave Ron an envelope with my name on it. Since this appeared to be our first substantial contribution, a modest celebration was planned at our headquarters at 340 S.W. 5th. With this financial boost, the campaign would be launched.

When we opened the envelope, there was a long pause. Higgins had donated all of one dollar to the McCall campaign. To the Old Guard, I was apparently still on Mrs. Gerlinger's "dreadful persons" list.

In the primary, I was opposed by Dan Mosee, a Portland businessman who later became a Democrat and is now a Multnomah County commissioner. At joint appearances in the spring of 1964, I would attack him as a John Bircher and he would grab me by the tie and say, "What's wrong with the John Birch Society?"

I carried 35 of 36 counties against Mosee. Oddly, the only county I lost was Malheur County where I had my most powerful chairman, State Senator Tony Yturri. I could never figure out what happened until Tony explained that everyone in that center of Basquedom thought Mosee was Basque. It was just a quirk.

My Democratic opponent was State Senator Alf Corbett. Alf was truly first class competition, the kind of man you don't like to drive from public life. He was wise, honest, and had a calm approach to government. But he didn't have much color and spark.

Since I was heading the state Republican ticket, Alf did his best to associate me with presidential candidate Barry Goldwater. He kept asking, "Do you support Goldwater or Johnson?" He asked the question far too many times because people began rooting for me and saying it was none of his business and it was my right as a private citizen to cast a private ballot. Taxi drivers and people I saw on the street would shout, "Don't ya' tell him!"

I had strong misgivings about Goldwater and felt compelled to speak out. Wade Newbegin of the R.M. Wade Company, the biggest manufacturer of irrigation pipes in the country, confronted me in my office one afternoon. We had a really wild shouting match on Goldwater. I finally conceded, "All right, I won't attack Goldwater—but I'm not going to support him."

Goldwater was a tremendous albatross to moderate Republicans. He pulled Charles Percy down to defeat in the Illinois gubernatorial race and torpedoed Robert A. Taft, Jr.'s senate bid in Ohio. In Oregon, he lost by more than 250,000 votes, yet Oregonians were perceptive enough to realize that Goldwater was extrinsic to the Secretary of State election and the purpose of that office. I was elected by a comfortable margin and Republicans won control of the Oregon House of Representatives. Still, I had campaigned so hard that I had to spend the final week of the campaign in the hospital in Klamath Falls. In those final days Audrey and Wendell Wyatt campaigned in my place.

Ed Westerdahl had been an extraordinary campaign manager. Our personalities were opposites. I thought he was a bullheaded right-winger. He thought I was a flabby liberal. Westerdahl was so well organized and so effective working on the issues that I found him indispensable in the campaign. But we had some heated exchanges.

One Saturday, Audrey and I went to a University of Oregon football game in Eugene. After the game, Tad came over with a young friend of his and they wanted a beer. So we had a couple of beers in our motel, and Ed came in. The next day, Ed was driving me down to the beach in his station wagon. We were about half way between Eugene and the coast when he said, "You shouldn't have done that. That's dangerous. You could get in trouble."

I said, "You rotten s.o.b., stop this car! I've taken the last criticism I'm ever going to take. Get out! Fight!"

Then, to show the power and control of the man, he just took it and kept driving. I said again and again during that campaign: "There never was a man my age with such a young Dutch Uncle, and I'm fed up to here with it!" A few days after my election, Ed was sitting under an apple tree in my front yard. He asked if he could be my Assistant Secretary of State.

I said, "God, we couldn't stand any more of each other. It just wouldn't work."

I picked Clay Myers, who had been vice president of the Insurance Company of Oregon, as my Assistant Secretary. And I retained Harold Phillippe, a career official with 44 years in state government, as the other Assistant Secretary of State.

Howell Appling had a good image as an administrator. He appealed to many conservatives. He was great on the old shibboleths that you run on economy. What he did was to set up a fee operation in the Secretary of State's office so the agencies for which his office was performing services would pay for them. Thus, instead of his budget going up, it went down. He was really a tremendous economizer.

One of the first things I did was to allocate funds for the restoration of Willson Park. The park, just west of the Capitol and owned by the City of Salem, had been destroyed by the October 12, 1962 Columbus Day Storm. Because the city couldn't afford to fix it up, I made arrangements to do so—even though it was going to cost $73,000. One of the main duties of the Secretary of State is being custodian of the Capitol building and grounds. I negotiated with the city and with the legislature, got the necessary appropriations and some federal funds for the storm damage, and took over the park.

Both Bob Straub, who had just been elected State Treasurer, and I took the position that our jobs weren't as narrow as the duties that were listed in the Oregon *Blue Book*, that we were indeed concerned citizens of the State of Oregon. Straub and I got into a big advance of the concept of quality of life.

Hatfield had introduced the phrase "livability." The most courageous statement he ever made and certainly the most accurate on the environmental front was his attack on the "twenty miserable miles" on the Oregon Coast. His record on land-use planning had been undistinguished. He was a grabber for payrolls at almost any cost. Straub and I brought a more rational approach to economic development, putting the balance between economic development and the environment into focus.

"The idea of livability alone is an incentive for big industry to move to Oregon," I said in a 1965 interview. "We will be able to pick what industries might settle in our state—specifically those that won't pollute our air and water."

Straub and I had the wider duties also of the State Board of Control memberships, as well as the Land Board. Corrections and Mental Health fell under our jurisdictions. We both took leadership in those fields as well as in education and the environment. The two of us were broader in our approach to serving in those offices than any of the occupants had been prior to that time.

In my first 100 days as Secretary of State, I did not miss a day at the office—including Saturdays and Sundays. I gave a report on my "First 110 days" in a luncheon speech before the East Portland Rotary Club. I told them the state office was so time-consuming that I didn't know as much about what went on at the Capitol "as I did back in the days when I got around as a newsman."

Howell Appling had enjoyed considerable success cultivating an image as a ruthless watchdog of the public treasury. And I retained his billing procedures. There was no use being suicidal about it, yet I felt a responsibility to do some things—like Willson Park, which he wouldn't touch. I believe that Appling would have been forced to recognize, had he continued in office, that his economy drive had bottomed out and some upward adjustment was necessary to improve essential services. Appling thought there was at least inferential criticism of the way he ran the office in the way I ran it. Within a year after he had urged me to run for his job, Appling was heading a committee to support House Speaker F. F. "Monte" Montgomery of Eugene for the governorship. Appling's support made Montgomery, an able legislative leader, a formidable challenger for the Republican nomination.

Gerald W. Frank, a Salem businessman and former head of the Salem Meier & Frank Co., who was Governor Hatfield's closest friend, fervently wanted to succeed Hatfield as governor. *News-*

week's "Periscope" column disclosed that Hatfield was setting the stage for Frank's candidacy. Frank, instead, chose to manage Hatfield's 1966 campaign for the Senate.

The most experienced and politically astute contender for the governorship was Senate Minority Leader Anthony Yturri of Ontario. On December 9, 1965, Yturri suddenly announced his withdrawal from the race "for health and personal reasons." If there ever was a "Mr. Republican" of Oregon it was Yturri. We had been classmates at the University of Oregon. My brother, Harry, and Yturri had been classmates at the university's law school. A month after Tony's withdrawal, Harry and I were having dinner at Chuck's Steak House in Salem. We hadn't seen Tony for some time and there he was. All the old buddies got together. It was really warm and friendly. Midway through the evening I said, "How about a hand, Tony, old boy?" He came through with a rip-roaring endorsement that broke the back of Montgomery's conservative support.

On January 31, three days after Yturri's endorsement, Montgomery dropped out of the race. Monte had talked about a target date—something like 180 days—in which he was going to build up his standing in the polls. Apparently, he was not doing as well as he had hoped. That, combined with the Yturri announcement, was probably decisive.

I always liked Monte. Had he been a candidate for governor, we would have kept to the issues in a clean, hard-fought campaign. When I declared my own candidacy in January, it was an exhausting day with news conferences in Portland, Oregon City, Salem and Eugene.

"There is only one real reason to seek the governorship—or, for that matter, any public office," I said, "and that is to reach a higher vantage point from which to come to grip with the issues."

Bob Straub was my Democratic opponent. Although our polls showed me leading him from the start, I felt it would probably go right down to the wire. Straub had amazing resiliency. He had served as Lane County Commissioner, State Senator and Democratic State Chairman. In 1962 his political fortunes seemed to be declining when he finished third in the Fourth Congressional District's Democratic primary. Bob came back in 1964 with an aggressive, hard-hitting campaign and upset Republican State Treasurer Howard Belton. Straub's candidacy could not be taken lightly. He was a strong person, physically. He could plod the campaign trail day and night and hold up. Moreover, he was running as the candidate of the party which had a great majority of the voters registered. I looked at him as solid-caliber competition.

Both sides conducted the campaign on a high level. The press described our campaign as the "Tom and Bob Show" because we agreed on so much, yet there were certain periods of nastiness. I remember Straub's people had Joey Tompkins take a picture of what were allegedly discarded Voter's Pamphlets—discarded by the printer because we had laid them out wrong. But instead of taking the picture of the Voter's Pamphlets, they took a picture of all the excess from one of the printing houses. They had a great debate over whether to use it or not. Better judgment prevailed and they didn't. It would have been a falsified ad and Oregonians have never looked kindly on political dirty tricks.

The Voter's Pamphlet is almost always a great issue to use against a Secretary of State because it is impossible to get it published with all the variations you have to make in a relatively short time frame.

I gave Straub credit for first enunciating from the platform the Willamette Greenway concept. We both had gotten material on it from the same man, Dean Karl W. Onthank of the University of Oregon. Onthank, who was an avid outdoorsman, had sent us both a file on the American River Greenway near Sacramento. He was a friend of both of ours—so he made it available to both of us. I had been keeping it and thinking about it and considered it a good idea. Straub and I both were speaking to the Parks Association in the Eugene Hotel and that's when he said we ought to have the Willamette River Greenway. He did it in the morning and I followed him the next day. There was enough interval in between so that the *Oregonian* attacked him for proposing such a far-out

Oregon Secretary of State Howell Appling, Jr., briefed his successor, Tom McCall, after the 1964 election. Appling had been considered a heavy favorite to win the governorship in 1966 prior to his decision to leave public office. He urged McCall to run for Secretary of State, yet later became a bitter critic.

"The Tom and Bob Show" was what the Oregon press nicknamed the 1966 McCall-Straub debates. "They saw that there was great substance to what we were agreeing about," McCall recalled. Straub makes a point during their joint appearance before the Oregon State Employees Association.

idea, not worthy of consideration. But the Eugene *Register-Guard*, being more reflective and having worked with Straub when he was county commissioner and state senator, said it was a great idea. So I went over to the *Register-Guard* and said, "I think it's a great idea, too."

The editors were really relieved. They said, "God, we just thought we were going to get chopped up in the campaign because one guy brought it up and usually in politics the other candidate has to attack it. That's what makes the issues." My grandfather, in a 1917 address to the Massachusetts Legislature, talked about preserving the greenery along scenic highways with a greenway, and I had talked about greenways in the parks' sense. But I have always made it clear that Straub first endorsed the concept from the platform.

The Oregon press was very discerning. They could see that there wasn't much substance to what we were fighting about and there was great substance to what we were agreeing about. That's why it was substantially a campaign of general agreement on what the objective of governance ought to be for the office.

Both of us endorsed Senator Maurine Neuberger's Oregon Dunes National Seashore bill. I notified Senator Alan Bible of Nevada, chairman of the Senate Interior Subcommittee on Public Lands, of my support of the bill, reiterating a position I had taken in a 1959 commentary. Straub also wrote to the Interior Committee. He suggested a joint statement. I checked with Mrs. Neuberger, who indicated that our previous efforts already had made the impact of a joint endorsement. The separate expressions were probably more effective because they were individualistic and spontaneous. We made our point that Oregon's next governor, whoever he was, favored the National Seashore. Senator Morse, who was very jealous of the Neubergers, blocked the Dunes National Park bill. We now have a sort of seashore area that doesn't receive the protection or the funding that the Dunes National Park envisioned by Dick and Maurine Neuberger would have had. Florence was the center of fulmination against Dick

Neuberger's idea. It was the epitome of the narrowness and the backwardness of coastal developers.

An issue I stressed in the closing weeks of the campaign was more citizen participation in state government. In Medford, I announced that if elected governor, I would make periodic visits around the state to discuss local problems. "It's a big state," I said, "and sometimes there is an awesome gap between the Governor's Office and the people in far-flung parts of Oregon." I proposed bimonthly visitations with citizens in their hometown. The plan was inspired by the late President Kennedy who said, "Every citizen holds office."

A few days before the election, President Johnson was scheduled to visit Portland where he would endorse Straub and senate candidate Robert B. Duncan, who was in a close race with Governor Hatfield. Johnson was forced to cancel. But Vice President Humphrey was among several nationally prominent Democrats to come to Oregon that fall.

It was my view that such visits were counterproductive. Senator Robert F. Kennedy of New York endorsed Duncan in a speech at Oregon State University. Vietnam was the great issue between Duncan and Hatfield—and Kennedy made it clear that his position on Vietnam was indistinguishable from Hatfield's.

When former Vice President Richard Nixon was speaking at a dinner at the Memorial Coliseum, I was campaigning in Albany. Many Republican legislators eagerly gathered around Nixon to have their pictures taken for local newspapers and their campaign brochures.

"We Oregonians welcome such dignitaries and are always glad to have them come, except when they come to try to tell us how to vote," I said. "For, then, in effect they are meddling in local and state elections. I would hate to think that my election would depend not on my record, my friendships, my campaign workers and the issues, but on the endorsement of some dignitary who perhaps had never seen me before. I will rest my case in this election on the dialogue between Tom McCall and the people of Oregon—without outside pressure or interference."

Nixon demonstrated the shallowness of the barnstorming campaigner that night in urging Oregonians to elect, "as your next governor, Bob McCall."

On November 8, I was elected Oregon's governor. I received 377,346 votes—a record for an Oregon gubernatorial candidate— to Straub's 305,008. My percentage was 55.3, roughly the same as Hatfield's had been eight years earlier against Governor Holmes.

The next day I began to consider selections for key positions in my administration and to devise a program to make the transition with the outgoing Hatfield administration as smooth as possible. I asked Travis Cross, Hatfield's former press secretary and administrative assistant, to serve as my consultant through Inauguration Day.

On Friday, November 11, I named Assistant Secretary of State Clay Myers, as my successor. The appointment came as a complete surprise to everyone. Many political leaders thought it would have been a great healing thing for me to have appointed House Speaker Montgomery, but Monte would never ask me for it.

There was never a spoken agreement with Clay. He was certainly aware that I intended to ask him to take an important post in any McCall administration. I had worked with Clay since our Young Republican activities in the late 1940s. Later, when I moderated View Point at KGW, I would get Clay when I wanted a bright, modern point of view to be argued well on any topical issue. He was and is probably the top person on reapportionment in the United States. He was co-author of Oregon's legislative reapportionment constitutional amendment approved by the people in 1952. He had the kind of mind Oregon needed to handle the intricacies of the election process. He also had management ability and much familiarity with the Department of State.

When I made the announcement, the press corps gathered in the Secretary of State's office. They kept waiting for the candidate, for the successor, to show up. Clay was standing there with me all the time. The appointment was generally applauded. The Eugene

Register-Guard said Myers was "probably the most qualified man in the state to hold that office."

There was some bitterness and jealousy. State Representative Lee Johnson, who later served as attorney general, had long nurtured gubernatorial ambitions. He was really outraged by Clay's appointment and called me. We proceeded to tear each other up.

I said, "All you're saying is that he's just too god-damned short!"

"Exactly!" he replied.

"If they start running campaigns on that basis," I said, "you're so stupid looking, fat and dull, you wouldn't get anyplace!"

The selection of John Mosser as director of the Department of Finance and Administration was an obvious choice. He was a Republican state representative from Washington County and chairman of the Legislative Fiscal Committee. John had been of great help during the campaign. In announcing Mosser's appointment, I said he would "bring to the position a perspective possessed by none of his predecessors—that of service as a member of the state legislative Ways and Means Committee."

Ed Westerdahl, whom I had rejected as my assistant secretary of state, had returned to manage the gubernatorial campaign. We began to understand each other and saw that we could work together. We still had our conflicts, but we were able to mediate and come to a solution. Shortly after my election, I asked him to become my executive assistant. He was 30, as was Ron Schmidt, whom I named my administrative assistant. They were nicknamed the "Kiddie Corps."

Before appointing Schmidt, I had given some thought to offering the position to Travis Cross. It came down to a choice between a skilled veteran or a young man of great promise. Much as I respected Travis, I chose to go with Ron. He had worked effectively in both my statewide campaigns. Moreover, he had been involved in many areas such as the Oregon Shakespearean Festival, where he had served on the board of directors, and Portland's Lloyd Center, where he had been director of public relations for five years. Where Westerdahl was the pragmatist, Schmidt was the idealist. It was a perfect combination.

Some of my appointments were made quickly. I can remember sitting in the Secretary of State's office with Mosser and Westerdahl, trying to determine who should be my administrative assistant for legal affairs.

John said, "You ought to have Ed Branchfield." Branchfield, a Medford lawyer and Purple Heart veteran of World War II, was a state representative from Jackson County.

As John was making this suggestion, he said: "You know that figure that went by that glass door was about Ed's height."

I shouted, "Hey, Ed, we've got an appointment for you!"

That was how we filled one of our key positions. Branchfield severed a tremendous potential for financial reward over the years in leaving his private law practice to enter full-time state service. He was a man of remarkable equanimity.

I named Wanda Merrill, who had been executive secretary to me in the Secretary of State's office, to the same position in the Governor's office. Like Ed Westerdahl, she was quite conservative. She had strong convictions and had no fear of making them known. A few days after my election as governor, I wrote a letter to Governor-Elect Ronald Reagan of California. Since Reagan had virtually no experience in state government and had run on a rather simplistic platform, I was offering some advice. It was a sort of Dutch Uncle letter, noting that I had been around government a long time and that he had a great challenge and opportunity. I thought Reagan was just going to shorthand it in Sacramento with all these shibboleths of the right wing. I urged him not to knee-jerk it, explaining that he couldn't possibly succeed with telegraphic thoughts from *National Review* or *Human Events.*

Wanda would not type my letter to Reagan. She absolutely refused. She said, "You'll just destroy the relationship between two states, and he's more right than you are!" My letter was never sent.

From the start, I had a friendly relationship with Democratic legislators. Among the first meetings I had, as governor-elect, was an hour session with House Minority Leader Jim Redden of Medford and Minority Whip Jason Boe of Reedsport. I told them of my intention to bring Democrats into key positions in my administration. "I will pick my key people on the basis of their merit, rather than lean on party label," I said.

As a veteran political reporter and analyst, I knew where the experts were and so was able to fashion a team of drive, imagination, daring and skill such as no state Oregon's size had ever seen. The party label of prospective appointees was the last item on the checklist that I looked at, if at all. No Democratic governor of Oregon had ever named so many able Democrats to high state office as I did.

At the same time, some shakeups were required in various administrative agencies. There had been many problems with the Oregon State Fair under its manager, Howard Maple. After careful checking, we determined that he would have to be replaced if the situation was to be corrected. Ron Schmidt drafted a letter of resignation for Maple to make his departure as graceful as possible, but Maple resisted and said he would not resign.

I bluntly explained that the state audit would present the facts of his troubled administration if he stayed on. The high cost and inefficiency of the state fair would be exposed. So he resigned, effective January 9, 1967. It is never pleasant to fire anyone. But if a state administrator is unable to do his job, the governor must intervene.

The remaining days of the transitional period were spent working on my Inaugural Address. I spent many hours at the typewriter in the study of my home and in the Secretary of State's office. There, seated beneath a portrait of the late Senator Charles L. McNary, Oregon's progressive Republican leader for a generation, I went through a number of drafts of the speech. Schmidt, Westerdahl, Myers, and Cleighton Penwell all read the speech in rough form and made many helpful suggestions. I knew, however, that when I rose to address the Fifty-Fourth Legislative Assembly, I would be on my own.

CHAPTER 5

Year of Decisions

My administration began on the cold, clear morning of January 9, 1967. Before I spoke, Mark Hatfield made his farewell address and Clay Myers was sworn in. I took the oath of office on a 107-year-old Bible which had been carried across the plains to Oregon in 1865 by Clay's great-grandfather.

In my Inaugural Address, I attempted to outline my philosophy of government, my conception of the governorship, and the goals of the McCall Administration.

"An imperative of progress in these years is a rapport between the executive and legislative branches," I said. "If differences there be, let them not arise from any fault in communications, and I pledge to you, for my part, to keep the lines of availability and cooperation constantly open."

I proposed the independent office of "Ombudsman" to serve as a citizen's advocate against "unjustifiable inaction, inefficiency, arrogance or abuse of authority" by state government officials. An additional reason for this new position, I said, was to "offer the citizen still another protection of his rights."

"Civil rights is a principle deserving of unflagging support," I said, "despite the rise and ebb of controversy. The lack of demonstrations on the part of Oregon's nonwhites should not induce the apathetic belief that our state is free from racial disadvantage and bigotry."

I quoted Governor John Whiteaker, who delivered Oregon's first inaugural address in 1859. He had described the state as "one of the most attractive portions of the North American continent." I said strengthening the State Sanitary Authority was essential if Oregon was to "continue to qualify for Whiteaker's description."

Another environmental reform I proposed was "the Willamette Greenway, suggested by State Treasurer Straub and endorsed by me." I also stressed the need for the state to acquire Oregon's beach lands. Few realized that the state owned the beaches only up to the median high-water mark.

In closing my address, I said: "A few weeks ago I said 'the over-riding challenge—the umbrella issue of the campaign and the decade—is quality: quality of life in Oregon!' I respectfully suggest that the proposals this administration has submitted to you today will meet the challenge and further dramatize the significance of that issue. Your oath of office and mine mark the moment of truth."

An informal reception was held in the Governor's Office after the ceremonies. Four of Oregon's former governors—Hatfield, Robert D. Holmes, Elmo Smith and Charles A. Sprague—joined me during the reception. When I came into the paneled Ceremonial Office through a side door, Governor Holmes pulled me aside. His eyes were moist. He put his arm around me and said: "This is the first time I've been invited to the Governor's Office in years. I just want to thank you for having me down. This demonstrates why you won so overwhelmingly. You think of other people and not just yourself."

I was touched by what Governor Holmes said. All too often former governors become forgotten souls. It was my good fortune to have Holmes as a friend and an advisor. When I needed his counsel, I would send a state car and driver to bring him to the Capitol. Later, I was to appoint him to the State Board of Higher Education, where he performed a service that equaled his gubernatorial career in stature.

As the reception was ending, I received a remarkable gift from my campaign staff—a model of the schooner *Thomas W. Lawson*, which was named for my grandfather and was the only seven-masted schooner ever built. Ron Schmidt had found this replica in a San Francisco bookstore.

It had been the proudest day of my life. Having covered state government for so many years and worked in the Governor's

Office during the McKay years, I had watched similar ceremonies many times, but this had been much different. It was awesome suddenly to take responsibility for more than two million people.

A few weeks later, I broke a precedent by testifying before a legislative committee. Straub and I had frequently testified when we were state treasurer and secretary of state, especially in matters dealing with Board of Control institutions. There had always been a sort of line drawn between the governor and the legislature. Traditionally, the contacts were on a one-to-one basis with legislators—or delegations coming over to his office. Governor Hatfield always maintained a shield between himself and the legislature. The only time he walked across the hall was to give his biennial message to the legislature. I wanted to shorten the distance between the two branches of state government. So, when the Senate Air and Water Quality Committee invited me to testify, I accepted without hesitation.

I told the committee, "We must draw a line beyond which existing pollution cannot come and then work out rollback schedules between the Sanitary Authority and the industrial or municipal pollutor. As a companion action, we must notify any industry planning to expand an existing facility, or any new industry coming into the State of Oregon, that a permit to build must come from the Sanitary Authority and only after the determination that the facility in question would not contribute to pollution in Oregon. It will help Oregon now and benefit future generations of Oregonians if we can establish that Oregon has propounded— and enforces to the hilt—an 11th Commandment: 'Thou shalt not pollute.' "

The State Sanitary Authority had been criticized sharply in a report on the Willamette River Basin by the Federal Water Pollution Control Administration. Members of the Sanitary Authority were further embarrassed when the report was leaked to the press prior to the time it was made available to them. I thought the report was somewhat inaccurate in discounting the work of some dedicated public servants, but it was obvious that the job of pollution control in the Willamette Basin was far from done.

Harold Wendel, a Portland businessman, had been chairman of the Sanitary Authority since it was created in 1938. Ed Westerdahl thought it was time to let Wendel give up the chairmanship.

"Can't we get a more dynamic guy?" Westerdahl asked.

"Absolutely not," I said. "I know you would like to have a more colorful personality who would be more dynamic, but Harold has served steadily and with courage."

Several days later, Wendel suddenly and unexpectedly died.

"See," I told Westerdahl. "Don't be so impetuous. There are some things you can't do."

It was a great lesson to Ed. If we hadn't reappointed Wendel, he would have dropped dead anyway, and we would have been blamed for being insensitive, inconsiderate and ungrateful to the point that we had caused his death. Wendel was a highly capable person. There are many ways of serving and not all of them have to be sensational.

My first inclination was to offer Wendel's chairmanship to John Mosser, but he was too busy with the state budget to take on still another assignment. So, to dramatize my commitment to the cleanup of the Willamette and to show that I really meant business in pushing some 20 bills dealing with the environment, I made myself chairman of the Sanitary Authority. No Oregon governor had ever before appointed himself to a state board or commission.

"As governor of Oregon, I know there is no more important task than to involve myself directly in the campaign against air and water pollution," I said at a meeting of the authority in Portland. "Therefore, I am in effect appointing myself as a member and chairman of the State Sanitary Authority for a period to end November 1, 1967. The course I have chosen will enable me to become thoroughly conversant with the ramifications of the most significant long-range problem facing the state. Moreover, my serving as chairman will apply the prestige of the governor's office squarely to the complexities of this vast issue. . . . Many will ask, 'Why assume such a thankless responsibility?' There is only one

McCall is sworn in as Oregon's 30th governor.

Gerry Lewin

David Falconer, *The Oregonian*

After inaugural ceremonies, four former governors congratulated McCall. "I can use all the advice you can give me," McCall told them. (Robert D. Holmes, Charles A. Sprague, Elmo Smith, and Mark O. Hatfield)

answer. I know from some 100 days in office that the buck, having to stop somewhere, stops at the governor's desk."

My appointment provoked considerable controversy. State Senator Lynn Newbry of Ashland called it "a tremendous political blunder." House Speaker F. F. Montgomery expressed concern that I was leaning too hard on industry.

State Treasurer Straub strongly supported my action. "I think it's good," Straub said. "It identifies publicly and openly the true situation, that the governor must make the decisions in pollution problems."

In my dual positions, I worked well with legislative leaders in putting together the greatest bulk of environmental measures, the largest one-whack commitment of any state in history. The most singular accomplishment of the 1967 Legislature was its comprehensive program to curb air and water pollution. Unlike previous legislative sessions, this session faced the menace of pollution squarely and took decisive action to roll it back.

When I signed the pollution abatement bill, I said it reflected "the desire of the legislature and this administration to see Oregon's open spaces clean, the air unsullied, the water uncontaminated and the scenery unblighted. We have not solved the problem of air and water pollution, but we have set up the machinery to facilitate tremendous strides towards its eventual eradication."

One of the most critical conservation questions ever faced by a governor and a legislature came in 1967. A circuit court decision confronted us with the possibility that the dry sands of the ocean shore might not belong to the public after all.

Governor Oswald West had made the Oregon Coast a public highway in 1913. West was perhaps as extraordinary a public servant as ever held a governorship in the Pacific Northwest. In his one term (1911-1915), the maverick Democrat set historical "firsts" galore, including a solo horseback ride from Salem into Idaho, a distance of some 300 miles. His most lasting legacy was the law he promoted through the 1913 Legislature, which made Oregon's beaches a public highway from the California boundary, north to Washington State. But the 1966 court decision indicated a strong possibility that this more than 300-mile strip of the "people's beaches" was far less than it seemed. The court's ruling was that while the people owned the wet sands, there was some question about title to the dry sands between them and the vegetation. When the legislature convened, every politician rode off wildly in every direction, each determined that he would be the "new Os West"—the 1967 saviour of the "people's beaches." It was only human for everyone to want to emulate West and be revered for the rest of their lives as Os West was.

As each legislator scrambled for position and chaos was mounting, my Nature Resources coordinator, Kessler Cannon, suggested, "Why not try the oceanographers at Oregon State University? They think they have a formula to settle this whole dilemma."

The next day, Kessler and I joined a team of oceanographers on the cool sands of the central Oregon beach near Salishan, to conduct a test. (We also went to Manhattan, Seaside, Cannon Beach and Garibaldi to repeat the ritual.)

The tide was all the way out, and an oceanographer took a slender, 16-foot pole down to the water's edge and set it down exactly perpendicular.

"Where the string running straightly horizontal from the top of this pole landward touches down should be the vegetation line," one of the oceanographers said. He was right. Except for swale and headland, that 16-foot line delineated the people's own beach all the way from Washington, south to California. The legislature quickly passed a "beach bill" based on that measurement—later confirmed by Highway Commission tests the length of the Oregon coast. It was later upheld by the Oregon Supreme Court in an opinion which truly reflected the way the world really ought to be.

As I signed the bill into law, I said: "This fulfills the dream of Governor West that, 'In the administration of this God-given trust, a broad protective policy should be declared and maintained. No local selfish interest should be permitted, through politics or otherwise, to destroy or even impair this great birthright of our people.' "

The 1967 Legislature provided appropriations for the Willamette Greenway program after I submitted a plan for this important project. I named a Greenway Committee, consisting of residents of every county bordering the Willamette, from Eugene to the Columbia. It worked with the State Highway Commission in developing its comprehensive plan for the preservation, public access and permanent recreational enjoyment of the Willamette. State Parks Superintendent Dave Talbott arranged for committee members to take a three-day boat tour of the Willamette, with stops at Harrisburg, Corvallis, Salem and Oregon City for public meetings. I joined them at Armitage State Park north of Eugene for the first leg of the trip.

Because of the great strides taken by the legislature and partly because of my heavy workload, I resigned as chairman of the State Sanitary Authority on July 10. In my place, I appointed John Mosser. John had completed his tenure as director of the Department of Finance and Administration and had been the man I had wanted all along for the Sanitary Authority.

During my 10 weeks as chairman, the Authority adopted sweeping statewide water-quality standards and began to break the stalemates on houseboat- and wigwam-burner pollution. In addition, it had put the muscle of the Governor's Office more effectively behind the pollution fight.

Pardons and extraditions are among the most sensitive issues that a governor must deal with. An early extradition crisis occurred when four escapees from the Tucker Prison Farm in Arkansas were arrested in Baker. The conditions of brutality and bestiality at that institution were probably the worst in the United States.

A 1966 report by the U.S. Justice Department indicated that Arkansas prison farms were infested with "inmate abuse and official corruption including death, threats, shooting of prisoners, gratuitous beatings with rubber hoses, blackjacks, brass knuckles, torture, stompings, lashings, kickings, sexual perversion and other forms of punishment."

When Arkansas Governor Winthrop Rockefeller asked me to extradite the four prisoners, I said, "Win, I can't do it. I'm not sure these men won't be done in if they are sent back."

I always thought Win Rockefeller appreciated my stand because the Arkansas Legislature allocated more money for corrections. They brought in a new corrections chief, a new warden and whole new approach. Rockefeller had been candid with me about his earlier inability to guarantee the four men against physical abuse once they were back at Tucker Prison Farm. Rockefeller later sent Robert Scott, his legal counsel, to Oregon to discuss their reforms and renew their efforts for extradition. Scott brought a letter from Governor Rockefeller which said in part:

"Your spirit of cooperation is deeply appreciated and I certainly want you to understand that I feel your concern about the conditions of the Arkansas State Prison has been justified in view of the recent disclosures of conditions and treatment of personnel." After conferring with Scott in my office and talking with Rockefeller by phone, I agreed to extradite Calvin Smith, James Pike, Richard George Emory and James Edward Stephens.

"My conclusion to extradite the four escapees is based on assurances tendered to me today by Governor Rockefeller and the governor's legal aide, Robert Scott," I said at a news conference. "Lacking these assurances, I had been reluctant to return the men to a situation which even Governor Rockefeller conceded contained the potential for cruel reprisals against them. He now informs me that he is ready to provide protection against brutal treatment. Protection has been made possible through removal of an assistant superintendent and three of the four wardens and employment of a professional penologist.

"The conflict between my conscience and duty under the U.S. Constitution to extradite the men has now been resolved. I feel certain that the four will be spared the inhuman treatment that has made Tucker Prison Farm notorious. I hope that the furor surrounding my prior refusal to extradite has helped spotlight the appalling conditions at Tucker for all America to see and that I have done at least a little to accelerate prison reform in Arkansas."

There were so many tangible accomplishments that came out of the revelations of barbarism that I thought a modern governor like Win would always regard me as his ally. But a year later, when I was among a group gathered in Nelson Rockefeller's Fifth Avenue apartment, the Oregon State Penitentiary riot broke open. We were all there to urge Nelson to run for President. Not until that night did I realize what Win's feelings about my role in the extraditions really were: "Before we start I just want to say one thing. Governor McCall, in the history of Arkansas, there has never been a prison fire or a prison riot." Win was mad as hell.

Such episodes can be politically costly. My grandfather, Governor Samuel McCall of Massachusetts, was asked to extradite a black murder suspect who had escaped from a Georgia prison. Grandfather McCall sent investigators down to find out what would happen if he signed the extradition order. He was told that the man would be lynched the minute he stepped off the train. So he refused to extradite him. As a result of this, the South blocked his appointment as a delegate to the Versailles Peace Conference.

My conflicts in interstate relations did not prevent me from getting a fair share of presidential appointments. In the summer of 1967, President Johnson asked me to observe elections in South Vietnam. Among those on the panel were Ambassador Henry Cabot Lodge, civil rights leader Whitney Young, Senator Edmund Muskie of Maine, Senator Bourke Hickenlooper of Iowa, Governor Richard Hughes of New Jersey and Governor Bill Guy of North Dakota. There was much cynicism about the elections. Critics said that Johnson had forced the elections to legitimize South Vietnam's government and that South Vietnam's military leaders were going through with the exercise to legitimize the war to the American public. Eleven slates of presidential and vice-presidential candidates were running. General Ngueyen Van Thieu and Premier Ngueyen Cao Ky were generally conceded to be the favorites. The ten civilian tickets boycotted campaign appearances

President Johnson wrote McCall on April 10, 1960. "Your leadership and friendship have been an unfailing source of strength to me in many times of great trial and decision. Our partnership has helped to create much that will endure for our people."

in the early months of the campaign, charging that the military was rigging the election.

As a white-knuckle flier, I did not look forward to the prospect of a long and potentially dangerous flight. My decision was further aggravated by the haunting picture of myself—tallest of all the 50 governors—mounted as a trophy over the fireplace of Ho Chi Minh.

"This is ridiculous," I told a staff meeting. "I don't have the courage to go. I probably wouldn't be able to do any good." They convincingly argued that it was an important recognition from the White House. I also knew that it was just about impossible to turn down a presidential request.

On the eve of my departure for Vietnam, I wrote an interoffice memo to my staff: ". . . . As for the mission to Vietnam, I am praying that it won't be dismissed as 'Operation Futility.' . . . While the detractors and the complications on the scene may make our trip seem like 'Operation Futility,' we'll keep our fingers crossed and heads down and try to make sense out of confusion. The odds are against much of a result—but the potential, slim as it is, for setting off some kind of settlement process challenges us onward."

There was good companionship and fellowship among the American delegation. Ambassador Lodge recalled that our grandfathers had been contemporaries in Massachusetts politics. Indeed, Lodge proudly recalled that Grandfather McCall had once given him a Boy Scout award.

Ed Muskie, whose environmental work I had long admired, became a good friend. When we stopped at an Air Force base outside of Tokyo, he bought two dozen Titlist golf balls. He was just taking up the game. Muskie was one of the hardest working members of the observation panel. He went into villages to meet with opposition leaders. He wanted to get the views of the counterforces. Muskie met with General Duong Van ("Big") Minh, the opposition leader who enjoyed a considerable following among Buddhists, students and intellectuals.

I roomed with Bill Guy at the Ambassador's house in Saigon. A jeep blew up below our window one night and the explosion knocked us out of our beds. We were still trembling at breakfast and neither of us could get the spoon into the jelly. We suggested that the Ambassador do it for us.

During my mission, I met with many Vietnamese including political candidates, peasants, village chieftains, election officials, and others. They seemed to have a dogged faith in this democratic exercise. It permeated everything they felt. They said it was the kind of thing to do in order to start building a strong, free country.

I thought it was an appealing outpouring of feeling. Even though the Viet Cong had been engaging in preelection terrorism, designed to scare away voters, there was an 83 percent turnout. A number of polling places were blown up and people shot at on election day, September 3. There were also kidnappings and general harrassment. So those who turned out seemed truly committed to a dream of democratic government. I don't know if they exercised their franchise with much consciousness or intelligence, however, for there were 500 candidates on the ballot for president and vice president and the 60 senate seats.

Thieu and Ky were elected with 34.8 percent of the vote. Finishing a surprisingly strong second with 17.2 percent was a Buddhist layman named Truong Dinh Dzu who had campaigned as a peace candidate. Among other things, Dzu had urged recognition of the National Liberation Front and immediate peace negotiations. I wrote an article for the *Oregonian* about the elections and Associated Press put it on their worldwide wire.

President Johnson met with the observers in the Cabinet room on September 6. We all gave our reports. Bill Guy said, "Too much attention has been placed on the possibility of irregularities and not enough on the other aspects. These people with great courage came out with a moving and profound example of desire for self-determination—as much as I have seen anywhere. We visited a precinct at which a bomb went off and killed three and wounded six during the voting. They closed it for forty-five minutes and then reopened it for more voting."

I had met with Thieu several times and reported that his aspirations seemed to reflect those of the Vietnamese. As it turned out, he was too much of an authoritarian. He wasn't willing enough to let a free democratic system function. Most of his political rivals were imprisoned. In terms of the war, Big Minh would probably have been a better leader, but I doubt if any government could have saved South Vietnam. It was a military defeat.

My own interest in the war was deeply personal. I had deep reservations about our involvement in Southeast Asia. Yet I also knew that I might end up with two sons in the war. I felt it was the worst deal any young generation of Americans had ever been given. They were offered an impossible alternative—to serve in Vietnam or serve in prison. I knew it was going to be a terrible thing to say to my sons, "If you go, the nation will curse you. And if you don't go, the other half of the nation will curse you."

People who didn't have children in the same age group as my sons never really understood my position. On this issue, there was a difference of opinion within my own staff. I once told a staff meeting when Vietnam came up: "Go your own way on this. But don't hit me too hard."

I wasn't about to tell my son, Tad, "I'm sending you into a no-win situation and half the nation is going to hate you." I fumed and sometimes exploded publicly because we at home failed to give our men over there moral support and backing.

My position was really as a supporter of our people who were in the war. Tad wouldn't break the law and avoid going because I was governor. Tad was a hero in Vietnam. He was known as "Mr. Swim" because he taught every member of the crew how to swim. There were real efforts made to relate to the Vietnamese people. If everyone had left something positive behind—teaching a craft or a skill—then we would have had a plateau of strength in terms of peaceful adjustment.

It was a war that everyone grew to hate and a war that no one truly won. When the cease-fire agreement was finally signed in 1973, I said: "It is far preferable to a conflict that has generated a blood-bath in Southeast Asia and international endemic neuroses and hostility. The immediate implications aside, this occasion and this agreement must be made a point of departure from the protracted tragedy of Southeast Asia—a point of departure toward achieving a world where Vietnams, because of mutual understanding, can never happen again."

If Vietnam was our national quagmire, property-tax relief remained Oregon's quagmire. I had proposed to the 1967 regular session of the legislature a property-tax relief program based on higher income taxes. The House of Representatives summarily slapped it down. Representative Lee Johnson's Tax Committee wouldn't even give it a hearing. An economic recession later made it evident that passage of my plan would have produced a budget tens of millions of dollars out of balance.

Still convinced that the people wanted and deserved property-tax relief, I called a special session. In my proclamation, I said: "There is a compelling need for property-tax relief which can be accomplished only by the Legislative Assembly, and it now appears that revenues for the current biennium will not be as great as were estimated at the regular session of the 54th Legislative Assembly, and it is desirable that the Legislative Assembly have an opportunity to make appropriate revisions."

I dropped my longstanding opposition to a sales tax and suggested it as a method of property-tax relief. The Senate Tax Committee struck it down. I then suggested that the legislature offer voters a choice of taxes—higher income or a three percent sales tax—to raise $100 million for property-tax relief. Such relief, I maintained, offered "a shift, not a gift."

I asked our state tax commissioners if this would be a proper choice. Their unanimous opinion: it would be complete misrepresentation to offer the two as equals because Oregon was already using the income tax right up to the hilt and to produce an additional $100 million would require us to have the steepest rates in the nation. Besides, they pointed out that the legality of a multiple-choice tax ballot measure was doubtful. So nothing was resolved in either legislative session.

Such frustrating setbacks made it tempting to run for the Senate in 1968. Democratic Senator Wayne L. Morse, who was seeking a fifth term, trailed me in several polls. Senate Minority Leader Everett Dirksen told me I ought to make the race. State Representative Bob Packwood, an eager challenger for Morse's seat, said "I haven't made an irrevocable decision to run. Governor McCall would be the most formidable opponent for Morse. I would not run against McCall."

CHAPTER 6

On the Firing Line

When the Republican Governors' Conference met at Palm Beach, Florida, in early December, I was urged to run for the Senate. Dirksen came down to see me at the fashionable old Breakers Hotel. In his whiskey-baritone voice, he said I would, in running, be making a contribution to the state, the nation and the Republican Party. Senator George Murphy of California, head of the Republican Senatorial Campaign Committee, made a special trip to Palm Beach in an effort to push me into the race. Murphy pledged me strong financial backing.

Senator Murphy unfolded a poll, which had been taken for the Republican National Committee. It indicated that I was the only Republican who stood a chance of defeating Morse or his primary election rival, former Congressman Bob Duncan. Murphy's assistant and the Republican campaign committee's executive director, Lee Nunn, had previously made a visit to Oregon to formally suggest that I run against Morse. Nunn, the brother of Governor Louie B. Nunn of Kentucky, accompanied Murphy to Palm Beach for our talks.

On this same trip, I went to Washington, D.C., to meet with members of Oregon's congressional delegation. I asked Hatfield about the transition from governor to senator.

"You wouldn't like it," Hatfield said. "You'd be so frustrated. You don't want to come here and be part of a committee of 100— and be 30th to speak. You might only make one decision where you made 50, and it's a committee decision." In a very nice way, without being impassionate, Hatfield talked me out of running. My wife, Audrey, and my mother warned me against trying to go too far too fast.

The most compelling argument of all came from Mayor John Lindsay of New York, a colleague in many a liberal battle. "Tom, it is the mayors and the governors who are under the hammer and the day's great problems," he said. "Stay among us. We need all the problem solvers we can put on the firing line. Don't go to Washington and just become an empty showboat."

Oddly enough, the same Lindsay who talked so persuasively about the duties of governance was the first applicant to Governor Rockefeller when Robert Kennedy was assassinated. Rockefeller said, "Tell me, John, why do you want to be a Senator." Lindsay hotly retorted, "Stop treating me like a child!" He did not get the appointment.

Even though the polls showed me running well against Morse, the campaign would have been hard on my nerves. I told friends, "I could beat Morse. But what would be left of me—nothing but raw hamburger." Morse was such a hard-charging, bitter opponent that he could outdebate me without trying and chew me to pieces.

It was not just my respect for Morse's rhetorical abilities that held me back. I really wanted to finish my term as governor. On January 18, 1968, I sent Senator Murphy my answer:

"I have tried to stack the pros against the cons as dispassionately as possible. Certainly no man in public life could easily resist the challenge of service in the world's greatest deliberate body. This, of course, would be my last chance to seek a Senate seat as I would be 60 before the next opportunity presented itself.

"But there also is an immense challenge to the life of a governor who wants to restructure government to help make the states more visible and vigorous in the federal system and increase their problem solving capability.

"Association with my fellow governors has encouraged hope that the state capitols will exert a growing influence on American public affairs. The governors are an engaging group of realists— brilliant, in the main, and alert to the need for fresh approaches to the complexities of a turbulent society. More specifically, I simply have too much to do in the governorship—too much started and too little time to finish it—to permit me to entertain prospects of seeking some other office.

"I have been close to state government for nearly 20 years, and I am convinced that it is here that I can do the best job. This is, after all, the prime consideration. Besides, I like living in Oregon and don't relish the prospect of living in Washington, D.C. Perhaps that is a selfish thought.

"Remember, though, that a governor's daily grind can get pretty rough. He stands right in the thick of all a state's problems. But there's a warm gratification in feeling that your people want to have you around to help them with their public cares and responsibilities.

"This is why I have been reluctant all along to run for the Senate in 1968. This is why my firm decision today is against making the race."

Packwood announced his candidacy one month later.

In not running for the senate, I had the flexibility to participate in the presidential campaign. Governor George Romney of Michigan had been the acknowledged front runner after the 1966 elections. Romney led President Johnson in major public opinion polls and, according to the same polls, appeared to be the choice of rank-and-file Republicans. Romney had been untested on the national and international stage, and I had misgivings about him as a presidential figure. Much to my disappointment, Nelson Rockefeller threw his personal and financial support behind Romney. Because I wanted to keep the door open for a Rockefeller candidacy, I sent letters to 19 Republican governors on March 22, 1967, asking them to delay endorsing a candidate until we could "consolidate behind one man—who would then almost certainly be the presidential nominee and the Republican who would have the best chance of success in next year's election." On Rockefeller's letter, I scrawled a postscript asking him to be our candidate.

"I'm out of it," Rockefeller responded. "If we moderates want to preserve any chance of nominating a candidate who can win, we'd better stay united behind George Romney. Any move to undercut

Nelson Rockefeller and McCall rode together in the 1968 Albany Timber Festival. "Rockefeller was the best campaigner in America," McCall said. "He could turn on the crowds." McCall was unable to persuade the New York governor to enter Oregon's GOP presidential primary that year.

New York Mayor John V. Lindsay, a longtime McCall friend and confidant, urged the Oregon governor not to run for the Senate in 1968. "Don't go to Washington and be another showboat," Lindsay counseled. "Stay with us, stay among the problem solvers." McCall agreed.

him would simply deliver the nomination to the other side on a silver platter."

A majority of the governors I wrote, however, agreed to remain uncommitted until "things jell a lot more." I thought the Republican governors could act with considerable effectiveness if we held together. In 1952, the governors launched the Eisenhower campaign and their backing proved to be decisive in enabling General Eisenhower to win the nomination. If the 1968 Republican governors were to move with near unanimity, I felt we could get Rockefeller going and stop Nixon.

Rockefeller's loyalty to Romney amazed me. When we were at a Republican Governors' Meeting at Jackson Hole, Rockefeller asked me to call a meeting of all the governors. He wanted a test of how many pledges there were for Romney. I think there were five or six. "He's dead in the water," I said. Most of those present asked, "Why not you, Nelson?"

"No, never again," he said.

Rockefeller was sincere in backing Romney. He had been through the bruising battle with Goldwater in 1964 and said he was a lightning rod for conservatives.

As Romney's campaign plodded on, it became more and more evident that he was not presidential timber, although he had been an admirable governor of Michigan. Travis Cross was his press secretary. Travis may have joined the campaign too late to salvage it. In any event, Romney's credibility diminished sharply when, in explaining an apparent reversal of position on Vietnam, he said: "Well, you know when I came back from Vietnam, I just had the greatest brainwashing that anybody can get when you go over to Vietnam."

Romney was never able to regain the momentum. The *Detroit News*, which had supported him in the past, editorially suggested that he was an incompetent and urged his withdrawal in favor of Rockefeller. He became something of a laughingstock for his "brainwashing" statement. Eugene McCarthy, perhaps the most acerbic wit in American politics, suggested in Romney's case "a slight rinse" would have been adequate.

Romney's first Oregon trip was a disaster. He was unable to persuade any Oregon Republican of stature to head his campaign committee. A few days earlier, Nixon had shrewdly picked Howell Appling as his Oregon chairman. Romney's most important appearance was at a fund-raiser at the Sheraton Hotel. An overflow crowd of Republican moderates had gathered to hear their new standard bearer. Most of them left disappointed and even bored. "It's beginning to look like we'll have to reconcile ourselves to Nixon," I said a few weeks later at Palm Beach.

But suddenly a Rockefeller bandwagon seemed to be moving. *Time* magazine featured a cover story on a "Rockefeller/Reagan: Republican Dream Ticket." Spiro T. Agnew, then governor of Maryland, was talking up Rockefeller with me in the gilded hallway of the Breakers Hotel as Governor Jim Rhodes of Ohio walked by. Rhodes grabbed me by an arm and Ted by an arm and said, "Boys, come on out to the putting green. We're going to put the presidency together for Nelson."

Romney's reluctance to face political reality made it difficult for us to promote Rockefeller. On December 11, when I shared the head table with Rockefeller, Nixon and Henry Cabot Lodge at a re-election dinner for Senator Jacob Javits, I seized the opportunity. "Republican New Yorkers are popular in Oregon," I said. "Nelson Rockefeller scored a historic win in the 1964 primary election. Parenthetically, I hope he repeats it in 1968."

It brought the house down. Mary McGrory, of *The Washington Star*, wrote a dramatic column about how this Lincolnesque figure stood amidst this room of black ties, expensive furs and painted faces and addressed the real issue at hand. She wrote, "It ruined the evening for Richard M. Nixon."

If Rockefeller was still a non-candidate, his mind appeared to be more open to a draft. George Hinman, New York's long-time Republican National Committeeman and Rockefeller's confidant, asked me to meet him at the San Francisco Airport in early January. We talked for three hours. Hinman was interested in what Rockefeller's chances were in Oregon. I told him they were most promising and that Romney had almost no chance against Nixon.

Romney returned to Oregon in February as the featured speaker at the Dorchester Conference in Lincoln City. His spirits were high and his performance was far more impressive than in earlier visits. His long weeks of shaking hands in the snows and blizzards of New Hampshire had made him a better campaigner.

On February 28, at the Mid-Winter Governors' Conference, I encountered Romney in the middle of the lobby in the Washington Hilton. His fists were clenched and his face was white.

"George, what is it?" I said.

"I've just now come awake about Nelson," he said. "What you have been saying about him is absolutely right. I'm going to have a news conference in a half hour and rip him from end to end."

By the time Romney showed up at the press conference, where he terminated his presidential candidacy, he was more subdued. He did not directly attack Rockefeller, but he pointedly did not endorse him. Romney felt betrayed because Rockefeller had admitted that he would accept a "draft" for the nomination. Rockefeller had, in fact, been his most stalwart ally. Yet Romney thought he had been used and, in the end, turned on Rockefeller. Romney, whose presidential hopes were fueled by his strong showings against President Johnson in the polls, suspended his campaign when his own pollster showed that Nixon was going to beat him six-to-one in New Hampshire.

Rockefeller had the opening we had all been waiting for. Yet he hesitated. In early March, Secretary of the Interior Stewart Udall called me and said he had become so fascinated with the Willamette Greenway, and impressed at our start, that he was going to give us $1.8 million from his special discretionary fund. Udall wanted me to come to Washington so that he could give national publicity to the Greenway concept. Nelson Rockefeller then called and offered to pay both ways of my trip if I would come to New York for a meeting his family had suggested.

A huge group had gathered in Nelson's opulent apartment at 812 Fifth Avenue. Former Secretary of Defense Tom Gates was there. Some of the others included Agnew, Governors John Love of Colorado, John Chafee of Rhode Island, Ray Shafer of Pennsylvania, Harold LeVander of Minnesota, and Winthrop Rockefeller of Arkansas; Mayor Lindsay and Senator Javits from New York; and Senator Thruston B. Morton of Kentucky.

There, surrounded by the works of Picasso, Calder and other great modern artists, we all urged Rockefeller to make his move. "Nelson go downstairs," Tom Gates said. "The press is there. Announce tonight."

Bob Price, an utter jerk who had managed Lindsay's mayoral campaign, suggested that Nelson could win the nomination without running. He vetoed and repudiated the unanimous recommendation of this committee of party notables. Price's idea struck me as stupid. Nobody could win the nomination without going into the primaries.

It was at this meeting that I learned of the riot at the Oregon State Penitentiary when Winthrop made his outburst. I immediately called my office. Bill Newell, one of my assistants, had been unable to reach me earlier in my room at the New York Hilton. The desk had given him the wrong room number. I was in my room watching "Mission Impossible," and the phone never rang. I was stunned when I learned about the fire and explosion and riot. I had never felt so helpless. I spent $48 in taxi fares going back and forth between LaGuardia and Kennedy airports, trying to get a flight home. All the flights were fogged in. If Newell had been given the correct information by the hotel, I would have made a flight and not attended the Fifth Avenue conference. When I was able to ascertain that the hostages were out and the fire trucks were in at the prison, I went on with the trip to Washington.

On my return flight, we stopped in Seattle. And I had a lucky break. I began visiting with another passenger and he turned out to be Charles Hagen, assistant director of the U.S. Bureau of Prisons. When I arrived in Portland on Monday night, I introduced Hagen as a special trouble shooter. Everyone said, "McCall is really on the job bringing in that man." They didn't realize that I never knew Hagen was on the plane until that chance conversation.

I had terrible guilt feelings about not having been in Salem when the riot occurred. Straub was also gone. He was visiting relatives in Arizona. Myers and State Senate President (and acting governor) Potts were in Grants Pass. My legal counsel, Ed Branchfield, was in Medford. Ron Schmidt was at Lake Tahoe. Fortunately, Ed Westerdahl was in Salem and once again demonstrated his coolness under pressure. He immediately contacted Myers and Potts, both of whom quickly returned, as did Schmidt and Branchfield.

When the Marion County Grand Jury issued its report on the riot, it was particularly harsh on the Governor's Office for not having more people on the scene. Westerdahl had explained to the investigating district attorney that everybody had been away on official business. "Where was Ron Schmidt?" the attorney asked.

"He was out of state on official business," Westerdahl said. Ed's attempt to protect Ron came back to haunt all of us. The man questioning him had been gambling and partying with Ron at Lake Tahoe!

The rioting probably would have been averted if House Speaker F. F. "Monte" Montgomery had used more discretion in his criticism of the penitentiary. Monte was trailing Clay Myers in his race for Secretary of State. He apparently thought that a dramatic issue—such as the prison—would revive his campaign. I was sorry to see Monte leaving the legislature where he had worked so constructively. The stridency and shrillness of his primary campaign were to have disastrous consequences. Monte charged that the Board of Control—McCall, Myers and Straub—were "sitting on their hands while there have been continuing reports of weapons and narcotics in our state prison." He sent me an inflammatory letter, demanding an investigation of the prison, and made the letter public.

Monte should have come to discuss the problems with me over my desk instead of releasing his letter to 25 newspapers. From my experience in Corrections, I knew that when a few men were screaming behind prison walls, it didn't take much to set things off. Prisoners are alert readers of newspapers and radio listeners. They know when the mush is being stirred is the time to strike.

In my reply to Monte, I wrote, "I know that in seeking public office it is very easy to seize upon issues without analyzing all the potential repercussions. Recognize in this instance that an outstanding public servant, Clarence Gladden, and an outstanding penal system, Oregon's, can suffer as a result of magnifying problems through a political attack."

One of the tragedies of the riot was the collapse of Warden Gladden. He was 73, well beyond retirement age, but Gladden was so revered by everyone that the legislature passed a special "Gladden Bill," enabling him to stay on as long as he wanted to. Like J. Edgar Hoover, Gladden stayed on too long. I had, in fact, raised questions whether Gladden could still administer. Schmidt, who knew Gladden quite well, pushed to keep him. What neither of us realized was that Gladden had cancer and no longer had the strength to control the prison. He kept telling us that he never felt better.

Gladden finally told us about his lung tumor three days before the riot and tendered his resignation. I told him that I couldn't toss him to the wolves by accepting the resignation during this controversy. Before Montgomery began his assault on the prison, plans were underway for Gladden to retire. Hoyt Cupp, the deputy warden at the Oregon Correctional Institution, had been alerted that he would succeed Gladden.

Ironically, the first demand of the prison rioters was Gladden's resignation. Gladden resigned hours later. It was a sad end to a distinguished career.

A lot of people were sore because there weren't some prisoners mowed down. There had been $1.8 million in property damage during the riot and fire. Attica exploded in New York State three years later, demonstrating how truly horrible prison riots can be. Forty-three persons were killed in that prison disturbance and another 80 were seriously wounded. The commission investigating Attica called it "with the exception of Indian massacres in the 19th century. . .the bloodiest one-day encounter between Americans since the Civil War."

When the smoke cleared and the ashes cooled, the Oregon riot had ended peacefully. Not one person had been injured. Clay Myers, as the senior Board of Control member on the scene, was doing his damnedest against an absolutely uncontrollable situation.

Montgomery's campaign self-destructed. People began to perceive his tactics as unfair, especially when he tried to exploit what was a catastrophe. Clay defeated him by a handsome margin in the primary.

Another casualty of the riot was State Corrections Director George Randall. The Marion County Grand Jury report was a hatchet job. It contained misleading and inaccurate information about Randall's qualifications for his job. The report, which was written under the supervision of District Attorney Gary Gortmaker, ripped into the innovative programs Randall had brought to Oregon.

Randall was a good man. He had brought corrections along quite far in a relatively brief period. His rehabilitation programs in North Carolina had won national recognition. Straub and I argued vigorously for his appointment when we came to the Board of Control. Hatfield had some reservations about him. His rehabilitative efforts seemed to some too avante-garde.

The climate after the prison riot was uncomfortable for Randall. I encouraged him to start looking for a job where he could make a fresh start. It was sort of like getting rid of a losing football coach. You have to bring in someone new to start a new spirit and generate a new movement. The new man may not be as good a coach technically, but, psychologically, there has to be a change. I was pleased that Randall was able to move to West Virginia and resume his effective work. Amos Reed was brought in to succeed him. Amos was able to build an exemplary program from the ashes he inherited.

I cut back my out-of-state traveling after the prison debacle, cancelling plans to attend the Republican Governors Conference and the National Governors Conference. Although these conferences were valuable experiences, my commitments in Oregon took priority.

Tension and excitement mounted as the March 21 deadline for the Oregon primary approached. If Rockefeller entered, it loomed as *the* primary battle of the year—an old-fashioned western shoot-out with Dick Nixon. On March 18, I sent Rockefeller a special-delivery note calling Oregon "your last train that will soon depart."

On Sunday, March 17—St. Patrick's Day—the "Oregon Draft Rockefeller Committee," led by Bill Moshofsky of Georgia Pacific, Alan "Punch" Green, Bob Ridgley and Ted Bruno, called on their candidate in New York. They presented him with 65,000 signatures placing his name on the ballot. They cited Rockefeller's firm lead over Nixon in the Bardsley and Waterhouse polls. Rockefeller was visibly impressed by their presentation. The Oregonians left New York confident that Rockefeller was about to throw his hat into the arena. The *New York Times* reported he was going to do just that.

Spiro Agnew, national chairman of the "Draft Rockefeller Committee," was so certain Rockefeller was going to run that he invited Maryland's capitol press corps to join him for the telecast of Rockefeller's March 21 press conference. Agnew's jaw is said to have dropped two inches when Rockefeller said, "I have decided today to reiterate unequivocally that I am not a candidate campaigning directly or indirectly for the Presidency of the United States." It caught all of us off guard.

I called Agnew and said, "I'll bet you are sitting there like a great turkey gobbler with your wattles absolutely purple!"

Agnew was fuming. He swore. He had been humiliated in what he had hoped would be his moment of glory. This is where he began moving into Nixon's camp.

Rockefeller had sent word that he was going to call both Agnew and me just before his news conference. But the calls were inexplicably cancelled. I was very surprised and extremely disappointed by Rockefeller's announcement. It was an enormous blunder not to have entered the Oregon primary.

Rockefeller would have defeated Nixon in Oregon. Everything was going his way. Since Oregon would have been the only contested primary, it, in all probability, would have determined the nomination. Watergate might have been remembered as the name of a luxurious Washington, D.C., apartment house if Rockefeller had gone after Nixon in Oregon. His failure to do so made Nixon the party's inevitable candidate.

In late April, Rockefeller changed his mind. It had been a month that shook the world—the assassination of Martin Luther King, the greatest pacifist since Mahatma Gandhi, followed by a wave of bloody riots; and the abdication of President Lyndon Johnson on the eve of his rejection in the Wisconsin primary. Rockefeller declared his candidacy on April 30 and, on that same day, won a remarkable write-in victory in the Massachusetts primary. A massive write-in effort was orchestrated in Oregon. Mayor Lindsay came out and campaigned for him. Audrey and I cast our write-in votes for Rockefeller, yet we knew that he had missed his chance. Nixon was campaigning throughout the state. Appling and Maurice Stans had raised $500,000 for their state Nixon campaign.

Nixon invited me to visit him at the Portland Hilton during his first 1968 campaign swing in the Pacific Northwest. He knew Oregon better than many Oregon politicians did. Since 1952, he had made at least one speaking appearance a year in the state. He had carried Oregon over President Kennedy in 1960. As a newsman, I had found Nixon somewhat calculating but not fully deserving of the Herblock cartoon of a heavy-bearded political mudslinger.

It was a more relaxed, more self-assured Nixon whom I met that day at the Hilton. He had a great deal to say. It was the most impressive array of knowledge I have ever heard from one man, a virtuoso performance. I could see how he was about to pull off the greatest comeback in the political record books. I resisted his efforts at courtship, although not completely.

A cluster of reporters were waiting in the lobby as we came down. Our conference had lasted for an hour and 40 minutes.

"It's been a very impressive contact with Dick Nixon, whom I've known for years," I said. "And I'd now put him number two on my list of presidential possibilities."

Nixon's face fell a little bit. What he did not know was that he was number 15 when he began our conversation. So he really made some headway. Rockefeller, of course, was still my choice.

Undaunted, Nixon continued to lobby for my endorsement. He wanted to line up some governors. I was viewed as a showcase liberal. Because I had been linked with Rockefeller, my conversion to Nixon would have been perceived as a breakthrough.

The Nixon forces made it clear that I was high on the list of those being considered for Secretary of the Interior. Bob Ellsworth, the former Kansas congressman who was Nixon's campaign manager, had a telegram they wanted me to send to all the Republican governors in the very probable event that Nixon would overwhelm all opposition in the Oregon primary.

I held the telegram in my hand. It said: "Dick Nixon, a great American, has won Oregon's primary. I urge you [Wally Hickel, or John Love, etc.] to join me in helping him move into the White House with a magnificent Republican victory in November."

If I had been expedient, like everyone else is in politics, I would have sent the telegram with visions of sugar plums and Cabinet meetings, but I was still hoping that Rockefeller might somehow have a chance at the convention.

When I wouldn't send it, they settled on another western governor—Wally Hickel of Alaska. Hickel met with Nixon at the Ramada Inn in Milwaukie, Oregon. Wally subsequently made a major initiative on behalf of Nixon and later became western director of the Nixon campaign. As his reward, he was appointed Secretary of the Interior. So, months afterward, I discovered how close I missed getting into the Cabinet. Wally Hickel, a plain-spoken, rough-hewn businessman, was the most courageous member of the Nixon Administration. He was fired for his forthright criticism of the gutter campaign tactics of Vice President

Agnew and for warning Nixon that they were alienating America's young people. Hickel's dismissal was, as Democratic Senator Ernest Gruening said, "both unjust and stupid."

Nixon won the Oregon primary with 65 percent of the vote. Rockefeller received 11.6 percent as a write-in. Nixon said many times that he won the Republican nomination on May 28 in Oregon. Rockefeller forfeited his last best hope.

Mark Hatfield also had national aspirations in 1968. For years, he had been promoted by the Republican National Committee as one of the "fresh new faces" in the party. Actually, Mark had held office continuously since 1950. Among the presidential hopefuls that year, Hatfield had been campaigning longer than any of them —except Nixon. In states less independent than Oregon, Hatfield might have started his candidacy as a "favorite son," but Oregon voters have never thought much of local candidacies. The only time an Oregonian won our presidential primary was in 1940 when Senate Minority Leader Charles L. McNary did it. McNary, however, was a major national figure, the highest ranking Republican officeholder in the United States. And he became the GOP vice-presidential nominee on the ticket headed by Wendell Willkie. In 1960, Senator Wayne L. Morse ran in Oregon's Democratic presidential primary and got walloped by John F. Kennedy. It was hailed as a signal victory for Kennedy. The defeat caused Morse deep embarrassment.

Hatfield correctly saw the presidential primary as a no-win situation. If he won, people would say, "So what?" If he lost, his inability to carry his own state would ruin his future as a national politician. His hopes were more realistically focused on the vice-presidential nomination.

Hatfield visited me at the Capitol not long before the primary. We talked about the presidential contest and assorted state issues. He began discussing the way our delegation to the Republican National Convention should be set up.

"I want you to be the chairman of the delegation this year," Hatfield said.

"Thank you," I said. "That's very nice of you. Isn't it generally true that the Governor is?" (Hatfield, as governor, had been chairman in 1960 and 1964. McKay had been chairman in 1952.)

"That's so," Hatfield said.

We were having a very polite talk. I asked, "What can I do in return?"

"I'd like to be on the Platform Committee," he said. Hatfield was actively involved in the great debate over the Vietnam War and said this committee assignment would be very important to him.

"Fine," I said. "Let's just consider it done."

In the primary, a Nixon landslide, my support of Rockefeller cost me some votes. There were 42 candidates for delegate-at-large. I ran slightly behind Hatfield—fewer than 4,000 votes separated us. I didn't hear from Hatfield after our meeting.

When the delegation was organized, Hatfield made himself chairman. It was a rigged election. Wendell Wyatt raised the question of honesty and propriety, knowing what the circumstances had been. Wyatt protested the repudiation of Hatfield's own proposition. Congressman John Dellenback leaned over, tapped Hatfield on the shoulder, and said, "I'm with you, Mark."

Perhaps Hatfield went back on his proposition because he felt the chairmanship would give him greater exposure. You really can't have much respect for somebody who does that. I went to the convention as the lowest ranking governor who had ever attended a national political convention. Always before, they had had some honorary title or an important committee assignment. I had nothing.

Hatfield threw himself at Nixon after the primary. He was so interested in the vice-presidential nomination that everything else seemed secondary. All of his liberal brethren in the Senate—Chuck Percy, Edward Brooke, Jacob Javits, Hugh Scott, Thruston Morton—were helping Rockefeller. Rockefeller minced few words over Hatfield's defection to Nixon. "Mark Hatfield just repudiated everything he's ever said about Vietnam," Rockefeller said.

In spite of Hatfield's maneuver which had denied me the chairmanship, I supported him for the vice-presidential nomination. It would have been a rare honor for the state. He was as experienced and qualified as any of the candidates who were being mentioned as possible Nixon running-mates. His seconding speech of Nixon was widely viewed as his Broadway tryout. The *Miami Herald* published an exclusive story by Don Oberdorfer, saying that Hatfield was Nixon's choice. John S. Knight, the newspaper's publisher, had been the first newsman to report the vice-presidential nominations of Richard Nixon in 1952 and Lyndon Johnson in 1960. To many observers, it seemed that Hatfield was about to enter the history books.

Ronald Reagan's forces tried to puncture Nixon's conservative Southern bloc by playing up the Hatfield story. Nixon operatives countered by dismissing the newspaper story. To show they meant business, Nixon people removed some "Nixon and Hatfield" posters which had been brought to the Convention Hall by Oregon delegates.

It later became known that Hatfield never really did have a chance. Dr. Billy Graham, a mutual friend of Nixon and Hatfield, urged Hatfield's selection because he was "a man of God." But the Southerners, who saved the nomination for Nixon, vetoed Hatfield, Lindsay and Percy for being too liberal. Ralph Cake, who had played a hand in getting Nixon on the ticket in 1952, said that Hatfield had also been ruled out by a conservative northern senator. Cake made no effort to help Hatfield; Nixon may have misled Mark. Hatfield is too smart to have gone for Nixon as far as he did unless there had been some kind of arrangement.

I believed Hatfield had gotten a rough deal from Nixon. The Oregon delegation all felt that Nixon had played us for suckers. We resented the way Hatfield had been treated, so we joined the floor movement against Spiro Agnew, Nixon's surprising choice. Hatfield would not allow his name to be placed in nomination. Neither would John Lindsay. Indeed, Lindsay gave a seconding speech for Agnew. George Romney permitted those of us dissatisfied with Agnew to support him. It was a principled gesture on Romney's part. Agnew rolled over him by a 10 to one margin.

After the convention, I was asked to campaign for Nixon in a number of western states. As a freshman Republican governor, I went along. They misused me in California. I campaigned for the national ticket in Los Angeles and in San Francisco. Then, they had me go to Sacramento to speak for a Republican legislative candidate. It was an intolerable abuse of a surrogate campaigner. They had me campaigning against a well-entrenched Democratic legislator who was an outstanding environmentalist. I was just another barnstormer giving an absolutely empty endorsement to a candidate I knew nothing about.

It bothered me that so few political leaders were addressing the threat posed by American Independent Party candidate George C. Wallace, whom I considered the shrewdest of southern demagogues. So, in my campaign travels, I spoke out about Wallace. "He is a frightening sideshow of magic and monsters," I said. "The Know-Nothings ride again."

The greatest danger of the Wallace candidacy was throwing the election into the House of Representatives and having the presidency determined by the Alabama segregationist. Fortunately, Wallace was not able to deadlock the democratic process.

Wallace won five states, more than nine million votes and 13 percent of the total vote. His candidacy denied Nixon a popular mandate. Indeed, Nixon's winning percentage was the lowest of any incoming president in more than 50 years.

Oregon's senate election was also a cliffhanger. Packwood, running one of the best organized campaigns I had ever seen, upset Senator Morse by 3,400 votes out of more than 800,000. Although I had endorsed and supported Packwood, I made no personal attacks on "The Tiger in the Senate." Morse had been a giant in American politics and I admired his outspoken independence. His willingness to risk political defeat and sacrifice his career on the Vietnam War was a profile in courage. Morse once told me, "I served with the idea that each term would be my last."

Morse did not accept defeat readily. One of the options he pondered after losing his Senate seat was running for governor. I was relieved when The Tiger chose not to take me on. I had enough problems without such a tenacious adversary. As things turned out, we resumed our friendship and were to become allies on a number of critical issues.

CHAPTER 7

Modernizing State Government

Over the years, Oregon governors had talked about making major changes in state government but little had happened since Os West's pre-World War I reforms. State Representative Rudie Wilhelm, Jr., a Portland Republican, made some recommendations as chairman of the "Little Hoover Commission" in the 1940s. Governor Holmes devoted much of his term to encouraging reorganization. He was very interested in giving the governor the proper tools to manage state government.

Governor Hatfield's Blue Ribbon Committee planted the seeds in 1960 for many of the changes which were enacted during my administration. Hatfield had sought, without success, a cabinet form of government. He was able to get through some of his programs. The Department of Commerce, for example, was created out of several independent agencies in 1963. As members of the Board of Control, Hatfield and I worked closely together in establishing the Corrections Division in 1965. But Oregon government, for the most part, remained a federation of loosely supervised baronies and fiefdoms, each agency and department concerned with its own self-perpetuation.

There was little, if any, coordination. We thought there were 175 state agencies, boards and commissions. After closer examination, we discovered about a hundred more. The governor had control of only a third. This made it possible for two-thirds of the state agencies to ignore or defy administration policies, yet the public expected the governor to take responsibility for every agency. It was a highly frustrating situation.

I appointed a special study group called "Task Force 70's" to investigate the ways and means of reorganization. Their study outlined how a governor could provide more thorough and efficient services on matters that were so often directed to him. Their analysis uncovered agencies, boards and commissions that previous governors had never heard of. They revealed that the governor was chairman of the State Power Agency. I had been intimately involved with Oregon's government for 20 years and never even knew it existed.

Whenever there had been a new problem, the Legislature or the Governor would create some new agency to take care of it. Year after year, these agencies kept proliferating. It was a topsy-like growth which had gotten out of control. To curb this trend, I inserted automatic self-destruct clauses in most of the Executive order committees and commissions that I appointed. The agency would go out of existence after it had completed a specific mission.

Many of the committees and commissions exemplified the Oregon system—the employment of public-spirited citizens as non-salaried volunteers in service of their state. On the Land Conservation Development Commission, seven people worked almost full time, without pay, taking terrible abuse. The Hatfield Blue Ribbon Committee had recommended that this citizen participation be continued even if Oregon did move toward a better coordinated state structure. If reorganization did anything, it forced us to look at these various entities and find out which ones, in a contemporary sense, were really necessary and had a job to do.

So even though we were trying to streamline government and put those segments together which had become so fragmented, we worked to retain this public participatory function. I'm not sure how thought-through this hybrid system was, but I think it has worked out fairly well. By tradition, the professionals say they are impeded by these citizen bodies, yet citizen participation ventilates the thinking of the professionals who sometimes get too close to the grindstone on the nitty-gritty of their problems and lose sight of what is in the public interest.

In creating the Transportation Department, we dismantled the Highway Commission. It had been the most desirable and sacrosanct of all the commissions. If you asked the businessman or farmer, who knew state government, which commission he would like to serve on, the Highway Commission was always his top choice. In terms of prestige and clout, the State Board of Higher Education ranked number two. Modern highways were, in a sense, born in Oregon. We were the state which, in 1919, invented the gasoline tax that pulled America out of the mud and launched the greatest highway system mankind has ever known, a more important event than even the building of the railroads.

We were faced with the ordeal of putting together a department where one partner, the highways, had $200 million, and the others, such as ports, had $20,000. The disparity in financing was such because of the historic pattern of the highway as the main form of transportation.

I began by having the commissioners—such as the heads of transportation and the head of highways, ports and aeronautics—meeting on an ad hoc basis. Finally, I recommended that they formally become a Transportation Commission. It knocked out all those commissioners, except one, in each of the five divisions.

The Transportation Department is now working toward a comprehensive, long-range transportation system for the state. In addition to managing the old Highway Commission, Board of Aeronautics, Department of Motor Vehicles and the Marine Board, it includes a new division which works with port authorities throughout Oregon.

The 1969 Legislature shared my commitment to government reorganization. In addition to approving the Transportation Department, it adopted my recommendations for centralizing other departments. The Executive Department became the management agency for the state government, which merged budget, accounting, and data processing systems; and included personnel division, the economic development division, and a Local Government Relations Division. I was always conscious of the importance of local government. And, in creating this division, I enhanced its capability to act. This division had the support and counsel of the League of Oregon Cities and the Association of Oregon Counties. It marked the first time that local governments had been brought into the dialogue of state policy decision-making.

Ed Westerdahl headed the Executive Department in its early years. He was wearing two hats because I still needed him as my executive assistant. Finally, Cleighton Penwell took over the Executive Department and kept it operating smoothly and effectively. Another innovation was the Department of Environmental Quality, which dramatically expanded the duties and responsibilities of the Sanitary Authority. It was given policing powers for air and water pollution, solid waste disposal and environmental controls. This really marked a new era in the battle to preserve Oregon's scenic beauty and livability.

As the session was closing, I was satisfied that more changes had been approved in those several months than had ever before been passed in a single legislative session. At my request, the legislature had redesigned state government. State Senate President Debbs Potts, a man of good sense who never broke his word, called me. "Governor," he said. "You've got the votes for your Natural Resources Department but won't you let up on us? We're beginning to look like a bunch of patsies. We've given you so much reorganization."

This was the informal, low-key way my proposal was blocked. If we had gotten the Department of Natural Resources, we could have averted many a bitter fight by consolidating the fish-raising activities of the Game Commission and the Fish Commission. They have more than 30 hatcheries between them which should be operated under a single head. We let Debbs—one of the most decent public men, anywhere—have his way.

Another legislative compromise involved the creation of the Ombudsman. This had not only been a pet project of our administration but it was also very dear to the heart of State Senator Ted Hallock of Portland, fiery liberal and chief sponsor of the bill. Unfortunately, State Senator Glen Huston of Lebanon let his personal feelings about Hallock get the better of him. Both were Democrats and they loathed each other as much as any two legislators ever did. Huston was chairman of the Senate "President's" Committee. The senate president would put bills there and Huston could arbitrarily kill them. We had a bill before Huston's committee to increase the compensation for injured workers. Our office had labored particularly hard on the workmen's compensation bill.

Huston came to me and said, "Are you going to support that son-of-a-bitch? Are you going to support his Ombudsman bill? If you are, your bills for workmen's compensation are dead."

I swallowed hard. We had to take the greater immediate good. Since Huston had life-and-death power over both bills, we had to go along with his ultimatum. Even if I had sided with Hallock, with whom I was often allied, I would still have lost both bills. Huston would have been sufficiently outraged to have held both of them in his committee, so we were able to get the workmen's compensation improvement. Politics is indeed the art of the possible.

The compromise with Huston did not in any way dampen our enthusiasm for the Ombudsman. I felt that government was getting larger and more insensitive. There were too many cries from the public which were not being heard. Some legislators had been wary of an Ombudsman because they felt their "hero role" in solving problems might be taken away from them, but after we got the office going, legislators were referring their constituents to the Ombudsman.

I created the Office of the Ombudsman by executive action on July 1, 1969. Though there was some whimpering about government by executive fiat, it was, I think, a sound decision. Setting the office up posed unique problems. We knew the Ombudsman sometimes was going to have to be anti-McCall administration, anti-agency, and the governor would still have to keep peace in the family. He had to have the independence to swing a fist on behalf of the downtrodden member of the public against the most powerful figures in state government. My idea was to let the chips fall where they may.

Some observers said the Ombudsman would have been more independent if he had been appointed by the legislature. If that had been the case, the Ombudsman would have been serving 90 masters. I thought he maintained his independence and autonomy far better as an arm of the Governor's Office run by an independent.

To walk this tightrope, I wanted someone who was independent, outspoken and bighearted. Grace Peck would have qualified but she was a member of the legislature. Marko Haggard fit the bill perfectly. He was a political science professor at Portland State and a Democrat. He was a man of great humanity, yet streetwise enough to know the structure of government and devise answers to most of the problems that were brought to him.

Marko would slash indiscriminately at the state's power elite— without fear of repercussions. He once came to the conclusion that the Highway Commission was arbitrary. I had telephone calls from two of the three members tendering their resignations. I talked them out of quitting under fire. Marko put me in a difficult position because everyone knew I had created the job and he was my appointee, attacking other appointees. At times, he may not have been tactful or diplomatic enough. But we wanted him to prove indeed that he was an independent operator and not a token functionary whose mission was to protect us from criticism. Marko kept on the job as long as he could. The position wears you out after a couple of years. You can only stand it so long. A certain percentage of the cases are unsolvable.

Marko was succeeded by Bob Oliver, a Harvard-trained lawyer who had been my legislative counsel. Bob performed brilliantly, but after a couple of years, he asked to be relieved. You just get exhausted and frustrated in trying to combat all the miseries of life —broken homes, starving people, old people without shelter. However, just having the Ombudsman on the job raised expectations and hopes for many. Moreover, the Ombudsman generally got results.

Another important first was the formation of a State of Oregon office in Washington, D.C. This vastly strengthened Oregon's voice in federal affairs. Establishing the Washington office was a delicate operation. We did not want to threaten the congressional

McCall conferring with State Senator Ted Hallock of Portland. The liberal democrat was a McCall ally and confidant although their personalities sometimes clashed.

delegation by implying that they weren't doing their jobs, in terms of casework for their constituents. So the choice of a person who understood the subtleties of politics, and, at the same time, could play a very strong role in state-federal relations, was vital.

I appointed Dale Mallicoat, whose breadth of public service uniquely qualified him for this assignment. He had been Howell Appling's assistant secretary of state, assistant state land commissioner and executive director of the State Land Board. Years earlier, he had been executive secretary to State Representative Frank Farmer of Polk County. He was the most even-handed, best-wearing person I knew. Another advantage was that his brother, Sam, was Senator Hatfield's administrative assistant. Dale encouraged cooperation among the state's congressional delegation and assisted them on state-federal issues. He'd bring things to their attention and was a great liaison between Salem and Capitol Hill.

Some critics charged that old Tom McCall just wanted a place to hang his hat when he was in Washington, but Dale's office was tremendously valuable to many state officials who used it as their headquarters during business trips to Washington. Chancellor Roy Lieuallen, for example, used it when he went back to testify on higher education. So did state legislators and people from the attorney general's office. Dale could often brief them on whatever issue had brought them east.

Having this office in Washington enhanced my capacity to be effective in federal affairs several fold. When I went back, Dale and I kept an exhausting schedule which would start with breakfast meetings and run through the evening. These sessions were with cabinet members, White House staff, and other federal officials. Dale cultivated relationships with most of the cabinet and sub-cabinet, developing important contacts which were of great benefit to Oregon.

Early in my term as governor, I learned that sending a telegram on a matter of significance made little impact. Former Florida Governor Farris Bryant, who was President Johnson's emissary to the statehouses, said a governor or team of governors should always testify in person. Where telegrams were dutifully filed in the hearing's record, a personal appearance often led to discussions which illuminated the problem. Dale kept his finger on congressional happenings of particular interest and prepared regular summaries for us. When I was unable to testify, he was an eloquent advocate.

As a direct result of Dale's work, Oregon received millions of extra federal dollars for patients in mental health hospitals, in special unemployment funds, and rent money for federal offices in state-owned buildings. When Oregon's pear growers were in a tremendous financial bind with massive surpluses, Dale put together groups of congressional and administration people to meet with a task force of Oregon growers. He knew how to make the federal bureaucracy serve the Pacific Northwest.

The best appraisal of Dale's work was probably a report by the Indiana governor's office. They surveyed the 14 states which then maintained offices in Washington. Their conclusion: "If we could set up an office like Oregon's, the program would be 100 percent worthwhile. Oregon's is the model set-up."

The Straub Administration scrapped the Washington, D.C., office, so they no longer have a direct pipeline to Washington. Members of our congressional delegation now find themselves explaining the same piece of legislation to different members of the governor's staff. There is no substitute for doing your homework.

Of all the reorganization changes, the hardest to achieve was the Department of Human Resources. It involved the elimination of the Board of Control which had been set up by Governor West in 1913 as a means of bringing the clout of the constitutional offices into the administration. Over the years, this had enabled the secretary of state and the state treasurer to broaden out in an official function other than managing fiscal affairs or being chief elections officer. They were charged with administering state mental and correctional institutions. It gave them considerable statewide exposure. In 1958 all three members of the Board of Control ran for governor. Most of the time, however, the board members tried to keep political considerations out of their official meetings.

Clay Myers was the man in the middle. He had been deeply committed to the improvement of state institutions. Regular visits to all the institutions were required. All of us made these periodic checks. While Clay enjoyed serving on the Board of Control, he also wanted to be loyal to me.

Straub fought the breakup of the Board of Control. He had been a good institutions man. But Bob's gubernatorial ambitions probably figured in his fight to save the board. He thought he was losing his forum.

There was a deadlock in the state senate over the board's fate. Finally, Senator Tony Yturri persuaded Senator Vern Cook to change his vote. This broke the stalemate, abolishing the Board of Control and enabling us to proceed with the Department of Human Resources.

This was a mammoth undertaking—a department with 10,000 employees and a $600 million budget. I said that a configuration of such size and scope would take time falling into place. Indeed, I predicted it would take a decade. It was so vast that parts were going to creak and even break down. Still, my feeling was that instead of having these problems scattered around in scores of agencies that were working independently of each other, we should put all of them under one roof.

Our consolidation made it possible for a family to go into one building to get vital services. The department handles some 250 programs for more than 500,000 clients. We extended the services to multi-purpose centers around the state.

I chose Jake Tanzer as the first director of Human Resources. Tanzer, who had been an assistant district attorney in Multnomah County, was a very compassionate lawyer. He had been a civil rights activist in Mississippi and was a great humanist. I put a good program man, Nick Peet, in as Tanzer's deputy.

Later, we changed that team to bring in Cleighton Penwell— who, as director, knew more about state government than anyone else. Former State Senator Cornelius Bateson, a Marion County

Democrat, who was head of our Health Division, became Penwell's deputy director. In time, we would have transferred Penwell and Bateson from Human Resources. It is probably the most difficult assignment in state government. The department became an issue in the 1974 gubernatorial campaign. Straub and Atiyeh brought up some of the things which were not working well. I told them to go ahead and debate but asked them to remember that this was a long-range project which would ultimately lead to better delivery of state services.

CHAPTER 8

The Nerve Gas Threat

On December 1, 1969, I was called to a military briefing at the Benson Hotel. Under Secretary of the Army Thaddeus Veal, Generals W. W. Stone and John Franklin—who was Commander of the Sixth Army—had made a special trip to Oregon to tell this onetime Seaman First Class that they were planning to relocate a substantial amount of lethal chemicals, used in warfare, to the Umatilla Ordnance Depot. They advised me that similar chemicals were already being stored at the Eastern Oregon military installation. I was taken aback when they solemnly reported the shipment was coming in from Okinawa, where the populace had protested until the Army had to move it. So, these men were simply telling me that the military was going to dump these deadly chemicals in Oregon. I swallowed hard and told them my office would have to check into their proposal to insure that no Oregonian would be jeopardized by the transport and placement of dangerous chemicals within our state. I knew I had no veto, and told them we would probably have to cooperate.

The next day, I flew to Washington for a presidential conference on drug abuse. Dale Mallicoat had arranged for me to meet with officials at the Pentagon and the White House so that I might learn more about the chemical shipments. Their comments were less than reassuring.

They told me that the Oregon shipment involved the most terrible chemical deterrent of all—nerve gas. I was stunned because President Nixon had just signed a resolution banning biological warfare materials from American arsenals, and this seemed to fit into that category. Apparently, to the Dr. Strangeloves of the world, you can get around almost any resolution. The military was eliminating germ-warfare toxins and substituting them with poison gas.

When I returned to Portland International Airport, I went to make a speech at a motel a short distance away. As I was going over my notes, a busboy came up to me and said, "You're not going to let them do this to us, are you?" Right then I began to see that I was entangled in an issue that was as emotional as any ever confronted by a governor.

Westerdahl and Schmidt told me there was no choice. "You've got to fight them," Ron said.

I knew they were right. There was no time to wait for Pentagon studies. I wrote President Nixon on December 5, urging him to cancel the shipment and to "consign nerve gas and like horror weapons to the limbo they so richly deserve." I also suggested that the Pentagon work on preparing a detoxification factory aboard ship to neutralize the fearsome chemicals. When there was no immediate reply, I called the White House the following week to repeat my message. I was curtly informed that the National Security Council was preparing an answer for the President's signature.

The only hopeful sign was that the Army, acting on my request, had postponed the shipments to make further studies on the risks involved. In making that announcement, I said: "I hope that the study will prove that these chemicals are no longer useful as a deterrent and that we will not be subjected to their storage within our state of Oregon."

State Treasurer Straub joined me in this effort. On December 10, he wrote President Nixon: "I strongly support the governor— both in his opposition to using the State of Oregon for storage of this unwanted gas, and in his recommendation for the manner in which it should be done away with." Since Straub was once again to be my opponent for the governorship, his action made the anti-nerve gas drive a truly bi-partisan effort.

The only announced Democratic candidate for governor when this crisis struck was Dr. Arthur Pearl, an outspoken University of Oregon professor. Pearl said that if he were governor, he would go and lie down on the railroad tracks in front of the train. "You don't have to be governor to do that," I said. "Be my guest."

Defense Secretary Melvin Laird wrote me on January 8. Laird insisted that the Nixon Administration was firmly committed to the Army's plan:

". . . The decision selecting the Umatilla Army Depot in Oregon as the relocation site was based on several factors, among which are its geographic location and its relative proximity to a deep-water Pacific port. I made these decisions with the interests of national security in mind.

"I do not believe that the transportation to and storage of these items at Umatilla is an unreasonable burden to ask of American citizens in light of the precautions that will be taken."

The White House called me after Secretary Laird's letter was released, wanting to know if it posed any problems. I told them it was unacceptable and that I resented Laird's cavalier attitude. Laird was contradicting Army Secretary Stanley Resor, who had told me that the Army would have detoxified the gases on Okinawa if it had been given the time and money to do the job. So it was obvious that the nerve gas was nonessential.

My office had received expressions of opposition from 23,360 Oregonians by early January. The *Oregon Statesman* and Eugene *Register-Guard* published strong editorials against the storage and shipment of the nerve gas. By mid-January, Dale Mallicoat had delivered these petitions, letters and clippings to the White House. We were assured that they would be given top-priority consideration at the next White House staff meeting.

"This is the strongest and broadest-based protest to develop in such a short time in Oregon," I said then. "It takes in the philosophical spectrum from peace marchers to military personnel and includes doctors, bankers, the elderly, students and employed adults of all ages.

"I am not trying to win a popularity contest on this issue, nor will I exceed the law and call out the National Guard or lie across the railroad tracks to stop the proposed shipments. The point to the great surge of sentiment against these munitions is that it supports my feeling that their shipments and storage did special violence to Oregonians' exceptional sensitivity to the environmental and moral issues involved.

"I had hoped for a more flexible position on the part of the Department of the Army. Now we have found that Secretary Laird's position is inflexible, we have appealed to the White House to review that position—to review it in light of its harshness from the standpoint of the people of Oregon. All Americans hope, of course, that the day will soon come for the utter renunciation of weapons of mass destruction by every nation. While we struggle in that direction, let us who disagree on the immediate problems be more charitable about one another's motives."

Governor Calvin Rampton of Utah urged me to keep up the fight. Rampton served notice on the Pentagon that no such shipments would be welcome in his state, either. Our battle seemed futile. When Straub announced his candidacy for governor, on January 26, he said, "I believe McCall has done all he can do."

Still, we had to keep trying. I spoke on a television program in Washington State—and 63,000 persons signed a protest petition. By the first of March, there were 40,000 signatures from Oregonians. I delivered more than 3,000 letters from University of Oregon students to Secretary of the Army Resor. Our meeting was no more productive than my three earlier sessions with him. If anything, he was more implacable in his determination to ship the nerve gas. I wrote President Nixon again, requesting his intervention.

In Eastern Oregon, there was some parochial bitterness over the controversy. Some people thought they were being discriminated against economically. It was like the old Albany proverb about the pulp mill: "It might have stunk to the tourists driving by. To us, it's the smell of greenbacks." The Umatilla Army Depot would be expanding its payroll to handle the nerve gas, but the money-grubbers were greatly outnumbered. Stacks and stacks of petitions kept coming into my office.

The U.S. Surgeon General posed some disturbing questions in his April 3 letter to Secretary Laird. Governor Dan Evans of Washington and I sent Laird a joint letter on April 18:

Gerry Lewin

McCall spoke at an anti-war rally and urged demonstrators to keep the pressure building against nerve gas.

McCall sent petitions to the White House to protest the shipment of lethal nerve gas to the Pacific Northwest.

Above: Senator Henry M. "Scoop" Jackson
Washington put pressure on President Nix
to stop the nerve gas shipment to the Pac
Northwest. McCall said Jackson's intervent
turned the tide.

Left: Secretary of Defense Melvin Laird was
unresponsive that McCall initiated a l
suit against him.

"Governors of Oregon and Washington urgently appeal to you for early decision regarding shipment and storage of chemical munitions from Bangor, Washington, to Umatilla, Oregon. We wish to inform you of serious problems which render the shipment unwise. It is our earnest hope you will be able to review these problems and cancel the shipment prior to court action now ready for filing by our states."

Among the considerations we cited were these:

"The U.S. Surgeon General recommended that you 'satisfy yourself and me of the capability of providing emergency medical treatment and evacuation of members of the public in the event of an unforeseen accident or other incident in the course of the transportation.'

"Red Hat OPS Plan places responsibility on the states for 'Preparation of Evacuation plans, to include evacuation routes and reception centers' and 'to establish contingency plans and procedures for care and feeding of evacuated persons including coordination with the American Red Cross and other agencies.'

"The states of Oregon and Washington have each notified the US Office of Civil Defense that large-scale evacuation is not practicable and such a plan cannot be prepared at the state level. Large urban areas, on or near the route, present insoluble transportation problems, and great if not insuperable difficulties in housing the aged, the lame, and the sick in remote medical facilities.

"Due to the impossibility of the states' satisfying the Surgeon General's concerns on the above points, we believe his letter of April 3 must place him in a position of opposing any shipment under the existing plan. . . .

"It is vital to note that the above situation, whose disruptive potential must be balanced against the need for chemical munitions, is to be taken most seriously even in the event no actual spill occurs. If there were a rupture, leakage, or explosion, the problems discussed above would be multiplied by many times through uncertain variables of weather, site of spill and containers.

"We most strenuously petition you to find an alternative disposition for the chemical munitions. It is our earnest hope that the decision to make the shipments can be reversed as a result of your personal decision."

Because Laird was as stubborn and unyielding as ever, we prepared to take him on in federal court. Attorney General Lee Johnson had been working with me since our office first learned of the shipment. Johnson, after much review, advised me that our chances were remote if the Defense Department complied with public safety regulations. But, upon reviewing the Army's final plan for shipment and storage of the gas, he concurred that it imposed duties on the State of Oregon which were constitutionally the exclusive responsibility of the federal government.

I instructed Attorney General Johnson to file a lawsuit against Secretary Laird seeking an injunction against the massive shipments of poison gas. At a news conference on Tuesday, April 21, I said: "Frankly, I am dismayed since receiving the Army's plan of shipment, April 6. We have been advised for several days running now that Secretary Laird is going to announce the go-ahead of the project. Each day we expect an announcement, we learn instead of a change in plans.

"The plan we received was inadequate, impractical and imposed responsibilities on the State of Oregon which we do not have the resources or the capabilities to perform. If the Secretary of Defense is intent on making this dangerous and unnecessary shipment, then the people of Oregon are entitled to the maximum protection humanly possible. Under the circumstances, I feel I have no other choice but to seek the aid of the federal courts to compel the Secretary of Defense to perform his responsibilities."

On May 22, a Federal District Court held that the Defense Department had satisfied all legal requirements on the nerve gas. It appeared that our long struggle had been in vain. I asked Attorney General Johnson to appeal the decision. I called the White House and all but demanded an immediate meeting with President Nixon. I would be accompanied by Governor Evans and the Oregon and Washington congressional delegations.

"My office," I said, "has worked nearly six months on this problem trying in every legal way to resolve it. We have not yet been successful, but we have not given up. We are told the Okina-wans are upset and afraid of having it around. We are also told the Guamanians would decline the storage of nerve gas because of the same fears, but as far as the U.S. Northwest is concerned, the people's opinion doesn't seem to elicit much Washington, D.C., interest. Never in the history of Oregon has its citizenry united in such an overwhelming majority. Every age group, every economic group, every occupational group—every possible kind of groups says NO!

"We have been told it will arrive, whether we like it or not. I strongly urge all concerned citizens to immediately write or wire our four Northwest United States Senators with support for their amendment to the Military Sales Act prohibiting use of any funds for shipping nerve gas to the United States. We must continue the fight in the federal courts and in the Congress of the United States."

Senator Scoop Jackson, a Cold War hard-liner who had been invited to become Nixon's Defense Secretary, came out squarely against the shipment in early May. Jackson took the Washington State petitions—written on a roll of paper as long as a football field—to the White House and was personally received by Nixon. When we delivered our petitions, a military attache picked them up at the back door.

Jackson flexed his powerful legislative muscles after the court decision. He went down to the White House and told Nixon that he'd better stop the shipment. I'm sure that Jackson told Nixon he was committing political suicide in the Pacific Northwest. So Jackson drove the point home. After his meeting with Nixon, Jackson broke the good news. We had blocked the shipment. Jackson gave Oregon credit for starting the agitation and for keeping it going.

It took some time before the White House press office got wind of what had happened. I called the White House after a wire-ser-vice report on Jackson's news conference. They would not con-firm the report. Governor Evans was irked that he had not been called, but we were all elated that our "Mr. Smith Goes to Washington" crusade had finally triumphed. Frank Capra could not have envisioned a more satisfying conclusion.

"Once again the people have spoken and their government has heard," I said. "For those who had serious doubts, let this be proof that the system does work; that the White House does and must listen; that the Pentagon ultimately is compelled to obey the citizenry. Never before have the people of the Pacific Northwest been so united in a single cause. Credit for this welcome change in plans must go to the people where, first and finally, power resides. It was the unified will of hundreds of thousands of Pacific Northwest residents that moved the national government to revise its direction.

"Oregonians—and their Washington neighbors—are extremely sensitive about the environment and any threat leveled against it. They have spoken and their will has been done. We can only hope that the message will be internationally noted and that this decade will see the utter renunciation of warfare itself."

CHAPTER 9

Vortex: The Governor's Rock Festival

Throughout the Vietnam War, Americans were polarized as never before. Most of the demonstrations during that turbulent decade went off peacefully, yet there had been notable exceptions, such as the 1968 Democratic National Convention where Mayor Richard Daley encouraged his Chicago police to use strong-arm tactics against anti-war demonstrators. Norman Mailer later wrote, "Children, and youths, and middle-aged men were being pounded and gassed and beaten, hunted and driven by teams of policemen who had exploded out of their restraints like the bursting of a boil." The whole world witnessed the bloody confrontation. We had entered a climate of white-hot tempers and it would take years for the nation to cool. President Johnson's National Commission on the Causes and Prevention of Violence termed the disorder a "Chicago police riot."

If demonstrators broke the law, it was generally a form of civil disobedience. There were, for example, sit-ins on many college campuses. Non-violence usually prevailed in such situations. A handful of radical activists sometimes tried to turn peaceful demonstrations into riots by provoking policemen. They were straightforward in saying their goal was revolution. This attitude was held by but a tiny minority. Most of the protesting masses wanted nothing more than peace and political reform.

When President Nixon astonished the nation by invading Cambodia, hundreds of demonstrations were called in protest. By comparing anti-war demonstrators to Nazi stormtroopers, Vice President Agnew was heating up the explosive climate still further. On May 4, 1970, National Guardsmen shot 15 students during a demonstration at Kent State University in Ohio. Four were killed. A nationwide student strike followed as 2,500 colleges and universities shut down. President Nixon declared a state of emergency and invited the governors to the White House for a meeting. I declined, pointing out that I was needed at home. My weekly open house, which normally took 45 minutes, ran nearly three hours because so many visitors stopped by to express their concern about America's course.

Many blamed the students for the Kent State tragedy. A Gallup poll indicated that 58 percent of those polled said "demonstrating students" were at fault. Tensions were mounting in Oregon. In Ashland, the townspeople were absolutely furious when President Jim Sours lowered the flag at Southern Oregon College. They were preparing to march on the campus. Everybody was cursing and moaning and grabbing rifles and pitchforks.

State Senator Lynn Newbry, a big, soft-spoken orchard farmer, said, "Fellows, does it really make a bit of difference whether the flag is a few feet lower for a few minutes today? Does it really make that much difference?" Newbry made it sound like such an over-reaction that the crowd just melted away. He truly had demonstrated grace under pressure.

It was a national trauma. In what may have been the most pessimistic analysis of America since Cotton Mather, John W. Gardner said: "Virtually all of us have failed in our duty as Americans. The failure goes to every level and phase of American life. . .and while each of us pursues his selfish interest. . .the nation disintegrates."

Vice President Agnew called the Kent State slayings "predictable and avoidable." The Scranton Commission would later ascertain that Agnew's rhetoric had helped set the stage for Kent State.

Not long after Kent State, I received word that Oregon seemed destined to be the next battleground. I felt shock waves as Attorney General John Mitchell said an explosive confrontation might occur in the City of Portland in September. The American Legion was holding its national convention at Memorial Coliseum. According to the U.S. Justice Department, some 50,000 young people calling themselves the People's Army Jamboree were planning to descend on Portland at the same time. Some of the group's members openly welcomed a riot. I could envision our state being pulled apart before the world's television cameras.

The Jamboree—first called "The Revolutionary Festival of Life" —was organized during the spring. It was activated and publicized through chapters of the Students for a Democratic Society (SDS) on college campuses all over the country. Their plans for a massive confrontation with the Legion were mapped out throughout the spring and early summer. Concerted recruitment of persons to join the Jamboree—primarily through underground newspapers—began in May, following the Kent State shootings.

On July 6, I asked the Jamboree not to hold their gathering simultaneously with the Legion. I warned of the possible violence, saying, in part, "I urge you to reschedule the People's Army Jamboree."

My request was summarily rejected. They accelerated their efforts. Periodic intelligence reports, evaluations and briefings from state and federal law enforcement agencies seemed to confirm what the Attorney General had said: there was no greater confrontation in prospect in the United States.

All of us who were trying to prevent this disaster had learned from the experiences of Chicago and Kent State. I vowed that every means available would be used to protect the citizens of Oregon. Ed Westerdahl became the coordinator of our efforts. He was the chief-of-staff and director of operations. A full-time, 24-hour command center was established on the 20th floor of the Portland Hilton.

A community group, "People for Portland," was formed to help try to find a way to keep things peaceful. A number of suggestions were made to avoid confrontations. I was asked to make land available so that the people coming to Oregon would have a place to go and things to do other than being swept into an angry mob. I remembered a Stanford University study which had shown that people were twice as likely to resort to violence when they were part of an emotionally charged crowd. So the idea of an alternative site had considerable merit.

When I decided to grant use of a state park for this purpose, I knew it would be controversial. "I've just committed political suicide," I told Schmidt. "But it's the right thing to do—and it's got to be done. We've got to save the people of Oregon and all these visitors from the agony of a bloody confrontation."

We selected McIver Park, 20 miles southeast of Portland in Clackamas County, as the location of a "rock festival," to coincide with the American Legion Convention. Our thought was that the young people could show their belief in peaceful expression of their views at such a gathering. It would also divert most of the masses from Portland and the potential confrontation. Because this idyllic state park is closed to overnight camping, there was much outrage and some fright in Clackamas County when I declared it would be open day and night for "The Governor's Rock Festival."

The town nearest the park is Estacada. A number of angry residents protested my announcement. They thought hordes of bearded long-hairs and pot-smokers were going to ruin the countryside.

One woman called me and said, "We're not going to put up with it."

I replied, "But many of those who will come are your children and your neighbors' children. Do you want them hassled in the city and beaten up and shot down simply because they wear long hair and beards? What would you propose to do in this confrontation?"

She said, "Goddammit, shoot 'em."

Mayor Terry Schrunk of Portland and Chairman Mike Gleason of the Multnomah County Board of Commissioners had great sensitivity to what was happening. City Councilman Frank Ivancie took a law-and-order stance. Ivancie was adamant against letting any of these young people into city parks. We thought some city parks should be opened up so that we could keep draining possible confrontations out of the center of Portland. Finally, Ivancie assumed such an absolutely obdurate position that Mayor Schrunk relieved him as head of the Bureau of Parks. The Mayor

Oscar Palmquist

McCall met with students at University of Oregon's Free Speech Platform in the fall of 1970. Carl Blackburn, later an assistant football coach at Oregon, is at left. University President Robert Clark is in the middle.

McCall went on statewide television and radio to explain his decision to sponsor a rock festival during the week of the American Legion convention.

McCall permitted the marathon rock festival, "Vortex I," at Milo McIver State Park, hoping to avoid violence in Portland. Though controversial, it worked. . . . "Vortex worked far better than any of us had dared hope. Some 35,000 young people went to the rock festival at McIver Park. There was some nude bathing and pot smoking. But it was peaceful and friendly. The whole episode was a great contribution to an understanding between the ages and generations."

Gerry Lewin

took the job over himself and made Delta Park available for the demonstrators.

The strategists for the "People's Army," from what we learned, were interested in having a huge mass of people in downtown Portland where they could be manipulated. We also knew that the great majority of demonstrators were not hostile or bloodthirsty. Most of them wanted merely to exercise their First Amendment rights by chanting and waving some signs.

A few demagogues, however, shouting out divisive rhetoric, were prepared to whip the crowd into a frenzy. With this mass of people running through the streets, a confrontation would be imminent. Arson and other acts of destruction were among the side effects that could have resulted.

A few months earlier, in Santa Barbara, California, a mob of student radicals had burned a police car, ransacked some real estate offices and firebombed a local branch of the Bank of America. I bore responsibility for protection of Oregon residents and property—and for the safety of our visitors. I had never experienced such strain and stress.

Secretary of the Interior Wally Hickel, the keeper of the federal park system, strongly endorsed my McIver Park initiative as "both a wise and responsible decision." Hickel had given President Nixon a stern warning after Kent State: ". . .if we read history, it clearly shows that youth in its protest must be heard." So Hickel's moral support was a great boost to our spirits.

I was in our Portland Hilton operations center when my old friend, New York Mayor John Lindsay, called me: "Tom, I'm in town for the national convention of the Municipal League and I've seen what you are doing to prevent violence next week. It is the only way to go to try to avert a bloody confrontation between the American Legion and the People's Army Jamboree."

Then Lindsay paused and framed his warning: "I'm afraid, though, Tom, no matter what your success as a peace-keeper, your voters will end up ripping you to pieces. You may be crucified." I told Lindsay that we had forgotten about the election, which was barely two months away.

Because of the urgency of this situation, I decided to carry my message before the people of Oregon in a statewide television address. It marked the first time that a governor of Oregon had addressed the entire state in an emergency. A direct appeal for peace and cool-headedness seemed the best course. I also felt the people should be given the background, the planning, and the possibilities of the upcoming events. I spoke from the KOIN television studio. It was a strong speech but not bullheaded. I also made a warm appeal to respect the hospitality of Oregon.

I said, in part: "Three days from now, Portland will host two groups. They could not be more dissimilar. Their simultaneous presence here has already generated tension—and could trigger violence. We will be tested to the ultimate.

"While the Jamboree's planning is directed toward confrontation, great numbers of young people attracted to Portland are *not* coming to riot. . . . They are coming to peacefully exercise their constitutional rights. Our reports were, however, that some would seek to manipulate the others as pawns to trigger serious and possibly violent confrontation. This was the setting for polarization facing Oregon earlier this summer. By then it was obvious that—should the anticipated numbers arrive—Portland could not deal with the situation.

"In consultation with civic, church and local government leaders, and with the advice and counsel of the FBI, I committed our resources. As Governor, I agreed to do all I could to prevent tragedy from breaking out in Portland. Out of those discussions over many weeks there has emerged a comprehensive plan. . . . It's a positive, effective and responsible approach to protecting the lives and property of all in Oregon. That, I believe, is what government is all about. In this situation we have prepared for the worst while hoping for the best. If the objective of averting conflict is not achieved, we are prepared to put down any violence that occurs. You may be assured that we are well prepared. . . . Our commitment to law and order has not tempted us to infringe upon the constitutional rights of Americans for peaceful assembly, freedom of movement and nonviolent dissent. That, too, is what government is all about.

"While we are prepared to *deal* with violence, keep it clear that our first priority is to *avoid* violence. It is within this framework —avoiding violence—and upon the strong urging of local, state and federal law enforcement officers that Vortex I emerged.

"Vortex is an activity planned and sponsored by a group of responsible young people, financially supported by People for Portland. This financial support has been committed from literally every major business in the Portland area. Law enforcement officials agreed that such an activity was needed. Upon their recommendation we surveyed the entire four-county area and granted the use of McIver State Park. They have advised me of the danger of thousands of young people roaming in bands through the residential areas of Portland at all hours of the day and night—restless, without a home base, without planned activity. Vortex was a conscious and direct response to the problem of suddenly trying to absorb these thousands of young people into the City of Portland—young people without a place to stay.

"There will still be some who want to thwart authority. With many of these, reason and option are of little or no value. To these people, I say: The State of Oregon, the City of Portland and the surrounding counties do not want violence, but we are fully prepared to protect our citizens. We have prepared the resources necessary to fulfill this commitment. This is not the rattling of swords, this is a statement of fact. The laws of this state and this community will be upheld. To those who understand this statement, alternatives are available. To those who choose to ignore this statement, less peaceful alternatives are in store. Vortex was authorized as a safety valve—as a defusing mechanism for reducing the numbers we may have to deal with in Portland. We can say to those young who are truly dedicated to peaceful disagreement: go to McIver Park or Delta Park. These are your alternatives to milling madness."

In closing, I addressed several different audiences. I told the Legionnaires: "As avowed targets of political confrontation, it is only reasonable to expect that some of you will become objects of taunting, of verbal abuse, of inflammatory gestures, of obnoxious provocation. The purpose of such acts is precisely to evoke your reaction; even, possibly in the hope you will react violently. Don't give them a victory. Don't let them use you. Don't be the tool of the radicals."

To Oregon residents, I said: "Just as the Legion may be a precise target for confrontation, the community at large is a general target. Many of you, too, will be subjected to the same provocations by those who seek to disrupt. Don't give the provocateurs a score. Just as I asked the Legion, I also ask you to resist the temptation to let fly. I also ask you not to let yourselves be used."

In a final appeal to the young people, I said: "Much of what I've said, by implication, casts on you the long and dark shadows of those who seek violent confrontation and world revolution. I know that most of you are just as opposed to violence as I am. I know that many of you are visiting here just to have a good time, or just to be where the action is, or just because you are curious. But let me point out that you, too, can be used by those amongst you who seek bloodshed. It is a deadly game. Don't be a pawn in that kind of game.

"Your presence in large numbers creates physical problems, housing problems, health problems, sanitation problems, and— perhaps most significant of all—your presence contributes further to an already tense situation. I ask that you respect the human rights and the property rights of others—that you show that you respect yourselves by your own conduct."

I ended the broadcast on an encouraging note: "Very recently intelligence reports have advised me that the tide of young people coming to Portland for confrontation may be waning. I say 'may be' because the reports are too scattered to be conclusive. The reasoning for this wane in the tide is that the word has gone out: Oregon's preparedness has dampened the fires of enthusiasm of those who would create chaos in our communities.

". . . For weeks now we have been doing those things best calculated to serve the public interest—perhaps not flawlessly, but to serve it so as to minimize to the greatest degree possible the risk to life and property—and to Oregon's image as a hospitable and law-abiding state. Hopefully, this will be the Columbus Day Storm that never came, but if it does, Oregon is prepared."

So I was letting the public know the whole story from beginning to end. My explanation was made and the events unfolded.

The poise and attitude of the law enforcement officials were reassuring. When I called out the National Guard, these citizen soldiers chose to name their assignment "Operation Tranquility." I had insisted that the Guardsmen would be unarmed. As the Scranton Commission would later warn, "The Kent State tragedy must surely mark the last time that loaded rifles are issued as a matter of course to guardsmen confronting student demonstrators."

I had a helicopter on call for crowd dispersal, but instead of loading it with tear gas, I had it filled with rose petals. Since Portland is the City of Roses, I thought this would serve as a friendly warning to overzealous demonstrators. If a crowd had persisted, the tear gas would have been utilized.

There was no confrontation. Vortex worked far better than any of us had dared hope. Some 35,000 young people went to the rock festival at McIver Park. There was some nude bathing and pot smoking. But it was peaceful and friendly. The whole episode was a great contribution to an understanding between the ages and generations.

I wanted to go to McIver Park and thank everyone for helping preserve Oregon's peace. Another reason was that if my administration was going to be voted out over Vortex, I wanted to be a witness to the scene that was responsible. Ed Westerdahl said, "Lord, no. You'll go out there and the members of The Family will see you and they'll all rush up and throw their arms around you. Television will take a picture of it—and you'll be dead politically."

So we went out when the rock concert was over. This group called The Family was cleaning up. Westerdahl was exactly right. They all ran up and threw their arms around me. It was a very emotional moment. We all held hands around a campfire.

The Family had been a sort of steadying force throughout Vortex. They were very sweet and kind people. I thanked them for helping to maintain order and looking out for the ill and for trying to keep people from overindulgence. It had been a remarkable effort.

When everything was over, the only damage of any kind had been one broken four-by-six-inch windowpane at Portland State University. Our prevention operation had cost time and money—$12,886 for the McIver Park Festival and $76,811 for other protective action. The U.S. Justice Department had established Portland as having the "highest risk of violence in the nation this summer." So this insurance had been cheap.

A survey of national violence during the week of Vortex indicated that the era of white-hot tempers had not subsided. In Madison, Wisconsin, a plastic bomb rocked the University of Wisconsin's Mathematics Research Center. The blast killed a graduate student and injured four others. In Minneapolis, a bomb damaged the Old Federal Office Building. At Harvard University a bomb was discovered in the John F. Kennedy School of Government. In Radford, Virginia, an army arsenal was rocked by an explosion which killed two people and injured four others. An American Legion headquarters was bombed in Seattle. A school was bombed in Rocky Mount, North Carolina. A journalist was killed in an East Los Angeles riot. Policemen were slain in Berkeley, Omaha, Chicago, and Philadelphia. And in Portland: one broken window.

I fully expected to get torn to pieces politically. A spring poll by J. Roy Bardsley published in the *Sunday Oregonian* had shown Straub leading me by one percentage point among registered voters. What I didn't know was that Straub had taken a later poll and learned that people thought my Achilles' heel was indecisiveness. When I went on radio and television, proclaiming that nobody was to be hassled in Oregon because, on the one hand, he was young and bearded, or because, on the other, he had fought for his country, people concluded, to my astonishment, that I could be very decisive after all, and they admired me for that—if not for my acceptance of grass smoking and skinny dipping. Twenty percent of the people still hate me because of the rock festival. But, to the great majority, it was a stirring demonstration of how tough problems can be—and how you can't always black and white them.

Straub became very pious about the pot smoking and other aspects of Vortex. Rather than give credit to the bipartisan and civic-minded team which had prevented violence, he went on the attack.

I responded: "It is easy now, after the fact, to find fault with the way in which we prevented violence in Portland during those critical days. It was not so easy for city, county, state and federal government at the time. Certainly, we must look for mistakes— but in a spirit of preparing ourselves better to deal with future crises, and not of demeaning those who tried to exercise their best judgment under agonizing circumstances."

The *Oregon Journal*, which had supported Straub in 1966, cited Vortex as one of its reasons for endorsing me for re-election: ". . . while nationally youth tends to gravitate to the Democratic party, recent days have presented the interesting spectacle of Democrat Straub accusing Republican McCall of excessive permissiveness in giving state sponsorship to the Vortex rock festival which was part of McCall's strategy for averting violence at the time of the American Legion convention in Portland last month. A majority of Oregon's citizens, however, we believe have accepted that McCall did what he had to do to keep Portland cool, and have approved his courage and inventiveness."

In any event, I won by a greater margin than I had four years earlier.

Gerry Lewin

Testifying before a legislative committee.

Gerry Lewin

McCall in reflective moment.

Gerry Lewin

The nation's tallest governor talks to a constituent.

McCall received an honorary degree from Willamette University.

McCall threw the first pass for the Portland Storm of the short-lived World Football League.

McCall and "Duffy," a longtime family pet. Unlike some politicians, McCall did not give speeches about his dog.

CHAPTER 10

Commentator-at-Large

One of the questions I heard most often after becoming governor was, "How do you like being on the other side of the microphone?" People were naturally curious about the transformation from reporter and news analyst to newsmaker. They soon discovered that once a commentator, one is always a commentator. When reporters asked what I thought, I told them.

My first experiences with the Washington press corps came at West Yellowstone, Montana, where the 1967 Western Governors' Conference was held. Montanans had wrought a miracle, refurbishing a long-dead railroad depot as their convention hall. I quickly learned that you didn't need to call a news conference to get national attention. Once I stopped to chat with Harold Hughes of the *Oregonian* and Doug McKean of the *Oregon Journal*, and I was pinned down for forty minutes by a group of more than thirty television, radio, newspaper and magazine reporters, analysts and commentators. The press, hunting in packs for angles on the Republican presidential contest, wanted my innermost thoughts.

I told them that there were twelve faceless souls from as many state capitols at the conference, twelve nobodies, plus very much of a somebody, regionally and nationally, Governor Ronald Reagan of California. I described Reagan as "the hottest political property of the Republicans" and "the best drawing card of either party." I made it clear that Rockefeller was still my candidate and that I disagreed with Reagan's political philosophy—but my comments about my California neighbor's rising stature made national headlines.

The next day Tom Mooney of the Lee Papers in Montana questioned me on the similarities of Oregon's and Montana's tax problems. Eight other interviewers moved into position. By the end of the conference, my commentaries had reached a wider audience than I could ever have imagined in my earlier television career.

Most Oregon editors seemed to like what they saw about West Yellowstone. An *Oregon Journal* editorial said:

"The recent Western Governors' Conference catapulted Oregon's Governor Tom McCall into the national limelight, not as a presidential figure, but as one governor willing and ready to speak out on any question that arose. It was his long apprenticeship as a newspaperman and broadcast commentator, which preceded his political career, that led to the national spotlight. Only the star appeal of California's Governor Ronald Reagan drew more attention.

"McCall is still at home in the newsroom, chatting in reporter-to-reporter style with old colleagues. Sometimes he is amazed to find his comments in the next day's newspapers and he has to remind himself that he is a governor now—and a very quotable governor, at that."

The editorial went on to say that I "left newsmen from other states, accustomed to a cool aloofness from their chief executives, shaking their heads, but grinning in gratitude."

Not everyone approved of my relationship with the press. Giles French, a former curmudgeon of the Oregon House of Representatives, and for many years the publisher of the *Sherman County Journal*, thought I was doing myself irreparable harm. Two days after I had been renominated in 1970 came this note from French:

"My dictionary defines laryngitis as an inflammation of the membrane of the larynx. It does not go into detail about its effects, which may in some cases be beneficial—for instance, in the suppression of logorrhea, which is a more disastrous disease than laryngitis. Incidentally, congratulations. There's only one man who can beat you and his name is not Straub."

Even though French was a newspaperman, he was emphatic that intricate public business should be conducted in secret, and in the 1940s and 1950s, when he was in the legislature, that was how business was done. I reminded him that I had been Governor McKay's executive assistant and press secretary, that he was forgetting that "I straddled the old days and the new."

I wrote Giles: "Life in Salem is much more precarious than in the one-party days when you and other Republican field generals decided everything behind Marion Hotel locked doors. For example, the press corps is four times as large today as it was then—and I try, perhaps too successfully for my own good, to operate in the open. Hence, there are as many as a dozen press contacts some days.

"Under like circumstances, were you governor in 1970, with your acid tongue, wit and pen, I suspect you would double me in spades in the art of mass alienation. It would be nice of you, then, instead of rattling under a tumbleweed, to give me some of your pungent advice now and then.

"Anyhow, thanks for the note of caution, but try to understand that in today's super-ramified government, a governor is bowed and buffeted by more damned-if-you-do damned-if-you-don't issues in a month than used to come down the pike in a year."

Giles disputed me in another of his letters, contending it was the illusion of every generation of politicians that its times were the most difficult and unmanageable.

My years with Governor McKay taught me much about press relations. McKay had always been accessible to reporters and willing to speak his mind on anything. He once told me, "Never get in a fight with a policeman, a reporter or your wife because you can't win." When I first joined his staff, he said: "You are going to hear lots of glowing appeals that sound very convincing on any given issue. Withhold your judgment until you hear all sides." So McKay had been a good mentor.

The first thing I asked Ron Schmidt to do, on the eve of my first inauguration, was to put out an advisory to the news media promising that we would always be available and honest with them. We worked hard to carry out that pledge for eight years. Our administration made candor its hallmark. As a result, we were probably the most thoroughly covered administration in the state's history. Indeed, we were covered in more detail than any government at our level in the United States. We even let the press know that it could come to our staff meetings, which we held daily. At these meetings, the germ of many ideas appeared for the first time. So the press would show up at staff policy sessions from time to time, usually on slow news days.

As a general policy, attendance by the press lasted only over a period of several weeks. I told A.P.'s Paul Harvey, who was the senior correspondent at the Capitol, that press attendance might be counterproductive. "It really doesn't work to have the press in at the incipiency of these ideas," I said, "because not everyone present feels free to discuss them. And, at my staff meetings, you have to throw up all sorts of ideas—idiotic or not—to get the thought process going. If somebody is there to take only the most sensational and far-out ideas, then you don't get an innovative thought process moving."

Harvey said, "I'm not coming any more to your staff meetings."

"I think I understand you," I said. "It's sort of like intruding on a lover's tryst, isn't it?"

He said, "Exactly."

Such intrusion sometimes did inhibit the development of ideas in an idea-prone administration. One of my department heads, Nick Peet, complained that having the press in the room turned informal sessions into a stilted television presentation. The talk became more guarded and restrained. The staff policy level was the seedbed of nearly everything we tried.

One of the most publicized pieces that came up in this open staff session emerged after I had vetoed a 50-mile limit for foreign fishing off the Oregon Coast. I was highly sympathetic to this cause, namely, protecting Oregon's offshore fisheries from the greed of foreign fishing fleets. But the Attorney General, Lee Johnson, held that it couldn't be done. Oregon couldn't extend the United States. Only the United States Congress had the power to do so, with presidential approval. My veto was greatly misread and I was attacked along the coast for not being sympathetic with our commercial fishermen or supportive of the resource.

The legislators, heading back for a brief 1974 special session, seemed hell-bent on an override. They appeared to have enough votes to undo my veto. At our staff meeting, I said, "This only breeds scorn for the law because this law would be unenforceable. But if it's on the books, I've taken an oath to enforce the laws of Oregon. So I'll have to do the best I can."

I directed State Budget Director Bob Smith to price an old Navy destroyer and crew, which would have involved converting part of the National Guard into a sea unit. The *Oregon Statesman* headlined its report on the idea, "McCall's Navy: Old Ironicsides." The irony was rust as far as the legislature was concerned—and the members thrashed the veto, forcing me to investigate several options.

One possibility seemed an innovative joint surveillance off the 400-mile Oregon Coast by Navy, Coast Guard and National Guard planes. I checked with the National Guard about the use of Mohawk airplanes to oversee the foreign fishing fleets, but this was overruled by federal authorities who said Oregon would be interfering in foreign relations. This unenforceable law is, then, unenforced.

The tongue-in-cheek talk about Oregon's own Navy had, however, produced considerable laughter and probably put a little steam behind congressional creation of a 200-mile U.S. fishery zone.

On more serious topics, I would never hesitate to raise a controversial issue. The press was ho-humming it through lunch after hours of committee debate by Oregon's progressive Republicans at their 1972 annual spring Dorchester Conference on the Central Oregon Coast. Suddenly eyes popped wide and there was a rush for cameras, microphones and telephones. I had departed from my advance text to cry out that our claim to being concerned human beings was hollow unless we addressed ourselves, positively but tactfully, to the nearly verboten subject, death with dignity.

This was the first such appeal for death with dignity by a major politician. My plea for humanity was immediately tagged "eutha-

McCall and California Governor Ronald Reagan provided a "Point/Counterpoint" debate at Governors' Conferences. At this 1971 meeting at Jackson Hole, McCall criticized Reagan for holding President Nixon "hostage" on welfare payments.

Gerry Lewin

When reporters asked a question, McCall was quick to reply. His responses were often controversial.

Vice President Spiro T. Agnew and McCall exchanged sharp words at the 1970 Sun Valley Governors' Conference.

nasia"—and the fight to bring rationality into still another explosive issue was on. Three years later, the tragedy of Karen Ann Quinlan (an attractive New Jersey girl), lingering in a vegetative condition, would pose a national dilemma on this very topic. *Newsweek* would devote its cover story to "A Right to Die." As is so often the case, the debate had begun in Oregon.

Since I had been frustrated and embarrassed when, as Governor McKay's press secretary, I would frequently learn of his appointments and policy statements in Larry Smyth's *Oregon Journal* political columns, I took pains to make certain Ron Schmidt always knew what was going on. Often I would call him to say, "Ron, maybe I'd better tell you what I just said at the airport."

To Schmidt's credit, he never tried to stand between me and the press. He played no favorites and didn't grant "exclusives" on major breaking stories. As he was leaving the Governor's office, Schmidt wrote about our open-door policy this way:

"We had a reference point, one which gave us guidance regarding what *not* to do: Ronald Reagan's administration in California. When I worked with the Capitol corps in Sacramento, or when I saw how the Reagan information team responded to national media, I got a vivid example of the other way. Reagan's staff protected him from the newsmen. He remained aloof and unreachable. His staff only unleashed Reagan when something was wanted—a package of legislation or re-election. It was a cold world in Sacramento.

"We never leashed Tom. Candidly, I'll admit I sometimes wish I had. But I do not think it would have been possible. As far as we were concerned in Salem, the press was our ally, not our enemy."

Most of the governors I served with were quite paranoid about the press. For example, Vice President Agnew gave the Republican governors a briefing in a private room, during which he said absolutely nothing that hadn't already been a matter of public record. But Governor John Love of Colorado, a good friend of mine, said gravely, "Gentlemen, before we leave, let's get together on our stories. Let's agree on no leaks."

I said, "John, you're being absolutely childish." It was the first and only time I saw John mad. He just exploded. I could never have agreed to such a silly ground rule.

The press would always turn to me as a conduit of information from closed-door sessions. There was nothing invidious I'd ever reveal. But, where it was newsworthy, I would commentate just as I had for a living for so many years—without necessarily having that represent advocacy. Governor Dan Evans and I always said there wasn't one of those sessions that couldn't have been held in public. We would relay the basic facts of what went on. To get to these remarkable resort areas where the conferences were held, the working press had to return something in the form of columns and stories to justify their spending that much money and travel. As a journalist on loan to government, I did my best to help them.

The roughest meeting I ever attended was the mid-December 1970 Republican Governors' Conference at Sun Valley. Shortly before the meeting, Interior Secretary Wally Hickel had been fired by President Nixon. And Vice President Agnew had successfully purged Senator Charles Goodell, a progressive New York Republican. "I think you'll find there'll be others," I said at a news conference. "The President is clearing his decks before going after a second term. Even the Vice President might be dropped, the way he's been running around the country carrying a knife under his shawl."

When I made that remark, the wind roared in my ears. I knew I was embarking on a trip that would probably take me into the national Republican wilderness as long as I lived. Some people talked about my foot being in my mouth. But it's an awfully big foot and you have to be somewhat calculating to get a foot of that size in your mouth. So I wasn't always rattling off without thought of the consequences. I knew of the tremendous risks. The press would set me up once in a while because they knew I'd give them something peppery if they framed the right questions. Agnew's gutter tactics and demagoguery made such questions unnecessary.

There were eleven fewer Republican governors after the 1970 elections. Six defeated incumbents were at Sun Valley. Some said that Nixon's and Agnew's unseemly campaign tactics had worked against them. Indeed, Winthrop Rockefeller blamed Agnew for his defeat in Arkansas. And Dewey Bartlett likewise in Oklahoma.

One of Agnew's assistants, C. D. Ward, told me that the Vice President wanted to see me when he arrived. Agnew came in the early evening and I went over to meet him. He poured me a pale scotch and said, "Tom, I'm mad as hell at you. What happened? We used to be great friends. Why have you changed?"

"Why have you changed?" I retorted. "You used to be one of the party's leading moderates. Now, you're just another win-at-any-cost politician."

Agnew seemed shrill and strident to me and Bob Davis when he spoke later that night. He criticized the Republican governors for second-guessing his strategy. Agnew described the Democratic landslide as an "ideological victory" for the Nixon administration. He gleefully noted that Albert Gore and Charles Goodell had been ousted from the senate. Agnew, in effect, was telling us, "I'm right and you're wrong." Every time he made a gesture, his smoldering eyes would burn right through me, where I sat directly in front of the podium.

Right afterward, Sander Vanocur of NBC caught me in the hallway. "There is a mistaken understanding of the mood and purpose of this nation in that rotten and bigoted little speech," I said, "the most divisive speech ever given by such a high official."

There was a three-hour private meeting with Agnew the next morning. Agnew took some gentle criticism from Governor Bartlett. "I told you," Bartlett said, "not to attack Fred Harris when you campaigned in Oklahoma." Bartlett had been upset by barely one percent of the vote.

It was a tense, no-holds-barred session. In the middle of all this, an aide handed Agnew a strip of yellow teletype paper. He looked at it, and his hand began to shake. Then he said, "Tom, you couldn't possibly have said this."

I asked him, "What is it?" My heart sank, knowing full well what the teletype was.

Agnew said, "You're quoted here as saying I gave a 'rotten, bigoted little speech' last night."

A terrible silence came across the room and everybody started craning.

"Ted," I said, "I'm not sure I said 'little.' "

Among most people this would have provoked a great guffaw and the tension would have been relieved, but because Agnew was so powerful and vindictive, nobody even cracked a smile.

Ronald Reagan broke the silence by saying piously, "In California, we have what we call the Eleventh Commandment—'Thou shalt not speak ill of another Republican.' "

Reagan said he faithfully observed it "except where John Lindsay is concerned." To the right wing, it never applied to Republican liberals. I felt Reagan was a hypocrite with his pretentious "commandment."

Agnew snorted, "Some of the problems with a lot of Republicans is they go out of their way to pat Sandy Vanocur on the ass and get on his boob tube."

Until this meeting, I had been all set to become vice chairman of the Republican Governors' Conference. The following year I would have been automatically elevated to the chairmanship. But after the Agnew confrontation, my candidacy suddenly disappeared.

One of the problems with politicians is that most of them cannot stand to be analyzed critically. You can talk about a great record someone has, but if you say one tiny thing that is adverse, he'll say, "Why have you turned into my enemy?"

The next summer, at Jackson Hole, there were more fireworks at the Western Governors' Conference. Audrey always had an understanding with me that she would press my foot when I was getting carried away or making a point with too much dramatic flair. She looked around while we were getting our luggage and found that I was gone. Squire Behrens, a political editor of the San Francisco *Chronicle*, had tagged me and said he was desperate for a story. By the time Audrey spotted me in this hangar, I was developing the story of the week—President Nixon was giving California more federal funds per capita than any other state, to keep Reagan's support. "For beginners," I said, "how would it be that we allege that Governor Reagan is holding the President hostage?"

Squire and a United Press International man with him started writing madly. Several other reporters had gathered here. (Some weeks afterward, Jack Anderson would confirm that Reagan was getting far more proportionately than any other state—some $600 million.)

Later, I had second thoughts about my terminology. I called Squire that same afternoon and said, "Maybe we ought to review your story before you send it in."

"It's already been published, Governor," he said. "And I want to tell you that you're big in California."

At San Clemente, President Nixon's press secretary, Ron Ziegler, said, "Governor McCall is apparently not aware of the good relations that we have with Governor Reagan. We consider the relationship between Governor Reagan and President Nixon very, very good." Of course Ziegler wasn't exactly an authoritative source. His denials about Watergate and his ignorance of the coverup indicated that he was out of his depth as a press secretary.

The next morning when Reagan arrived, I came out of my little chalet alone except for an NBC television crew who queried me about the Reagan charge. As we walked toward the main lodge, Reagan emerged from his chalet with a huge retinue. I shouted, "Hi, Ron!" He turned up his collar and just walked faster. When I said, "Hi, Ron!" for a second time, he couldn't avoid me.

So he drew me within his contingent as we hurried along and said, "Damn it all, Tom, why couldn't you have called me? I'd have told you there wasn't any sort of irritation or pressure between the White House and Sacramento."

"But, Ron," I said, "if I'd done that, there wouldn't have been any story."

Reagan just frowned. Like most governors he never understood the necessity of saying something provocative, but factual, to give reporters an excuse to come to our meetings and pick up something solidly interesting about governors, along with the political froth which they cherish so greatly. (Jack Anderson was to confirm the story, and Reagan's protestations ended his assualt on the White House.)

One of the tools the press has long relied on to remain strong and independent is the First Amendment. It is the essence of what constitutes liberty for many Americans. The difference between the United States and totalitarian regimes has always been most evident in the freedom of our news media to report any story without fear of state repression. To hold this freedom, we have always depended on the Supreme Court. Its interpretation of the amendment has defined freedom of the press. In the era of the Warren Court, Justice Hugo Black and a majority of the court were steadfast in their commitment to this constitutional right.

But the Burger Court, shaped by President Nixon, began to chip away at the First Amendment. I was troubled by Nixon's early court nominations. Chief Justice Burger hardly seemed an adequate replacement for Earl Warren, one of the giants of American legal history. The senate wisely rejected Clement F. Haynsworth and G. Harrold Carswell, the latter perhaps the most unfit person ever recommended for such a lofty position.

When Nixon was reportedly about to nominate another judicial mediocrity—which, in this case had been vetoed by the American Bar Association—I sent the President this telegram:

"Many shared your expressed concern about the role being assumed by the Supreme Court in our national government, and all applauded your expressed intent to appoint to that bench only men and women of demonstrated pre-eminence in the legal profession. Mr. President, I do not quarrel with the appointment of those who strictly construe the Constitution and laws. I am gravely disappointed, however, when I contemplate the qualifications of nominees reportedly being considered by you and compare them with the high standards you proclaimed."

In that October 21, 1971, telegram, I recommended the appointment of Senator Sam J. Ervin, Jr., of North Carolina. As a "strict constructionist" and a southerner, Senator Sam would have met Nixon's criteria. Moreover, Ervin was an ardent civil libertarian and protector of the Bill of Rights. It would have been a statesmanlike appointment. (Two years later, Senator Sam rose to national prominence as the wise old chairman of the Senate Watergate Committee.) Nixon named instead William Rehnquist, whose chief qualifications seemed to have been presiding over the

1971 May Day arrests which held thousands of demonstrators in prison for many hours without providing legal counsel or booking them for any offense. It was perfectly justified, Rehnquist argued, since martial law transcended the Constitution.

It was in this atmosphere that the Burger Court strangled the First Amendment. In the Pentagon Papers case, the court ruled that national security took priority over freedom of the press. And, in the Caldwell case, a *New York Times* reporter refused to testify about confidential information and sources he had gathered in covering the Black Panthers. The Burger Court ruled against him, citing the Executive Branch's right to investigate. In 1972 they rejected the appeals of five reporters from lower court decisions requiring them to name news sources. A federal district judge went a step further a year later by giving Vice President Agnew's lawyers the right to subpoena eight reporters for the same reason. The First Amendment had been snuffed out at the federal level.

I had long supported legislation protecting the identity of confidential news sources. During the 1966 gubernatorial campaign, a student editor of the University of Oregon's *Daily Emerald*, named Annette Buchanan, wrote a series of articles based on interviews with people who were using drugs on the campus. She was held in contempt of court because she wouldn't disclose her sources. I took a position strongly supportive of Miss Buchanan:

"The proceedings at Eugene reveal a conflict between the law and the journalistic ethic," I said then. "Since the ethic is useful beyond doubt to a free press, then it seems to me the law should be changed to facilitate the functioning of the ethic.

"Such a highly principled journalist deserves commendation, not abuse. Without the confidence of anonymous news sources, much of the news as well as answers and truths concerning criminal actions would be lost. It is not realistic to ask a news contact to jeopardize himself in order to expose a criminal or unjust action. As an active newsman for 25 years, I would estimate that 50 percent of my effectiveness was due to my protection of news sources."

State Treasurer Straub, who was running against me, took the position that Miss Buchanan was wrong. Oddly enough, she ended up endorsing him.

We finally got a press shield law in 1973—after the Burger Court had all but trampled the First Amendment. Bob Davis, my executive assistant and a former circuit judge and district attorney, did tremendous research in preparing the legislation. Its leading sponsors were Senators Ted Hallock and Victor Atiyeh, and Representatives Les AuCoin, a former newspaper reporter, and Keith Skelton. I had never dreamed that I would have to advance a bill authorizing freedom of the press, but when the Supreme Court nullified the true intentions of the Founding Fathers, the reaction of the Oregon Legislature was swift and carefully positive.

At the time I signed the bill, I said, "Oregon has uttered a decisive rebuke to those who would subvert the American press into becoming a servile vassal of government. It is particularly important that a state, noted for its independence and reverence for freedom, speak in no uncertain terms at this time of danger to an unfettered press. History must regard this action as a ringing hands-off warning to those who are fostering a climate of coercion threatening the vigor and effectiveness of a very precious democratic institution."

In the State of Washington, the press was ill disposed to accept a press shield law unless the protection from disclosure also extended to cases of slander and libel. When I was explaining our new shield law to a conference of Pacific Northwest broadcasters, I said that the press had an unqualified privilege against disclosure, with one exception. Protection from disclosure in libel cases bore the potential for a wholesale launching of McCarthyism with hidden accusers. A spokesman for the Washington State broadcasters stood up and said, "Well, that's where we held out for a purist law. We wouldn't submit to that exemption in our law for libel."

"All right," I said. "You got the hole and we got the doughnut."

We approached the shield law with pragmatism—not in the sense of deserting basic American principles—but in the sense of

what could be achieved. I was very proud of Bob Davis, who prepared the bill and guided it through the legislature. The publishers
of Oregon and some of the managers and owners of television
stations preferred to keep their faith in the First Amendment. Yet
when you got down to the working level, the working stiffs who
would go to jail for protecting sources, it was a different story.

There was, then, almost unanimous support for the shield law
from the working press. Davis effectively demonstrated that this
was the case during deliberations on his bill. I believe the Oregon
shield law is the strongest such law in the nation. The *New York
Times* v.s. Sullivan remains an adequate defense of the press
against the might and power of public figures, but I would like to
see every state and the congress pass an Oregon-type shield law.

There is considerable debate among journalists on a shield law.
At the 1973 National Governors' Conference, I asked a panel of
newsmen what they thought of a federal shield law—an unqualified law as proposed by Senator Mark Hatfield.

Elie Abel, dean of the Columbia University Graduate School of
Journalism, told me that the press's right to function in a free
society rested squarely on the First Amendment. Abel said if some
newsmen have to go to jail to validate that right, "then I would
submit to you that American journalists have been ready to do
that since the beginning of this Republic."

It was very high blown. Abel and conservative columnist James
J. Kilpatrick both said they would leave it up to the First Amendment. Neither of them, at their exalted levels, stood a chance of
being thrown into jail. David Broder of the *Washington Post* was
silent on the panel. I said afterward, "Dave, I inferred that you
agreed with them but didn't want to pound McCall down on it."

"Yes," Dave said, "no use making a rout out of it."

Abel's argument would have been persuasive prior to the Burger Court. But as matters now stand, the First Amendment has
been washed overboard and it will not resurface simply because
some news people are willing to go to jail. A shield law is not
merely a shield for reporters. It is a shield for the public's right to
know.

The ultimate test is the accuracy of the information, not the source. It is the responsibility of reporters to insure accuracy; and if any is consistently inaccurate, he will have no credibility and, appropriately, be shunned by his peers and the press. In the Watergate and Agnew cases, reporters met the test. They were correct in exposing criminal conduct. I don't think they rejoiced in discovering that our nation's highest officials were corrupt. All of us should be thankful that, because of such responsible reporting, we might get a better shake in the future.

CHAPTER 11

Defeat of an Ideal

From the moment I was sworn in as governor, I was entwined in controversial tax problems. They lasted throughout my administration in spite of our best efforts. The McCall-Mosser tax plan was presented to the legislature early in 1967. It was a system of property-tax relief based on higher income taxes. Our plan would have given a 50 percent state school support ratio. The Republican House of Representatives summarily slapped it down. We never even got a hearing.

Republicans in the legislature, at the time, were enthusiastic about a sales tax. I had opposed such a tax for many years, noting, "You can do everything with an income tax you can with a sales tax." But the legislature sent the message that I had better "bite the bullet" on the sales tax. So, in 1969, I went along with them. I had no emotional commitment to the regressive tax, but I supported it in the sense that unless the sales tax was voted up or down, Oregon was never going to get tax reform.

It was a poor bill that finally came out of the legislature. The bill squeaked through the Democratic senate by two votes—Betty Roberts of Portland and Al Flegel of Roseburg.

Senators Roberts and Flegel felt much the same as I did. They said, "We're never going to have any tax program and proper school financing unless we lay the sales tax to rest. We vote to send it to the people and we know the people will thrash it."

As the election drew near, and public indignation blossomed, there were only about three officials left campaigning for the sales tax and I was one of them. Some of the people who had pressed for it began hooting against "Old McCall's Sales Tax." The whole thing was very distasteful. On the weekend before the June 3 election, I rode in a parade at Brookings. I knew it was going to be a tough election when I got some boos and a dog barked at me. Returning to Salem, I thought the program would probably be defeated about two-to-one.

My estimate had been conservative. The sales tax was crushed by an eight-to-one margin. That shows how charismatic my leadership was. It also demonstrates how independent and contradictory Oregon voters can be. A year later I was re-elected. It was one of the few times, to my knowledge, that a governor hadn't been thrown out of office after advocating a massive new tax program—and getting whipped on it. I could never figure out how I survived except possibly the people felt I had done such a terrible job on the sales tax that I couldn't do any worse the next time around.

I was properly humble the morning after the sales-tax massacre. "I have heard from my board of directors," I said. "They tell me I'm all wet. I accept their verdict, and will now go to work on something else more acceptable that will do the job that still has to be done."

Giles French, the sage of Sherman County, wrote me this advice after the sales-tax debacle: ". . .and never call that bunch (the legislature) together again, not even if we're invaded. And if we are, send them to the front.

"Now we're getting someplace. We are the voters. We have told the politicians that we don't want a trick gadget like the one and one-half percent; now we've told the politicians we don't want a sales tax.

"We do not know how many other silly bills we'll have to turn down before we have a reasonably smart bunch of politicians, but we are willing to keep trying.

"Pretty soon it will dawn on the politicians that what we want is economy in government, fewer counsellors, fewer advisors, fewer experts, fewer smart guys that seldom have the brains of an old sheepherder. What we want is less restrictive laws that cause expense for local governments. I know that one of the hardest jobs in the world is educating politicians, but we are making progress.

"We're saying Oregon doesn't need new taxes, or a shift in taxes. Oregon needs some new politicians and sadly I admit there are none on the horizon."

As always, there was something in what Giles had to say. The people were often ahead of their leaders. Early in this century, Oregonians got fed up with government and adopted the initiative and referendum, a historic milestone of government by the people. In 1929, Oregonians found common cause again, and adopted an income tax as a property-tax relief measure. That might have been the time to have promulgated a property-tax limitation. But it didn't occur. The property tax was soon reasserted as the kingpin of revenue-raising methods and became a source of grief to many of our citizens.

In 1971 I said, "Let's go on the basis of gradualism." I tried everything to get basic school support raised to 35 percent. I was purposely trying to lower expectations, focusing on a more realistic goal. Back through the years, people were saying, "Here's our 50 percent goal." And the state would make a great leap and not go anywhere. If we had a lower perch to aim for, I thought we just might make it. We froze budgets and got a raise in the cigarette tax, but the effect was like trying to apply a Band-Aid to a punctured artery.

Oregon, quite simply, needed sweeping tax reform.

My staff set about with me to create a masterpiece. Briefly, we proposed that school operating costs be paid by ability-to-pay taxes instead of home taxes. The shift would represent equal increases on the individual and on business and the three quarters of a billion dollars thus transferred would go into an equalization formula guaranteeing no child would be penalized because he lived in a low- or semi-low-value school district.

I felt so strongly about this plan that my office conducted a survey of legislative candidates in the 1972 general election to get their views on my program. I did not actively campaign against any candidate who supported it. Only when I endorsed a candidate-supporter over a candidate-nonsupporter did I charge that the latter was unqualified. I asked the voters to screen the candidates on this critical issue. There was some grumbling among candidates over my efforts to produce such a strong consensus before the election.

My intervention may have been the decisive factor. The Democrats won control of the legislature for the first time in a decade while Republicans were winning four of five statewide races. I had supported a number of Democrats who were sympathetic to the tax plan. They ran hard on it and often defeated reluctant Republicans who wouldn't come out for it. The Democrats recognized my program as a concept whose time ought to be here. So my unusual proposition led to the election of the only Democratic Legislature I had while I was governor. It is my conviction that a Republican who knows what government is about is restive within the confines of the Republican Party because the majority of his party is not issue-oriented in a modern way. So, if I hadn't been a Republican in Oregon—with a tradition of progressive Republican leaders from Governor Sprague and Senator McNary to the Dorchester Republicans in the 1970s—I doubt if I could have stuck with the party.

When I addressed my first strongly Democratic Oregon Legislature, I drew heavily on Governor Sam McCall's 1917 inaugural message to the Massachusetts Legislature in my message to Oregon lawmakers. It was so modern in terms of consumerism, drug and price control and the environment that it popped their eyes to learn it not only came from a Republican but was written 56 years earlier. At a national governors' conference, State Senator Bill Saltonstall of Massachusetts told me, "We're still working to carry out your grandfather's massive blueprint for reorganization and constitutional revision."

Grandfather McCall's example showed them that Republicans weren't all fusty, musty stick-in-the-muds. I suppose it was the influence of the first Governor McCall that made me go so hard for a reformation of school financing and the tax program.

The Democratic Legislature enacted more than 90 percent of my recommended programs. The role of government, then, and now, is best served not through partisanship but through a cooperative procedure. When the House of Representatives approved my school finance program in February, I described their vote as "a momentous act of concentration, courage and conscience."

There was, however, a stumbling block in the Senate. Vern Cook of Gresham, one of the most irresponsible and whimsical people ever to have served in the legislature, was chairman of the Senate Taxation Committee. Cook set his feet down against it and vowed to block this program we had all worked so long to put together. So Senate President Jason Boe of Reedsport said, "I remove you as chairman of the Senate Taxation Committee." It was the most dramatic action ever made by a legislative leader in Oregon. It was an extraordinary rupture of all the mores of legislature, which had always operated like an old club. No matter what a member's political philosophy, they got along.

But Jason Boe was a strong leader and was not bound by old-fashioned customs. He quickly secured senate approval for the tax program, assuring a public vote.

Vern Cook took to the warpath against it. The opponents of our tax plan made a strange conglomerate ranging from Cook to Stafford Hansell, the conservative Republican legislator and pig farmer from Umatilla County.

Ours was such a superlative plan that it actually taxed incomes of up to $15,000 no more to have a better, fairer school system statewide. It did, though, slightly gore that ox known as The Establishment. Republicans and business came down on it hard, and spent heavily to defeat it.

I launched the formal campaign for "Tax Relief Now" at a State Street storefront headquarters on March 28. Senate President Boe, House Speaker Dick Eymann and State Treasurer Jim Redden, all Democrats, also participated in the program. They were to join me in campaigning from border to border for our program. John Piacenti, owner of Plaid Pantry markets, became chairman of our campaign committee.

Among the organizations which enlisted in the campaign were the Oregon Grange, the Oregon Farm Bureau, the AFL-CIO, the Teamsters, the Oregon Education Association, the Oregon School

Boards Association, Retail Clerks Union Local 1092, Schools for the City (Portland), and the Oregon State Employees Association.

Many prominent Democrats rallied to the cause. Bob Straub came out for it. Former Senator Wayne L. Morse sent word to me that he wanted to help. I knew that Wayne was considering a comeback against Bob Packwood in 1974 so I asked him if he knew the political risks of getting into the tax referendum. Of course, Wayne said, but he believed it offered justice to Oregon's young people and equity to the taxpayers, and he couldn't stand mute to that opportunity. So I went down to Eugene and we held a joint news conference. He was in magnificent form. It was a fairly complicated tax bill, made even more complicated by newspaper analysis of it, yet Wayne managed to wrap it up magnificently in about 90 seconds. He explained it with such force, clarity and logic that it was overpowering. Morse was so eloquent that some of my conservative friends refused to listen to him for fear of being converted to his liberal views. I was deeply grateful to the old Tiger for getting into this fight.

One of the last times I saw him was when we crossed paths in downtown Portland in late April. "Tom," he said, "you know what I've been doing today? I was in Columbia County campaigning for your school tax plan."

All of us fought hard for it. Bob Davis, my executive assistant and a former state Republican chairman, was a great advocate. He worked very closely with all the organizations supporting us and with the Democrats, too. The chairman of my own Board of Education, Eugene Fisher of Oakland, joined the opposition, but the state's leading education organizations were behind us.

I was a very pugnacious supporter of everything I believed in; I was not very tactful or subtle on an issue of this importance. When I was having dinner at our motel in Eugene, a doctor at the table next to me was moaning about the tax program. He said it would cost him about $800 more a year to have this program in effect. This was someone who probably was earning $60,000 a year. I said, "You son of a bitch, if you don't care any more than that about the schools of Oregon, why don't you go back to

California?" I'm sure he didn't vote for the tax measure. House Speaker Dick Eymann called our opposition, "That coalition of nitpickers, mostly millionaires." They consistently distorted our program and preyed on the fears of the people.

"Local control" was a volatile issue. We had written into the bill the strongest statement on local control and the most detailed statement ever put in a measure. Under the existing system, with school boards so dependent on the property tax, they are less a policy board than money-grubbers—running frantically trying to figure out how they can keep the schools open financially.

"The local school boards are still going to call the tune," I said in a speech at the University of Oregon. "But they're going to call a clearer tune."

In closing my remarks at Eugene, I said, "The school finance program offered to you will make our corner of the world a better place in which to live, and for that I promise you my word. I told another group that if it didn't work I would personally hang myself in front of the Capitol. They all clapped to beat heck." The university audience did the same.

One week before the election, I spoke before a League of Women Voters Public Forum at Milwaukie High School: "Some opponents treat tax reform as if it were like the new educational toy that's on the market. No matter how you put it together, it's wrong. What they're saying, of course, is that they like things as they are, and well they should. Many big corporations have gotten tax benefits for themselves in the past, and now they're opposing a new system that would benefit the middle-income majority of Oregon.

"At least 80 percent of all Oregon taxpayers will pay less if the tax relief program is adopted. Included among the beneficiaries are virtually all homeowners earning less than $16,000 a year, low and moderate income renters, and 90 percent of Oregon's small businesses. If you're waiting for me to drop the other shoe, there isn't any. This program provides a total of $130 million in tax relief from existing revenue sources, with no new taxes."

Gerry Lewin

"I was a two-bit Lyndon Johnson," says McCall of his penchant for giving bill-signing pens to state legislators. In this case, McCall made the presentation to State Senator Jason Boe of Reedsport.

Eugene Register-Guard

Their relationship was often stormy, yet McCall and Wayne L. Morse maintained a friendship for nearly forty years. McCall resisted GOP efforts to match him against Morse in 1968. "Maybe I could win," McCall said. "But what would be left of me—raw hamburger." Morse joined McCall in 1973 to campaign for the McCall tax plan. "I consider it a bill of tax justice," Morse said.

PRITHEE, FORSOOTH,
"QUACK-QUACK"?!!

william sanderson 1973

"I'LL GIVE YOU EIGHT TO FIVE AND TAKE THE TALL DUDE ON THE LAME DUCK."

Cartoonist Bill Sanderson portrayed McCall as a white knight on a lame duck in the 1973 tax referendum.

Opposition forces were clever with their advertising. One of their ads left people with the impression that no tax relief would be granted. Another advertisement pointed out that some large corporations would indeed get tax relief. And then, finally, they declared that business would be adversely affected. The response to my speeches had been so encouraging and the people supporting the plan were so enthusiastic that I was optimistic about the May 1 referendum.

So my spirits were high when I settled down in my living room to watch the returns with Audrey and Ron Schmidt. When the vote came in decisively against the tax program, I was shell-shocked. You really can't put so much into a campaign and get so tired and wound up in it and then lose it without a sense of repudiation and bitterness. Big business and the special interests had tipped the scales.

Ron accompanied me as I walked solemnly down Winter Street toward the Capitol mall. "I'm going to have to step down," I told my old friend and associate. "I can no longer lead Oregon. The people no longer have faith in me. It was not a school financing defeat. It was a defeat for Tom McCall. I think the state needs a new leader. If I can't give effective leadership on the most critical issue facing the state, how can I possibly lead in other areas? Call a news conference for tomorrow morning. I'm going to resign." Ron listened patiently and let me get the steam out of my system.

I called Secretary of State Clay Myers and advised him that he would be taking over as governor. Myers urged me not to act so abruptly. But I insisted. "You can finish out my term. I'm through." (Clay immediately called Ron Schmidt and said, "This makes no sense. We won't let him do it." Ron assured Clay that they would talk me out of it.)

Ron handled it with finesse. When I arrived at the Capitol the next morning, he said, "Tom, the news conference is all set up for your resignation statement. I've alerted the networks. It'll be a great national news story."

He caught me by surprise. During the evening, I had decided that quitting under fire would not help anything. I was determined to serve out my term, yet this was the low point of two terms in office. Red-haired Sue Robinson of United Press International put down her tape recorder and pencil, looked at me soulfully and said, "Governor, I just can't bear to see you so sad."

When I went to our morning staff meeting, I looked at Bob Davis and we both burst into tears. I was red eyed from exhaustion, pale and haggard from weeks of campaigning. I had committed body and soul to the cause and got clobbered. The tears were not a sign of weakness but an indication that we were human beings, with great sensitivity toward the problems we faced. As I left the room, still wet eyed, the staff rose and applauded.

Later, our plan received national recognition as a model tax system. The Department of Health, Education and Welfare was entranced by it. They asked us to present our battered prize to 600 experts on educational finance in Washington, D.C. Their consensus: It is so complex it would baffle any state's electorate but so wise and good and fair it ought to be enacted in states where the hair-trigger referendum reflex is conspicuous by its sensible disuse.

With such a complex program, it is almost impossible to have an intelligent vote. Our rational alternative might be a constitutional amendment which would empower the governor and the legislature to put the new tax into effect for a trial period. It could then be fairly evaluated at the next general election. This is probably the only way such complicated tax programs can be explained to the people. The school closures which plagued Cottage Grove, Eagle Point and North Bend in 1976 would not have happened if our tax program had been adopted. Oregon has always been in the front lines, strongly independent, not willing to roll over and die when other states have given in. The time has come to bring about substantial change in the state's tax structure. Unless we get such change, schools will continue to close and middle-income homeowners will be further imperiled.

McCall and Oregon Secretary of State Clay Myers in conference.

CHAPTER 12

A Mighty River Saved

The Willamette River is not only a major artery of the Pacific Northwest, it is the twelfth largest river in the United States. Lewis and Clark recorded some early impressions of the Willamette in their journals. They incorrectly reported that it reached south into California and provided access to Spanish New Mexico. Their misconceptions prevailed on American cartography for a half century. The settlement of the lower Willamette Valley in the 1840s marked the beginning of the modern era for the Pacific Northwest. John McLoughlin, the grizzled patriarch of the Hudson's Bay Company, was to dominate the region from his house overlooking Willamette Falls. Jason Lee founded a Methodist mission on the Willamette in 1834, which led to the first great migration into Oregon. Most of the pioneers came to farm. Steamboats were the major source of transportation and commerce. The river provided food for the settlers, particularly salmon and steelhead, as it had for the Indians for centuries. Tragically, the Willamette's Indian population had been destroyed by disease when trappers came into the region.

The industrial age took a high toll on the Willamette. By the 1890s, Willamette Falls was generating electrical power. Sawmills were transporting logs and lumber products up and down the river, and pulp and paper mills began dumping their wastes directly into the Willamette.

By the 1920s, the Willamette was an ecological disaster. Most of it was unswimmable. The great salmon runs were diminishing. Construction workers refused to work along the river because of the stench. The Oregon State Board of Health created an "Anti-Pollution League" in 1926. A year later, the Portland City Club investigated conditions on the Willamette. Their report characterized the river as "ugly and filthy" and "intolerable." The City Club also commissioned a public opinion poll which showed strong support for pollution controls.

In 1929, the first water quality survey of the Willamette was made under the auspices of Oregon Agricultural College. It showed that the waters downstream from such cities as Eugene, Springfield and Salem were becoming poisoned from the discharges of raw waste. There were no sewage treatment plants. But the greatest damage was being inflicted by five pulp and paper mills—at Lebanon, Salem, Newberg and Willamette Falls. The residue, mostly wood sugars and wood fibers, was discharged into the river, forming sludge deposits. These deposits often became floating, foul-smelling islands during the hot summer months.

Governor Julius Meier summoned the mayors of cities on the Willamette to a conference "responsive to a statewide demand for abatement of stream pollution." As a result of that conference, the pulp and paper industry began studying pollution. Two years later, the Stream Purification Committee of the Oregon State Planning Board made a comprehensive study of existing water pollution laws. They found some 35 separate laws. Their conclusion: ". . .promiscuous adoption of unrelated and uncoordinated nuisance and penal statutes. . .cannot form the basis of a concerted and direct effort to prohibit pollution of streams."

The 1937 Oregon Legislature passed a water purification and prevention of pollution bill in response to public outrage over the Willamette's deterioration. Governor Charles "Iron Pants" Martin, a fiscally conservative chief executive, promptly vetoed it. Martin contended the bill placed too great a financial burden on cities and towns. The governor may have underestimated the importance of this issue for he was defeated for renomination in the 1938 Democratic primary. In the fall of 1938, an initiative measure reinstating the "Water Purification and Prevention of Pollution Bill" passed by an overwhelming margin.

Under this new law, state water quality standards were established and, to enforce them, the State Sanitary Authority was formed. As its first priority, the Sanitary Authority decreed that cities were responsible for cleaning up their wastes. They recommended primary treatment and effluent chlorination to restore water quality to acceptable levels.

The Army Corps of Engineers was scheduled to build reservoirs on some of the Willamette's tributaries. These multipurpose storage projects assured the Sanitary Authority of increased stream flows during the summer and fall months when pollution was at its worst. World War II delayed construction of the reservoirs until the early 1950s.

Meanwhile, the pulp and paper mills continued to discharge concentrated sulfite wastes into the river. The Sanitary Authority ordered them to halt such dumping during the summers. The waste was impounded and released during high-water months. The fruit and vegetable industry emerged as a major polluter in the 1940s and 1950s. Its waste discharges, including strong chemicals, were threatening to finish off an already sick river. Fish began dying. The Sanitary Authority called for higher levels of sewage treatment, but such changes took time. Conservationists and sportsmen were becoming impatient. So were many other Oregonians.

In KGW-TV's 1961 documentary, "Pollution in Paradise," I shocked some people by referring to the Willamette as "an open sewer." Yet that is exactly what it was. Some of the big-time polluters threatened lawsuits. But none of them dared. Television had exposed them as no other medium could.

Oregon could not have afforded the demise of the Willamette. Seventy percent of the state's population lives in the Willamette Basin. There are more than 600 industrial plants on the river as well as 20 municipalities. And its food and vegetable farms serve an international clientele. So public sentiment was always behind efforts to preserve the river. The Sanitary Authority, while lacking the power to crack down on polluters, prepared the way for the cleanup of the Willamette in the 1960s and 1970s.

Pollution was a major issue in the 1966 gubernatorial campaign. Bob Straub and I both pledged to restore the Willamette. This was no idle promise. We both had long-standing commitments to this cause. In office, I assumed the chairmanship of the Sanitary Authority to signal that the McCall Administration was making the Willamette top priority. We secured new legislation which required permits for discharging pollutants into the river. This gave the Sanitary Authority real clout.

One of the first tests of the new law came in September of 1967. I was resting in Hawaii following my mission for President Johnson in South Vietnam. John Mosser, whom I had appointed to succeed me as chairman of the Sanitary Authority, telephoned me to report that, after exhaustive hearings, the authority was evenly divided on American Can Company's application to build a $40 million pulp plant outside Halsey. (Bob Straub had originally supported the plant, which was to be the turning point of the Willamette's cleanup. But he confessed that a friend, a Eugene professor, talked him into opposing it.) Mosser asked me how he should vote.

"John," I said, "you vote with the best decision-making machine anybody has—John Mosser's brains." Mosser's vote, for approval, marked a new era of industrial development with pollution controls. The Halsey decision compelled the older pulp and papermakers to install chemical recovery and secondary waste treatment plants. And the 20 municipalities which had long pumped sewage into the river were finally converted to secondary sewage treatment. A series of tax credits and state bonds made it possible for industry and local governments to install these plants.

Some industrial wastes were even put to constructive use. Hot waste water from a Weyerhauser plant was sprayed on nearby fruit orchards to prevent the trees from freezing. The same water, when used on vegetable fields, enabled farmers to produce two crops in one year. Water pollution was reduced by 90 percent in the aftermath of the tough regulations.

For the first time in 40 years, the river was swimmable. No longer were typhoid shots required for wading in the Willamette. Sportsmen didn't have to clean algae and scum off the bottoms of their boats when they took them out of the river. Even the Willamette's stock of virgin sturgeons burgeoned.

Nothing illustrated the restoration of the Willamette so vividly as the increasing number of Chinook salmon, trout, and other game fish. Construction of a $3.7 million fish ladder at Willamette Falls and the improved water quality produced record salmon runs—from 79 in 1965 to 33,000 in 1975. Some of the salmon made the spawning trip up Mill Creek at the northern edge of the lawn of my house in Salem. Fall chinook had never ventured into this stream until the Willamette was cleaned up. As Audrey and I watched them in our backyard, we were almost tearfully happy, agreeing we'd probably never again see anything so exciting.

There were, to be sure, moments of conflict in the struggle to save the Willamette. In the summer of 1972, the Boise-Cascade Corporation pulp and paper mill in Salem shut down under threat of court action. The plant had been discharging 150,000 gallons of sulfite waste into the river daily. During this controversy, more than 200 angry employees confronted me on the steps of the Capitol.

L. B. Day, the outspoken director of the Department of Environmental Quality, and I pushed through the Capitol's revolving front door, and a great jeer rose from the crowd on the marble steps.

"Hitler, Hitler," they chanted.

"They're referring to you, L. B.," I whispered hoarsely.

"No, Governor," Day said. "The honors are all yours." I missed few opportunities for confrontation on the Capitol steps, but this one the afternoon of July 26, 1972 was highly productive.

The Boise-Cascade employees were aroused enough, as were their hooting wives, to march on the statehouse. They milled there in the belief that the state had shut down their plant for not meeting repeatedly deferred pollution-control deadlines. When our bellowed explanations got across—that they were being used by their own management—worker spokesmen shouted, "Okay, Governor, you lead us and we'll picket our own plant and management!"

An hour later I was across the Boise-Cascade negotiating table from those managers. They admitted it was their decision to close the plant after a pipe conveying a volatile chemical broke. No one denied that the state's pollution fighters made a much more dramatic scapegoat, and were so used. But a new pipe was in place in five days, the mill re-opened and, as a side result, an explosive lawsuit settled.

Industry spent more than $50 million to modernize their facilities. The only casualty of the Willamette cleanup was a Crown Zellerbach Corporation plant at Oregon City. This great environmental triumph could prove to be a pyrrhic one if we don't keep the pressure on. It won't stay clean if we languish in the admiration of our own handiwork.

In May 1973, a pipe on Portland's East Side broke. It sent twenty million gallons of raw sewage a day into the river. It was a frightening lesson about the power of man's pent-up waste and how in a few moments it can nullify what it took nearly 50 years to correct.

Our efforts on environmental affairs, particularly the Willamette cleanup, received tremendous support from the people of Oregon and from the state's newspapers. In a 1969 editorial, the Pendleton *East Oregonian* said:

"Almost immediately upon occupying the governor's office, Tom McCall showed that he was in tune with Oregonians on livability. He understood that he could impose harsh controls on pollution and not exceed the desires of his constituents.

"He has known what they wanted before they did. He has written a great record on a subject that has evoked almost unbelievable public concern and enthusiasm."

Oregon's Willamette Greenway gained momentum from the strong backing it received from government, industry and the general population. Karl Onthank's proposal for a 255-mile-long river park captured the imaginations of planners and visionaries across the nation. The Greenway was defined by the task force in a report they prepared for me: "The basic objective is the preservation and enhancement of the river's natural environment while at the same time developing the widest possible recreational opportunities in a manner that injures no one and benefits all."

Gerry Lewin

Following the closing of a Boise Cascade plant for pollution, McCall spoke with angry workers and their families on the Capitol steps.

Gerry Lewin

McCall and environmental czar L.B. Day then met with demonstrators at the Salem industrial plant.

Gerry Lewin

Fishing on the rejuvenated Willamette.

From the report and other sources, we figured the Greenway would cost $15 million. Such funding would have permitted strips along both sides of the river, keeping it in virgin condition. What we got in 1967, after a great legislative battle, was $800,000. We also got a prohibition against condemnation of farm land. The farmers were uptight about condemnation. We later backed away a little bit from outright acquisition and suggested scenic easements. The farmers didn't want to lose access to the river. They also didn't want people pouring all over their land, leaving the gates open, tearing down their fences, and generally interfering with their privacy. We held a series of meetings and finally got the easement idea over. Public access would be prohibited if it conflicted with the farmers. Most of the farmers seemed cooperative. Then Bob Straub came in and jibed at us about what a puny effort we were making. His bull-in-the-china-shop approach turned the farmers against the Greenway. Instead of the moderate procedure we had followed, there came this setback.

Still, we continued our efforts. I spent three weekends on the Willamette, in freezing weather, helping to narrate a film about the Greenway. My sinuses could hardly take the cold. The film was produced by the State Highway Commission. In it I was explaining the Greenway to a young boy in the boat with me.

There were three distinct phases in the Greenway's development. In the first phase of the Greenway program, state and local funds matched federal money, mostly in metropolitan areas. Phase Two brought into the Greenway concept five state parks in five of the nine Greenway counties. Phase Three, made possible by a $5 million federal grant, involved state efforts to secure parklands. Each of the counties now has a major river park. The Greenway has combined state parks, county parks and cities, recreation areas, protected areas, hiking paths, bicycle paths, and scenic and historic sites, preserving the natural state of the Willamette similar to the river's condition at the time of Lewis and Clark.

Oregon has not yet realized the dream of Karl Onthank in getting a river-length park. The President's Council on Environmental

Quality recognized the urgency of Onthank's plan in its 1973 report:

"The original concept of the Greenway was visionary—an entire river bordered by a natural parkway. That concept has been altered to fit more modest goals. In the longer view, however, the initial vision may not be misplaced. Within 50 years, a strip city is projected to run the length of the valley. A parkway of the original scale would be an invaluable asset at that time. Delay in the present makes the future of such a park system problematic."

Willamette Valley residents want this unique park. Its completion is of the utmost importance to future generations of Oregonians.

Water pollution was not the only threat to the Willamette Valley. Air pollution, primarily caused by agricultural field burning, reached a crisis level in August of 1969. When the winds changed from an east-west wind to a south wind, they carried this mass of black smoke into Eugene. I got calls by the score saying, "For God's sake, Governor, save my children." People had their children in basements with wet cloths over their faces. The smoke became so oppressive that residents were forced to keep windows and doors closed at night during the most humid month of the year. Traffic crept on the freeway at a snail's pace; it reduced visibility, tragically resulted in one death, one serious injury, and numerous other traffic crashes.

I described the pollution as "completely intolerable," and asked the seed industry to give voluntary cooperation to end the emergency. In a statewide radio broadcast, I said:

"Field burning cannot be tolerated in any degree that encroaches so severely on the environment in Oregon. Other ways to handle the problems of the industry must be found. The industry is worth $30 to $35 million dollars annually to Oregon's economy, in its contribution to the marketplace. But there is no bartering of Oregon's livability."

When there was scant sign of improvement, I exercised the police powers of the governorship and prohibited the burning.

The public health and safety must always come ahead of the public economic interest. Attorney General Lee Johnson provided valuable counsel in drawing up my executive order. Johnson also served as my personal representative in presenting the field-burning order to the Environmental Quality Commission. My executive order of August 13, 1969 gave an updated report of the crisis:

"Smoke from the agricultural field burning in parts of the Willamette Valley has blanketed not only those areas, but regions to the south. Efforts to achieve voluntary restraints on this burning have failed. The Lane County Medical Society has represented to me that the continuing presence of this smoke constitutes a grave and imminent peril to the public health, particularly in the case of the aged, the infirm, and children. In Lane County, 11 doctors alone have reported to me 183 instances of aggravated respiratory illnesses this summer due to this increased air contamination. Law enforcement officers have advised me that reduced visibility caused by this smoke endangers the safety of persons on our public highways, and already has been a factor in numerous accidents. Leaving aside all aesthetic considerations, I find that an emergency situation exists requiring prompt and firm action to ameliorate a grave and imminent danger to the public health and safety."

On this basis, I turned out the fires. It was controversial. A year later, I was to lose what had previously been one of my strongest counties, Linn County, in my race for another term. It happened to be the center of the grass-seed industry which was doing the burning.

Always probing for a political soft spot, Bob Straub sent me a letter on August 27. He wrote, "Rather than knocking heads, interested parties should be working together to find a solution to field burning in the valley." In my response, I said: "Not only has a substantial amount of work been done in attempting to solve the agricultural field-burning problem, but day-to-day dialogue continues between this office and all persons coping with this complex dilemma."

Many different approaches have been attempted since then, but nothing has really worked in subduing the smoke. The big machines which were once thought to be the answer are too unwieldy and uneconomical. Research efforts must be escalated if the Willamette Valley's air is to be as clean and pure as its water.

CHAPTER 13

Visit Oregon, but Don't Stay

Thousands of Jaycees were assembled from all parts of the country at Portland's Civic Auditorium on a June morning in 1971. They were listening to what seemed a whimsical welcoming message from the Governor of Oregon, chuckling along with the warmth of the words and the usual one-liners. "We want you to visit our State of Excitement often," I said. "Come again and again. But, for heaven's sake, don't move here to live." I got stares of disbelief and a moment of silence. Then, the delegates burst into a clap of laughter.

To ease any tensions, I added a softener: "Or, if you do have to move in to live, don't tell any of your neighbors where you are going."

It was touch and go on that speech, because, tongue-in-cheek though it seemed, it violated a cardinal ethic known as Western Hospitality. But someone had to raise the point, somehow, sometime—and within 18 months we were wondering if Oregon's flora and fauna could stand even unlimited tourist visitations. Since then, similar official mutterings have been heard in a number of states, California and Florida included, but the Oregon shot was indeed the one heard round the world.

For years, some Oregonians had said that our state was getting far too many tourists. I saw merit to their argument. And, at the same time, I was skeptical of the development-at-any-cost policy which had been pursued by the Hatfield Administration. When I came on as governor in 1967, the state had an economic development quarterly called "Growth." I had it renamed "Quality" and it was later redesignated "Progress."

I minced few words about livability. When I spoke before a group of Los Angeles businessmen in March of 1969, I said: "Oregon has not been an over-eager lap-dog to the economic master. Oregon has been wary of smokestacks and suspicious of rattle and bang. Oregon has not camped, cup in hand, at anyone's affluent doorstep. Oregon has wanted industry only when that industry was willing to want what Oregon is."

In my first three years as governor, I appeared in films promoting Oregon for the Highway Department's Travel Information Division. I declined to do a film in 1970. I thought it was time to evaluate how many more tourists we could handle and how many we could absorb into our population. It struck me that there was little need to advertise for more tourists.

The rest of the nation really didn't begin to notice what we were doing until January 12, 1971, when I was interviewed on the CBS Evening News by Terry Drinkwater. I said then: "Come visit us again and again. This is a state of excitement. But, for heaven's sake, don't come here to live."

This interview generated a tremendous amount of mail. Most of it was favorable. People were very perceptive about what we were trying to do. D. C. Thacker of Vancouver, British Columbia, the editor of the B.C. *Lumberman*, wrote, "Your course is similar to one I intend to advocate in British Columbia. . . . Communities located on beautiful rivers or lakes are crazy to clamor for industrial development."

Thomas E. Dustin, executive secretary of the Indiana division of the Izaak Walton League, said: "How refreshing it is—at a time when most other states still compete in the insanity of quantity— to hear the head of at least one state speak of quality and stability. . . . We will all be in your debt if you stand by your views."

There were, to be sure, some negative comments. M. C. McCauley of Santa Barbara, California, wrote, "The personal freedom to live where we choose remains a cherished privilege."

Senator Mark Hatfield's response was defensive. He said, "My eight years as governor gave Oregon the highest economic growth and greatest progress on recreation facilities of any West Coast state. Now, when I go around the country, people ask me, 'Is it true your governor doesn't want industry or people to come into Oregon?' "

I was not surprised by the Hatfield criticism. The Senator has enough vanity that he hates to see anyone else from Oregon get attention, and he may have recognized that his policies had helped mark Oregon for the swarm. Another factor was that I was being mentioned as a possible challenge for his senate seat in 1972.

The national Jaycee convention was, as mentioned earlier, the next forum where I enunciated this new policy. As a result of that speech, the Governor's Office began getting letters about whether it was necessary for out-of-state residents to apply for special permits to visit Oregon. I would explain that all we were trying to do was to make sure that we preserved the kind of life that they would come to Oregon as vacationists to enjoy.

My "Visit, but Don't Stay" remarks were reported in the *New York Times* shortly before I was to address a luncheon audience of New York businessmen at the St. Regis Hotel. I told them that the often-quoted remark was not intended to seal Oregon's borders.

"We are being realistic," I said. "We know we cannot, at this time, support a human tidal wave of migration. We haven't the jobs for that kind of onrush—we haven't the facilities—and we are determined to maintain our magnificent environment. . . . When we say 'visit often but don't come to live,' we aren't being hostile or provincial. We are being prudent. It is not our intention to lure anyone to a promised land that becomes, instead, an environmental disaster.

It may sound presumptuous, or immodest, but the context in which I pitch to you is this: Oregon is accepting a few applications for location of branch offices by a carefully screened set of corporations with reputations for honoring the sanctity of the environment."

We were interested only in healthy, imaginative, nonpolluting industry. I could go to New York and say at the St. Regis Hotel, "If you want to become a member of our club we'd like to have you, but we don't like rattle and bang and smoke and dirt. If you abide by our rules, you can be a member of our club."

To a remarkable degree, it worked. I had great support from Oregon industry. One of my most prized possessions is an award which I received in 1970 from Associated Oregon Industries:

"To Governor Tom McCall, who has done more to restore, enhance and preserve the enviable environment of Oregon than any other man; whose concern for the state's economy has led to consistent cooperation with business and industry, knowing the health of one is the success of the other; whose driving goal is to bequeath the beautiful Oregon country, preserved from pollution and prepared for progress, to the generations to come."

I was criticized by tourist associations and motel owners for suggesting that we consider amending the welcome mat for tourists. They were outraged at the inhospitable tone of it all. I pointed out that we were hosting more tourists than ever before, and if they were not getting their share then perhaps they should look somewhere other than the Governor's Office. The downtrend at run-of-the-mill lodgings began long before my well-publicized statements.

One of the most vitriolic exchanges came when I spoke before a Kiwanis Club in San Diego. An indignant San Diegan wrote to the club, erroneously, that I was the guy that invented "Don't Californicate Oregon." He sugested that they reject me on a slogan, "Don't Oregonize California."

Oddly enough, the most protective Oregonians are former Californians. They seem to resent bitterly the intrusion of another Californian. Where members of the James G. Blaine Society, a group formed by Portland author Stewart Holbrook in the 1940s, would like to have a ten-foot fence around Oregon, these transplanted Californians favor a 50-foot fence against their former neighbors.

Much of our own effort had to be couched in humor because there was no way we could legally prohibit people from coming. The greeting-card industry was particularly helpful in injecting some comic relief into a controversial issue. Frank Beeson, an artist and humorist from Eugene, came up with the "Oregon Un-greeting Card." They became a great commercial success. Most of them emphasized the rain: "In Oregon, you don't tan, you rust!"; "You can tell when summer is near in Oregon. . .the rain feels warmer!"; "Last year in Oregon, 677 people fell off their bikes and drowned"; and "Oregonians never water their lawns—they simply drain them."

Another card said, "Tom Lawson McCall, Governor, on behalf of the citizens of the Great State of Oregon, cordially invites you to visit Washington or California or Idaho or Nevada or Afghanistan." I laughed heartily when I received the first of these cards.

At first, my statement seemed to work in reverse. More people were coming to see what it was we were trying to hide. The tourism numbers jumped from nine million to twelve million. A Salem *Capital Journal* editorial said, "McCall stayaway speeches draw more and more attention to the state and in the end discourage no one."

After this leap in tourism, I raised the question of how many tourists we could accommodate. I began wondering about twenty-four million feet trampling the flora and scaring the fauna. Someone said, "That's terrible for you to say when we depend so much on tourism." I retorted, "How'd you like to have a billion tourists if you depend on it so much?"

There is an optimum of tourists that you can handle without destroying those renewable resources and making the state unpleasant. Young California couples seemed to understand our concerned efforts to preserve the vacationland they came to enjoy. A newspaper survey in Southern Oregon indicated that younger Californians agreed that our environment was fragile and could be trampled by hordes of tourists.

I made many visits to California, assuring people that we were a friendly neighbor. When I appeared with San Francisco Mayor Joseph Alioto, I said: "We in Oregon love California. San Francisco is probably our favorite city outside Oregon. There are 700,000 people in San Francisco that Mayor Alioto is responsible for. Well, I was responsible for five million Californians last

THE UNGREETING CARDS . . .

Eugene humorists Frank Beeson and Jim Cloutier gave McCall's "Visit, but don't stay" doctrine a boost with their "Oregon Ungreeting Cards." Beeson sent McCall the first dozen cards printed. McCall said his message had to be "couched in humor" since his legal authority to restrict tourism was doubtful. "We're not inhospitable," McCall said, "just concerned about saving a few pieces of scenery and other resources."

summer. The care and feeding of Californians is something of great concern to any Oregon governor."

The Oregon attitude was noted in thousands of newspaper, radio and television commentaries. News analysts weighed it both wittily and solemnly. In December of 1976, almost six years after my initial warnings about encroachment and congestion, some thoughtful Greeks were questioning the price their nation was paying for record-setting tourism. "At one time we wanted to attract as many tourists as possible," said Tzannis Tzannetakis, secretary general of the National Tourist Organization. "But enormous numbers of visitors just destroy what they come to see." Greek authorities confirmed the same harmful side effects I had been citing—pollution, overcrowding and the abandonment of precious farmland for commercial development.

Oregon has been a major battleground for land-use planning. One of the reasons I tried to warn outsiders away was because we hadn't done enough planning to be able to know how to handle a major population increase. Oregon's population growth rate is twice that of California and three times that of Washington State. The one theme I consistently hit on was that we didn't want to be a link in the megalopolis spreading south from Seattle and north from San Francisco, because we would be committing some of the richest farmland in America to supermarkets and suburbs.

Oregon's first initiative in statewide land-use planning was Senate Bill 10, which was adopted by the 1969 Legislature. It required each city and county to begin land planning, with the provision that, if they did not, the governor would step in and do it for them. A coalition of developers, farmers and businessmen fought the law. I regarded it as a building block for the future and was a staunch defender of the concept. Opponents of land-use planning sought to force a referendum on Senate Bill 10 in 1970, although it was originally proposed by an interim committee composed mainly of farm interests. I was pelted with such bitter epithets as "King Tom" and "Hitler."

"Repeal Senate Bill 10," I intoned, "and you might as well throw me out too because I refuse to preside over the deterioration of Oregon's quality environment." The challenge was as brash as it was politically inept. Voters, when thus dared, would usually throw both the bill and the taunting official over the side. But this was a time of rising environmental consciousness and the monumental land planning and zoning legislation was kept on the statute books and I was re-elected.

After clearing that hurdle, I became more deeply involved in land-use planning. Although air and water pollution have received more attention, the desecration of our soil has been a national disgrace. The Indians of the Pacific Northwest had a much better understanding and appreciation of the land than succeeding generations.

The Duwamish Tribe in Washington Territory was stunned, for example, when the federal government asked to negotiate for the transfer of their lands. Chief Sealth wrote this moving letter to President Franklin Pierce in 1855:

"How can you buy or sell the sky—the warmth of the land? The idea is strange to us. Yet we do not own the freshness of the air or the sparkle of the water. How can you buy them from us? We will decide in our time. Every part of this earth is sacred to my people. Every shining pine needle, every sandy shore, every mist in the dark woods, every clearing and humming insect is holy in the memory and experience of my people. . . . The air is precious to the redman. For all things share the same breath—the beasts, the trees, the man. . . ."

Despite this eloquent appeal, the Duwamish and other Indian tribes were forced to sell their land and yield to the new Anglo-American way of altering the land.

There was no regulation of land use for more than a century. Only one political figure at the national level, Alf M. Landon of Kansas, in his 1936 presidential campaign, had recommended bold approaches to land use. Stewart L. Udall, Secretary of the Interior in the 1960s, became a forceful spokesman for wise land-use planning. His book *The Quiet Crisis,* included a superb analysis of the consequences of indiscriminate development and the necessity for rational planning.

Early in 1973, I testified for strong federal legislation to encourage state and local planning. I said that we could not save the environment unless we had sound land-use planning from the neighborhood to the pinnacle of the federal establishment. I urged members of the Senate Interior Committee to penalize states which lagged behind on land-use planning. "We need the threat of federal sanctions hanging over us," I said. "I don't think states' rights should be used as a shield for misfeasance by the states."

At this same hearing, Senator Cliff Hansen of Wyoming and I talked about compensatory zoning and he asked me to guess what it would cost. I estimated it at $300 billion. He looked at me benignly and commented, "We have had witnesses before this committee who put the estimate in the neighborhood of one trillion dollars." The day after my appearance, White House environmental counsel Russell Train telephoned me with thanks for standing by the proposed sanctions under considerable opposition from senators who had raised the states rights' argument.

"How do the governors split on the issue of the penalties?" I asked.

Train replied, "Right now, it's one for and 49 against."

Today there are other governors who favor the penalties, and a solid majority favor federal planning help without them. Oregon is still looked to, nationally, to hold up the torch. Yet Oregon hasn't always handled its lands right. Our coastal estuaries are not considerable in their acreage, but they are extremely important in maintaining biological systems. Former Council on Environmental Quality Director Russell Peterson says, "The work of an estuary amounts to about $83,000 an acre and is a producer of plant and animal life." In Oregon, this had not been understood and our estuaries had been treated cavalierly. When some cases of filling wetlands came before the Land Board, we turned them down. We also rejected some people's applications to establish marinas. In 1970 I prohibited state construction in estuaries. It would have been a double standard to ban private development, as the state was merrily filling them for bridges and highways.

The most abused land in Oregon is on the central coast. Developers carved it up with a buffalo hunter mentality. Lincoln City was a model of strip city grotesque. By the fall of 1972, the pelt skinners had moved in for the kill. Local officials had approved a subdivision of 1,400 lots with a drain-field area for only 600 houses. Thirty-nine of 60 water systems did not meet state standards. Department of Environmental Quality inspectors found 34 cases of raw sewage flowing onto the beach. I declared a moratorium on construction in Lincoln County, which brought heated protest from developers and real estate salesmen. But it sent them a message that hucksterism in land sales would not be tolerated.

Coastal planning is the area where most of the volatility is generated in Oregon, California, Texas, Alaska, or any coastal state. The closer you get to the ocean, the hotter the land-use planning issue becomes. Four and one-half percent of the people live along the Oregon Coast. This doesn't mean they should be overruled, unless their conduct of managing their resources is antisocial and against the best interests of balanced protection and development. This has often been the case. We've got some of the worst foul-ups on the coast, some of the ugliest coastal strips in the United States. One of the most respected federal officials in the Coastal Zone Management Program told me, "I worked in the South and was constantly frustrated by red-necked local officials. I came out to the Oregon Coast and it's just as bad."

The public is far ahead of these local officials who cater to developers and exploiters. They know how fragile the coast is.

The drawback of Senate Bill #10 was that it did not give local governments the tools and the technical help to draw up comprehensive plans. All it did was give them ten goals to go by—and no money to achieve them. So I found that it was almost futile to go in under these conditions.

I called for a new land-use planning law in what became known as my "grasping wastrels" speech, my opening address to the 1973 Legislature:

"There is a shameless threat to our environment and to the whole quality of life—unfettered despoiling of the land. Sagebrush subdivisions, coastal 'condomania,' and the ravenous rampage of suburbia in the Willamette Valley all threaten to mock Oregon's status as the environmental model for the nation. We are dismayed that we have not stopped misuse of the land, our most valuable finite natural resource.

"We are in dire need of a state land-use policy, new subdivision laws, and new standards for planning and zoning by cities and counties. The interests of Oregon for today and in the future must be protected from grasping wastrels of the land. We must respect another truism. Unlimited and unregulated growth leads inexorably to a lowered quality of life."

State Senator Ted Hallock, the chairman of the Senate Environmental and Land Use Committee, and State Senator Hector Macpherson sponsored Senate Bill 100, the most substantial land-use planning legislation ever proposed in Oregon. Opponents of the bill said the state was tampering with "private property" and would confiscate land. The Oregon Rural Landowners' Association said Senate Bill 100 was "the biggest land grab since our great-grandparents took this land away from the Indians 150 years ago."

I retorted that without a statewide law there was "a very real danger that uncontrolled development will clear-cut the state of its livability."

When the bill fell into trouble, former Department of Environmental Quality Administrator L. B. Day was asked to chair an ad hoc committee which would rewrite the bill. All points of view were represented. Several concessions were made. They deleted the "areas of critical state concern" clause, placing greater emphasis on local planning and citizen participation. Day said then, "We're talking about planning that basically comes from the bottom up, not from the top down." The Governor was no longer to be the enforcer. The Land Conservation and Development Commission was instead charged with this.

I went before a legislative committee on behalf of L. B.'s compromise. "In most respects," I told the Environmental and Land Use Committee, "it is more satisfactory than the original Senate Bill 100." After much debate and several other changes, the bill was passed by both houses of the legislature. I signed it into law on May 29, 1973.

The LCDC went into operation in February of 1974 with L. B. Day as its chairman. A conservative State Senator, Lynn Newbry, denounced L. B. as "public enemy number one" and me as "public enemy number two" for appointing him head of DEQ in 1971. L.B. was a Teamsters Union official who gave more to his state in time, agony, and hard work than just about anyone. We stood shoulder to shoulder in many a fight. In the spring of 1976, L. B. said he was tired of playing games with "two-bit elected officials who don't take responsibility." I told him that he was overestimating their worth, which couldn't be more than a nickel.

L. B. vigorously pushed local governments to prepare their comprehensive plans. Some said he was too abrasive. But he was also pragmatic. He told me that he hoped to have LCDC in place in five years. I said, "L. B., five years would be 1981. That would be twelve years after the passage of our first statewide planning act, Senate Bill 10. Why so slow?"

He said, "You can't move any faster than the people will let you move." Governor Straub accepted L. B.'s resignation in July of 1976 to appease backers of an initiative to repeal Senate Bill 100. It was unfortunate that Straub would not stick by this courageous administrator. To his credit, he did name an excellent replacement for L. B. in John Mosser. Happily, the repeal measure was defeated by an enlightened electorate. In the same election, November 2, 1976, the voters opted to retain regional councils of government which my administration had launched nine years earlier.

But we have to continue the hard work if we are to retain the paradise that's not yet lost and recapture the paradise that was. As I was leaving office, I helped organize a group called "1,000 Friends of Oregon" to serve as a watchdog on the implementation of land-use planning. It is the only single-purpose public-law corporation that I know of. Glenn Jackson, chairman of the State Transportation Commission, and Allen Bateman from Klamath County were among those who started the "1,000 Friends." Whenever the land-use law is threatened, the "1,000 Friends" have stepped in to make certain that it isn't gutted.

In the meantime, "Visit, but Don't Stay" has become official policy in the city of Petaluma in the east San Francisco Bay area. Their growth-control ordinance was struck down by a federal district court in 1974 because it interfered with people's constitutional right to travel and live where they wanted. However, this ruling was reversed by the U.S. Court of Appeals, which said that preservation of a rural environment was a legitimate government concern. The court said, ". . .the concept of the public welfare is sufficiently broad to uphold Petaluma's desire to preserve its small-town character, its open spaces and low density of population, and to grow at an orderly and deliberate pace."

Wording of the ruling sounded like a McCall replay. We talked of retaining these Quality-of-Life essentials on platforms in a dozen states besides Oregon. In 1976, the Midwest Research Institute published a study on Q-of-L factors which had been commissioned by the Environmental Protection Administration. Portland and Eugene in Oregon were the only cities in their respective large and medium-sized metropolitan areas to win perfect grades on a yardstick of livability, including the criterion of balanced economic and environmental factors. And Salem ranked 15th nationally in the small metropolitan area category.

Father Albert Foley, of Spring Hill College in Mobile, called me after release of the study. He wanted me to come to Alabama to explain why Portland and Eugene ranked first and Birmingham and Mobile last in the MRI findings. It was a ticklish assignment, but I pointed out that old cities in the East and South had grown too fast in eras of planning indifference and utter heedlessness of growth consequences, while most of the top-rated cities in the study were newer cities in the West.

A citizens committee in Mobile wanted to do better by the area's environment which, by the way, fully earned the MRI's flunk. Mobile is expecting a canal to reroute a heavy volume of the Mississippi River's barge traffic through Mobile Harbor by 1981—and, in the words of Mobile Attorney and Civic Leader Ben Kolborn, "We haven't yet done one damned bit of planning for it." Oregon and most of the South speak a different language when it comes to planning and reasonable growth restraints; yet our state and the South are under heavy population and industrial expansion pressures. Oregon can't handle them properly without the implementation of effective land-use planning goals; nor can the South, which is getting the cart before the horse in creating irreversible damage by making fast growth its idol.

As we put it in speeches: "Oregon, Queen Bee though she is, is not yet ready for the swarm."

In 1973 and 1974, in talks in Hawaii, including one to the Hawaiian Legislature, I warned that the island paradise was heading along a destructive course, even though it had adopted the first major land-use planning act in any state.

President Henry Walker, of the conglomerate AMFAC, wrote me a letter defending the wildly growing tourism and new-resident influx of Hawaii as necessary to the economy. True, that economy had been hurt by declines in sugar and pineapple production, but the very same warning I sounded has now been reiterated by Hawaiian Governor George Ariyoshi. Late in January of 1977, Governor Ariyoshi blamed Hawaii's fast population buildup for the state's high unemployment, rising crime and declining quality of life. He urged adoption of a constitutional amendment to stem the tide of new residents into Hawaii—"a national treasure but a very fragile treasure."

A joint session of the legislature heard him go on to say, "The program I am proposing will put this state in direct confrontation with the present laws of this land and possibly even the Constitution of the United States." Truly, Hawaii has been staggered by the swarm. It may well be too late to salvage this island paradise from a trend whose momentum is unstoppable, but, for heaven's sake, let her lesson be ours all across America.

CHAPTER 14

The Bottle Bill

It sounds silly—but the innovative highlight of my ten years in elective state office was the passage and implementation of the Oregon Bottle Bill. Nine Oregonians out of ten think it is a great law. We can see now, as energy and material shortages more clearly impend, that it was a visionary piece of legislation. This is true despite its centerpiece being the mundane returnable soda pop and beer container which had been a part of America's way of life until throwaways began to intrude on the scenery in the 1950s.

A law requiring cash deposits on soft-drink and beer bottles was near approval in the 1969 session of the Oregon Legislature. However, bottlers, brewers and manufacturers of cans and bottles asked for delay, promising to work with legislators in the interim prior to the 1971 session to resolve problems created by nonreturnable cans and bottles.

The legislative Rules Committee Subcommittee on Litter, created in 1969 and chaired by Representative Gordon Macpherson of Newport, held 219 hours of public hearings that produced the first Bottle Bill draft in 1971. Another coastal Republican, Representative Paul Hannemann, claims authorship, but my Natural Resources coordinator, Kessler Cannon, was also in on the act early.

I posed a clinching bit of imagery concerning steel and aluminum cans. Obviously, a crumpled metal container didn't have the utility of a returnable bottle, good for 30 to 35 trips.

"The chemicals in Jesse James' body were worth maybe $1.30, but the rewards on his head must have totaled $50,000," I asserted. "Also, for the reason of its anti-social impact—its despoilment of nature's esthetics—the can must have a reward on its head disproportionate to its value as a crumpled piece of metal."

The 1971 Legislature enacted the Bottle Bill, effective October 1, 1972, over the most intense opposition I had seen to any measure in my nearly 25 years around the marble halls at Salem. Lobbyists for container companies, breweries and soft-drink bottlers came from near and far. They fought the legislation every inch of the way with dire predictions of economic disruption and serious unemployment if the Bottle Bill materialized. Members of Glass Workers Union 740 left their jobs to buttonhole legislators at the statehouse and plead that their livelihood be saved from this threat of destruction.

When I signed the Bottle Bill, I said it was "one of the most significant legislative acts of any state legislature in the nation to turn us away from use and waste to a positive program of reuse and save."

After our Bottle Bill had been operating for more than a year, I pronounced it a "rip-roaring success." The following year, Governor Thomas Salmon of Vermont described his state's Bottle Bill in the same exuberant words.

Brewers, can and bottle manufacturers and soft-drink bottlers brought suit in 1972 seeking to have the Bottle Bill declared unconstitutional. Marion County Circuit Judge Val Sloper upheld the constitutionality of the law. His opinion was, in part, ". . .bold and forceful action taken by the Legislature is a major response to the concern that the citizens in Oregon feel and have demonstrated concerning their environment and its pollution and the problems presented by roadside litter and the disposal of solid waste. . .the Court would be ill-advised to interfere in any manner in this timely and necessary endeavor."

The plaintiffs appealed to the Oregon Court of Appeals. That court ruled on December 17, 1973, that the Bottle Bill is valid under the commerce clause of the U.S. Constitution since (1) it is a valid and reasonable exercise of the state's police power, (2) it is consistent with federal policy, (3) it does not impede the flow of interstate commerce, and (4) it does not discriminate against non-Oregon interests. The opinion also cited the Bottle Bill as valid under the due process and equal protection clauses of the U.S. Constitution, and under the Oregon Constitution.

The plaintiffs declared there were other means besides a deposit law to accomplish the desired reduction in litter and solid waste. Judge Jacob Tanzer said, "Each state is a laboratory for innovation and experimentation in a healthy federal system. What fails may be abandoned and what succeeds may be emulated by other states. The bottle bill is now unique; it may later be regarded as seminal."

The forces fighting the legislation—growing in cunning and abusiveness and amassing a huge war chest—turned their efforts away from Oregon. They had been defeated in the legislature and rebuffed in the courts. So their thrust changed. We were sneered at, in effect, for being "woodsy-weirdos." And they argued that if the bill worked in kinky Oregon, it was bound to fail in any really "civilized state."

Foes of the program rolled up victory after victory in legislatures, courts and elections on local referenda. I alluded to their formula for achievement as the "Four-Ds—distortion, deceit and dollars equalling defeat" for our cause. That the Bottle Bill is a momentous cause is true for a number of reasons. It inculcates a clean-up ethic in the citizenry of a Bottle Bill state, instead of government paying highway litter pickup crews to conduct "Let George Do It" operations.

Most importantly, though, it symbolizes the switch society has to make everywhere from profligacy to husbanding diminishing resources. It is a practical first bridge for this most wasteful of all countries to cross, in reducing a life-style often bordering on opulence to a level of relative affluence. And, mechanically, it does the job. It reduced litter volume 47 percent and beer- and soft-drink-container litter by 83 percent in the second year of the new law's functioning in Oregon. It resulted in a net gain in jobs in Oregon, was responsible for no increase in pop and beer prices or decrease in pop and beer consumption and saved enough energy annually "to provide the home heating needs of 50,000 Oregonians."

These quotes and figures proved unassailable when I cited them in my pro-Bottle Bill forays into other states. They were compiled objectively and scientifically by a young Portland engineer, Don Waggoner, who though an admirer of the legislation, was willing to let pure research dictate the way the chips would fall on this one.

My forays included three trips into Michigan, two each into Massachusetts and Colorado and solo missions into Hawaii, Connecticut, Virginia and Minnesota. In four of those seven states, I pleaded the Bottle Bill case before legislators. Kessler Cannon of my staff was almost as busy, and "Bottle Bill" Moore of the Oregon Liquor Control Commission also was active in the educational process.

Nearly every state wrote the Governor's Office to find out how it worked—and observers came from several foreign countries to marvel at the cleanliness of Oregon's beaches, highways and streets, streams and road sides. Tourist after tourist from out of state observed that nothing they had ever seen came up to Oregon's spotlessness. Polls found 91 percent of Oregon's citizens firmly behind the Bottle Bill, and a reputable public-opinion firm determined that, nationally, 78 percent of our countrymen favored the idea.

It was an idea whose time had arrived—but over the dead bodies of the container, brewing and bottling industry, if at all. Yet, there were breeches in the industry front. Oregon's leading Pepsi-Cola bottler, Ted Gamble, bought Christmas radio spots to thank the people of his state for making the Bottle Bill work so effectively. Industry house organs occasionally quoted bottlers who said they ought to go to refillables to bring down prices, move more of their product and give the Bottle Bill hassle a happy ending.

Schlitz mounted a campaign in Vermont to advertise the lower beer prices refillables made possible. A beer distributor in Benton Harbor, Michigan, slipped me one of his advertising ballpoint pens, told me he was with my cause and then pleaded, "But please

McCall and Secretary of State Clay Myers drank soft drinks from returnable bottles during a Salem bottle collection drive. Both officials fought hard for Oregon's bottle bill.

don't show the pen to anyone in Michigan." He was that scared of his peers' reaction.

President William Coors of the Coors Brewery at Golden, Colorado, sees a national returnable container law as inevitable but feels it ought to deal primarily with aluminum cans. A big soft-drink bottler in Minnesota, Jerry Yocol, took an airliner seat beside me, gave me his card, and as we shook hands, told me that returnables were making him a lot more money.

"But your Bottle Bill discriminates against the can and the freedom of Americans to choose the kind of packaging they want," he added.

My rejoinder was that "we ought to rewrite the Bill of Rights and include the damned cans."

"That's the trouble with your law," he said. "It polarizes. Every time it's brought up, there's a squabble." Squabbles grew into donneybrooks in the last three months before the 1976 general election. Four states had skirted unresponsive legislatures to put Bottle Bills on their ballots by initiative petition.

Industry came out in the open then with its big buy-and-lie technique of winning elections. The public wasn't aware of how low the container and beverage entrepreneurs would stoop to scuttle Bottle Bills, but I had followed their tactics in local elections in Florida and Minnesota. They were so raw I felt compelled to observe that "if their advertising account executives were lawyers, we could have them disbarred, pronto."

Audrey and I campaigned for the initiatives in Michigan and Colorado and I went by myself to beat the drums in Massachusetts and Maine. We ran into clouds of incredible guff in all four states—and extremely determined pickets in Michigan and Massachusetts. Placard-bearing United Steelworkers members circled our hotel in Detroit, and nine protesters from the Owens-Illinois glass plant in Charlotte, Michigan, paraded outside the Capitol at Lansing, where Governor William G. Milliken and I held a joint news conference.

The signs the objectors carried in Michigan—and Massachusetts —had an inhospitable theme. Some of them read, "Deposit

McCall in Oregon," "AFL-CIO and Teamsters Say McCall Go
Home—and Take Milliken with You." The head of the Michigan
Federation of Labor classed Milliken and me as "kooks" for supporting Proposal A, the Michigan initiative. A container-manu-
facturing union representative fifth-columned a news conference
at the State Capitol in Boston to pop up and brand everything I
had said that morning as "a batch of dirty lies."

I reminded him that his side, not mine, was gouging the truth
with its patently crooked advertising. He shouted back, "We have
only $62 in our local's treasury. We didn't pay for those damned
ads." Even enemies of the Massachusetts Bottle Bill were embarrassed by their camp's scandalous propaganda.

And the spending to defeat these initiatives was as huge as it
was blatant. In fact, it had begun to backfire when I campaigned
in Massachusetts in October. The Massachusetts Secretary of
State's official records showed that the Committee to Protect Jobs
and the Use of Convenience Containers in Massachusetts had
spent more than $1 million or some 25 times as much as the initia-
tive's proponents.

At least the Massachusetts anti's labeled their committee somewhat honestly. Foes of deposit-container legislation in other states
gathered under all sorts of misleading banners designed to put
them on the side of the angels. The most flagrant of these was
"Virginians for a Clean Environment," a title appearing on "a
question and answer fact pack" chock-full of tricky misinforma-
tion. In tiny, tiny type it was whispered that these self-styled
environmentalists were "concerned members of the Virginia beer
wholesalers and soft drink associations." Some people are indeed
without shame.

But in the fall of 1976 that ubiquitous Man in the Street was
beginning to awaken and come to the rescue. He was starting to
ask in Massachusetts, Michigan and Maine, "Why is so much
being spent to defeat the Bottle Bill?" His mounting suspicion
helped turn the tables in Maine, pad the Bottle Bill victory margin
in Michigan and vitally narrow the gap in Massachusetts to the
point the initiative lost by about 20,000 votes out of some

2,500,000 cast. Even the conservative Boston *Herald-American* surprised our side after I had visited the new publisher, and endorsed the Bottle Bill.

The disappointment of disappointments was Colorado. Audrey and I had been there only an hour or so before we agreed that "the smell of death" was on the initiative. The editorial boards of both the *Denver Post* and *Rocky Mountain News* told us in question-and-answer conferences, "If you find out where the governor stands on this, please let us know."

Richard Lamm of Colorado, one of the most ardent environmentalists ever elected to a governorship, was an enigma when it came to the Bottle Bill. Apparently, the man who led the fight to keep the 1976 Winter Olympics out of Colorado had been hedging on his environmental acuity to get closer to The Establishment and had fallen between the wheels, satisfying neither camp's hardliners. Lamm finally came on with a lunge for the Bottle Bill in a powerful endorsement which both of us signed in Denver. This followed a colloquy at the Governor's mansion between Bill Coors and me, moderated by Governor Lamm and audited by some 30 dinner guests. The president of the popular Colorado brewery and I ended up with considerable respect for each other.

His message was that Coors operated in 21 states and that if a variety of Bottle Bills and ordinances passed, his business would be handicapped to the point he would be forced to initiate a drive for national deposit-container legislation. His thought was that a congressional act ought to provide for a uniform five-cent deposit and allow ample transition time for the changes the industry— particularly the retailers—would be required to make.

Coors' pet theme was, and is, to "consider the poor grocer"; also the conviction that metal cans can compete economically with bottles. He waved his right arm toward the Rockies and beyond and pronounced that "a mountain of bauxite lies over there and billions of tons of coal."

Recycling a can requires only ten percent of the energy needed to make the original can—and aluminum cans are lighter than returnable bottles. Still, it is questionable whether cans can compete, costwise, with refillable bottles used and re-used 35 times.

At our big Boston rally for the Bottle Bill, a retired Coca Cola executive said he purchased glass for the company on the basis of a bottle being good for 35 trips. Vice president William Wessinger of Blitz-Weinhard, Oregon's only brewery, disclosed that one bottle among their 1976 returnees was manufactured in 1933.

These statistics may seem trivial but they are central to a multibillion-dollar argument that involves basic changes in the personal and business life styles of our nation. Oregon stepped into a thousand-megaton minefield when it passed the Bottle Bill, but we didn't know it for sure until the Great Bottle Debate of 1976. Research brought us the reminder that before 1958, more than 75 percent of the beer and soft-drink containers sold in America carried a deposit.

Incredibly, this thrifty, husbanding habit was deliberately smothered year after year by the industry. Throwaways enabled large beverage producers to penetrate distant markets at competitive prices—so to Hell with everything else, and on with breaking the traditional backbone of our nation's Free Enterprise system, the small business.

With a callous disregard for the importance of small breweries and mom-and-pop bottlers to their home communities, the juggernaut of ever-bigger profits rolled ahead. Between 1950 and 1974, 60 percent of the little soft-drink bottlers were driven to the wall, despite an increase in consumption of 276 percent. The jobs of 7,900 soft-drink workers went down the drain. The Environmental Action Foundation reported that a major soft-drink producer intended to replace 900 franchised plants across the nation with 78 centralized plants.

The same ruthless pattern is evident in the brewing industry. There were 184 U.S. breweries in 1958. There were 55 in 1974, with six companies winding up in control of 68 percent of the beer market. This narrowing-down process eliminated 26,300 brewing-industry jobs. Here, then, the beverage industries which inexorably got rid of more than 34,000 jobs, were in the forefront of the attack on Bottle Bills on the grounds they would increase unemployment. Such shoddy hypocrisy caused me to tremble with rage at every contact with its disseminators and their printed and broadcast trash in the 1976 fall campaign.

Some of their outrageous claims included:

The Bottle Bill would cost the average Massachusetts family $100 a year. (It would if each member of a family of five drank 400 bottles or cans of pop and beer a year and threw all their returnables away.)

If a $50 fine won't keep a slob from trashing, neither will a five-cent deposit. (Oregon's experience is a more than 90 percent return of beer and pop containers carrying a five-cent and two-cent deposit.)

The Bottle Bill in Oregon hiked the cost of beer and pop 25 percent. (The anti's in Colorado based their campaign on this falsehood, even though they confessed to *Rocky Mountain News* Reporter Steve Lang that they couldn't substantiate it. Still, the misrepresentation continued to run.)

Much was made in Colorado and other initiative states of the Washington State Model Litter Control Act of 1971 as an alternative to the Bottle Bill. This red herring faced the acid test a few days prior to the 1976 election. Don Waggoner induced the Washington and Oregon State Highway departments to scientifically test comparable stretches of highway for litter. Washington's were found to contain seven and a half times as much as the Oregon measurement areas.

I suppose, however, the fear of losing jobs will be massaged heaviest in future Bottle Bill contests, as it was in 1976. Effective counter-ammunition is found in a 1976 study. After a year-long study of the possible impacts nationally of an Oregon-type Bottle Bill, the Federal Energy Administration released an 800-page report on October 1, 1976. Bottle Bill supporters were jubilant over its findings. FEA discovered that such congressional legislation would conserve as many as 82,000 barrels of oil a day and result in a net increase of 118,000 jobs, hiking payrolls by as much as $932 million annually.

As for the argument that the Bottle Bill would destroy "skilled jobs," FEA determined that application of the law nationally would cause a net addition of these higher-paying jobs, plus creation of many thousands of entry-level jobs. Moreover, FEA statistics were based on only half or less of the 35 trips-per-bottle Coca Cola had used as a standard.

Pressures by industry and labor crushed Senator Mark Hatfield's Bottle Bill by a 60 to 26 vote on June 30, 1976. "The power of big business and big labor marching in lockstep simply overwhelmed us," Hatfield said then. But Hatfield said the FEA study should "lay to rest" arguments that had cost his legislation defeat twice—and his junior senator, Bob Packwood, chortled, "This is absolutely dynamite." As the new session opened, Oregon's congressional delegation vowed to renew their Bottle Bill fight.

Of all the combatants on our side over the Bottle Bill years, none was under greater pressure to surrender than Administrator Russell Train of the Federal Environmental Protective Agency. Empathizing with the cause early, this fine Southern gentleman and former federal judge built his case carefully and delivered a ringing endorsement of the legislation in a speech in San Francisco in November of 1973. Industry loudly protested. President Nixon's close friend, Pepsi Cola Chief Executive Don Kendall, rushed to the White House to insist that Train be muzzled. It is to Nixon and Train's credit that Train pressed on. His agency testified in May of 1974 on behalf of Hatfield's first Bottle Bill. In 1975, Train reiterated EPA's unswerving support of a nationwide mandatory deposit measure and his agency presented formal testimony to that effect in 11 states.

The same year saw EPA take its most courageous step of all in the returnable-container struggle. In November it published an agency regulation or guideline requiring returnable deposit cans and bottles for all federal military installations, parks, and other reserves and facilities. The next 60 days were designated as a comment period, and most of the 5,000 responses that came in were hostile and concentrated largely in the Southeast. EPA attributed the protest to "a massive industry lobby."

A 1975 Jack Anderson column reported that "the manufacturers of cans and bottles are spending $20 million to thwart the EPA cleanup scheme. Even more dismaying, the container tycoons have been able to pull strings inside EPA and to get inside information for their lobbying campaign." The *Washington Post* headlined the column, "EPA Sabotaged by Container Lobby." Sabotaged, maybe, but not crippled, for EPA formalized the guideline in September, 1976, under a procedure that would see it go into effect on federal premises a year later.

EPA worked out a trial run with the U.S. Park Service and a concessionaire for Yosemite National Park in 1976. This confirmed all the glowing claims for deposit-container programs, with a more than 70 percent rate of return on cans and bottles in the park. It was reported that everything was recycled at Yosemite, "even the chicken bones." In December, 1976, I contacted Interior Secretary-Designate Cecil Andrus and urged him to extend the Yosemite trial to every "feasible" park in the National Park system.

"Sounds like a great idea," the direct-talking Andrus responded. "I'll get right on it so it can be operative during the 1977 tourist season."

A coalition representing environmental voters graded Jimmy Carter at the highest level of environmental concern and Mr. Ford as "hopeless," but Mr. Carter, hailing as he does from the southeastern hotbed of Bottle Bill animosity, may need a little indoctrination on the legislation's merits. It is understandable that Southerners with their warm-water fishery (and Coca Cola's headquarters located in Atlanta) might not apprehend the symbolism and actuality of the salmon and steelhead (or of the Bottle Bill, either). I have perhaps overdwelt on the latter, but the condition of our runs of Chinook and coho salmon and the mighty ocean-going rainbow trout—the steelhead—says a lot about our priorities as a people.

If these anadromous fish resurge in numbers, it is proof we care about clean streams, ergo we care about clean air and clean open space and the totality of the environment, and about each other.

When the salmon are running strong, then all is right in God's world—at least in this magnificent corner of it where we must insist that people not crowd out the wild things that make life richly meaningful.

Gerry Lewin

Of all his awards, McCall most cherished this trophy as the National Wildlife Federation's "Conservationist of the Year."

CHAPTER 15

The Energy Crisis

The pack of men enfolding a microphone in the huge state fairgrounds auditorium faded back until only one remained to speak. He cracked the tension: "Governor, we want to be able to tell our customers whenever anything goes wrong that this is your scheme and you're to blame." A sound came from the throats of the 640 other service-station operators in the surrounding chairs that plainly meant "Amen to that." Without a moment's pause, I replied, "Gentlemen, be my guests."

So the vote was taken, with only two or three "nays"—and there was born the odd-even plan of gas rationing, later adopted in 13 other states and countless small jurisdictions and suggested by the federal government as a possible working alternative to growing chaos and detested coupon rationing of gasoline.

This scene, in January, 1974, was part of a struggle that ebbed and flowed from the beaches of Oregon to the heart of the White House. One interim stop was Stateline, Nevada, where the National Governors' Conference was in session in early June, 1973. I presumed and imposed by delivering every governor a copy of Oregon's energy prospectus, published only days before and based on the findings of a think tank that could only exist in Oregon—the State Energetics Unit. The exponents of this new science had begun strumming a life or death tune about "net energy."

Their computers figured out how many kilowatts and BTU's could be saved if, for example, housewives washed clothes and dishes by hand. A sullen-eyed Audrey greeted me at home after these measures were announced among 37 expedients for saving electricity and natural gas. Cumulatively, they would save a potful if everyone cooperated—but not enough, even so, to close the apparently impending massive gap between hydro-production need and availability in the brown-out-threatened Pacific Northwest.

Proceeding on the basis of a probable emergency was as ticklish a business as any elective executive in a democracy could undertake. So I called on the world from Israel in May, and from Nevada in June, to avoid Arab oil blackmail, and on America to forge a nationwide energy policy.

The energy research office, which helped prepare Oregon for the coming storm, had been part of our improvement of services with the centralization of duties in the Executive Department. By the beginning of my second term, I was starting to get distress signals about the energy situation in the Pacific Northwest. Oregon was particularly vulnerable since we were a completely importive state in terms of natural gas and oil, and since we were so dependent upon receiving a normal water flow. Eighty-two percent of our electric power was hydroelectric and our economic growth was hinged upon the Columbia River's dams.

The think tankers, headed by the cerebral Joel Schatz, disclosed that if we had a shortage of energy and it cut down the economy by 10 percent, the spinoffs would explode all through the government system and the economic system. Income tax revenues would go down sharply and welfare rolls would rise. They were remarkable researchers. They collected data and information on the status and future of energy. We were in the best position of any state to predict when the energy crisis would hit us.

In May of 1973, when the White House was insisting that there was no energy crisis, I said the nation was facing "a tremendous energy shortage, and I anticipate no brightening of the outlook for at least two years."

At a Capitol news conference, I said, "The energy crisis is real. It is obvious, when viewing the national ripples from Oregon's energy perspective, that it is time for the states to join together to press for regional cooperation and a national energy policy. . . . The problems faced by Oregon are faced by all states and by the planet."

One of the reasons that Oregon found itself as the Fort Sumter of the energy crisis was a traumatic water shortage, the most severe in the Pacific Northwest since 1943. That winter we hadn't had enough snow in the mountains to fill the reservoirs. There had been an unusually dry spring. There were 28 billion kilowatts in storage and we needed 41 billion in the Northwest. It was an alarming deficit.

Because of this grave shortage and the energy unit's research, we immediately moved into a program of austerity. I declared an energy emergency on August 21. "We've had the idea that energy in abundance would be forever at our fingertips," I said. "We've become careless. We've installed all the modern conveniences, used them without regard to energy supply, and now the piper must be paid. It takes six hundred pounds of coal to provide the energy to operate one sixty-watt bulb for a year. Turn off that bulb!"

I directed that Oregon's 32,000 state employees heed the danger —that they stop using office hot water and air conditioners and drive state cars sparingly and no faster than 55 miles per hour. To insure that there wouldn't be any cheaters, we took off the hot-water tap turners in the state's toilet facilities. State agencies were directed to cut electrical consumption by ten percent. There was tremendous cooperation, nearly a 30 percent cutback over the next month.

The response to our appeal for voluntary cutbacks was good but not good enough. In the meantime, our reports on the energy situation were gloomier by the day, so I had to go after the electricity usage practice that was at once the most wasteful and most visible. One of the things we kept running into when we asked people to turn off a few lightbulbs was an attitude of, "Why should I, when the used car lot across the street is so ablaze with lights that it could be seen from Mars on a clear night?" People wouldn't believe there was a crisis with the Golden Arches glowing away. At our staff meeting, Cleighton Penwell said, "Is there anything legal you can do to attract the public's attention?" Attorney General Lee Johnson and our office spent a week exploring our alternatives along that line.

I jarred the state in opening the 1973 Western Governors' Conference at Salishan Lodge, on Sunday, September 23, by announcing an executive order banning all outside display lighting except that of a most essential nature. I said that Oregon State Police would be reporting flagrant violations of the order and that Attorney General Lee Johnson would seek injunctions against violators. I added that a court test was likely and said if my action was invalidated, I would call the legislature into special session to give the state police authority on this matter.

I explained, "Blacking out the signs will save a lot of water behind our Northwest dams, and if we save enough water now, maybe we'll have enough juice to run our factories and keep our toes warm this winter. We've got to have more volunteerism, too. If we don't get it, we'll just have to order something more. We can't wait until the lights go out to wonder what we're going to do about it."

Other political leaders liked our direct approach. Governor Cecil Andrus of Idaho, who attended my press conference, called my executive order "politically courageous." Cecil had previously implemented a power cutback in Idaho state institutions. Governor Dan Evans of Washington said the Oregon outdoor lighting ban would dramatize the energy crisis in the Pacific Northwest and intensify voluntary cutbacks in his state.

Interior Secretary Rogers C. B. Morton, addressing the Western governors, allowed as how the move was "both daring and necessary. . .whether legal or not." Special interest harpoons came whistling in from everywhere. The message got through to the citizenry, though: McCall really meant it. The situation in the coming winter could be dire. So let's see what we can do at home.

Most of our mail was supportive. A letter from 16 Marion County students said:

"We, the students of the seventh grade at Brooks School, would like to tell you we think your idea about turning off signs that use up too much of our precious electricity is a wonderful idea. We

Gerry Lewin

checking his energy message at the 1973 Western Governors' Conference, McCall makes some final revisions.

Gerry Lewin

Call announced his energy conservation measures at the 1973 Western Governors' nference, which was held at Salishan. Washington Governor Dan Evans, sporting a well-trimmed beard, listened.

Oregon's odd-even gas rationing program was adopted by service station managers during this meeting with McCall at the state fairgrounds.

"YOU IN THERE! TURN OUT THOSE BLASTED LIGHTS OR I'LL HUFF AND I'LL PUFF AND I'LL BLOW THEM ALL OUT! AND IF THAT DOESN'T WORK I'LL ... UH ... SIC MY DOG ON YOU!"

"On questionable authority, McCall ordered lights out. The bluff worked."

are doing our share by turning off all unnecessary lights. We like your idea because we want to save electricity."

There was, however, considerable dissension about the blackout. Our people were aggrieved that we were setting an example, carrying the load for the West. They could go to California and get the impression that our neighbors were celebrating the energy shortage by turning on every light that they could. California was the most profligate, wasteful state you could imagine. Reagan said the idea of a blackout was too depressing. But Los Angeles Mayor Tom Bradley called me and spent an hour discussing the energy crisis; he came up with some of his own ideas. Shortly afterward, he delivered one of the most forceful energy messages of the year. He also initiated an energy conservation program in Los Angeles. It was reassuring that I was no longer the Lone Ranger.

We were disappointed at Washington State's inaction. It was irritating to Portland business people to see the neons flashing across the Columbia River in Vancouver. Evans had been given emergency powers by the Washington Legislature, but his energy advisory committee was stacked with old-line power company people. It was untypical of the normally progressive commissions of the Evans years.

State police notified all businesses found to be in non-compliance with the executive order. If they persisted in keeping the lights on, I told Public Utility Commissioner Richard Sabin to instruct private utilities to shut off their power. Sabin drew up a list of some 686 violators. As it turned out, they rallied behind our conservation effort and the names were never publicized.

Still, I had expected a test of my authority over this issue and welcomed a court battle. The Marion Dunes International in Salem was to have been our test case. The owner of the Dunes chain had defiantly kept their outdoor flashers on. Attorney General Johnson prepared the suit. But when the motel owner went to the hospital to see his mother, who was dying of cancer, she said: "I've been reading the paper, son. You obey your governor!" This grand old woman talked him into turning off the lights.

I caused something of a stir by suggesting that school boards consider the elimination of night football games, as an energy conservation measure. I said it was one option that could be considered if schools were to reduce consumption of electricity by at least 10 percent. Several districts did shift football games from Friday night to Saturday afternoon. And a number of districts rescheduled junior varsity games to daytime hours. As a onetime sportswriter, I well understood the importance of varsity football to the athletic programs of most school districts, so I emphasized that we didn't want to have districts lose attendance by a time shift and thereby hamper a district's ability to sponsor other sports. I did suggest that schools not turn on all lights during team warmups and that lighting be cut back at least 50 percent, if possible, immediately after the game, and turned off entirely as soon thereafter as practical.

The White House and President Nixon undercut our emergency measures with a September declaration that there was "no energy crisis."

In a letter to President Nixon, I wrote:

"I can't join in saying there is no crisis. . . . I say this from the perspective of a Governor of a Pacific Northwest state, where a major deficiency of electric power is forecast for this winter, and perhaps, for years to come.

"We have launched a campaign for energy conservation. . . . But we can't rely on conservation to keep our economy afloat. We must look for new sources of power, and for prompt completion of all viable Northwest hydroelectric generating systems."

Two months later, the Arab oil states stopped all petroleum shipments to the United States in retaliation for American support of Israel in the Yom Kippur war. The boycott suddenly brought the message home for the rest of the country. The stock market plunged. President Nixon ended months of indecision and, in a nationally televised address, recognized Oregon for taking the lead in the energy crisis. He called on other states to follow the Oregon example with "tough, strong" action. He announced a ban on Sunday gas sales.

President Nixon was also preparing a nationwide 50-miles-per-hour speed limit for cars and 55-mph for trucks and buses. I strongly felt that the different speed limits were both unsatisfactory and unwise. The Oregon Transportation Commission had already set a uniform 55-mph limit for our state. Congressman Wendell Wyatt wrote a bill setting the 55-mph limit for all vehicles. Wyatt, like McCall, favored a nationwide speed limit to bring about equal conservation efforts in all the states. We both opposed the two-level system.

On this issue, the governors of the Pacific Northwest effectively worked as a team. Dan Evans of Washington told me that the director of the Washington State Highway Department and the chief of the State Patrol "came to the conclusion that differential speed limits are totally unworkable." Dan had set a 50-mph speed limit for all vehicles. Since Dan was chairman of the National Governors' Conference, he possessed considerable clout. He summoned a meeting of the NGC Energy Committee to obtain a collective view.

Cecil Andrus of Idaho had imposed a 60-mph limit, and wanted to maintain that limit since new signs had just been printed. But Cecil said he did not like the two-level limit Nixon was proposing. He joined Dan and me in pressing for the uniform limit.

In November of 1973, a delegation of governors went to the White House for a meeting with President Nixon on energy policy. Nixon called us in so that we could endorse his moves in our states and get the public to cooperate. I was like the black sheep at the family reunion.

"Mr. President," I said, "we can't ask the public to cooperate and you can't expect the public to cooperate if buses and trucks are driving by passenger cars and splashing water, snow and everything in their faces! It's just unfair."

Nixon turned to Energy Czar William E. Simon and said, "Bill, don't all our studies show that this is the way it should be—a staggered 50 and 55?"

Simon said, "Yes." Despite this obstinancy, the governors prevailed. Oregon had been instrumental in suing for the unitary limit.

President Nixon told this same meeting some forboding news on another front. "We're going to have to go after coal," he said. "And it's going to drive the environmentalists up the wall."

"Mr. President," I said, "let me just remind you of your speech. Just remember your words—because there is apprehension on the part of the environmentalists about a collapse of the law and the regulations that we built up to try to clean up this nation and keep it clean. Here we've only gotten halfway to where we ought to go and you are talking about retreating.

"If you must relax them—set a limit. Allow only a certain period for relaxation, and review it every three months to see if the need is still there."

I had real fears that the oil companies might tear up the West in their quest for oil-bearing shale. Coastal oil spills from offshore drilling was another concern. The Nixon Administration finally did take a more careful approach to preserving ecological gains.

Not everything we proposed in Oregon succeeded, notably my mild suggestion that schools might well extend Christmas vacation to a month—December 15 to January 15—to save heating oil, electricity and gasoline. Working mothers exploded and educators and strawberry growers followed suit.

The state abandoned the proposal and urged instead that schools stage an Energy Week just before the holidays so that students could go home and imbue their families with arguments for kilowatt and BTU saving. Not only did it shape up as a chillier Christmas but a more cheerless one, too, for the display-lighting ban extended as far as home Christmas-lighting displays.

Scrooge McCall didn't have to ride that one all the way to bitterness, however. Nor did Education Energy Week have its full impact either. Torrential rains in November washed away the urgent justification for our emergency actions by cutting in half the region's expected late-winter hydropower deficit.

So the executive order for the lighting ban was rescinded in early December, 1973. The repeal was accompanied by a call to bear down, voluntarily, on every possible electricity-husbanding device, and citizen-level frugality continued at a high level; although for school-agers, prospects of taking some of the waste out of their parents' energy habits lost a lot of appeal.

While the hydropower emergency diminished, the gasoline crunch was coming on strong. More than any other state, Oregon caught the full smash of that precursor of what yet must become a vast change in American life-styles.

Oregon had the longest gas-station lines and the earliest. Harassed dealers increasingly referred to their business routine as "hand-to-hand combat." There were reports of people chasing service-station operators with tire irons. I met with service-station representatives to see what could be done. Don Jarvi, a young man whom I had appointed director of the Energy Information Center, suggested the odd-number, even-number license-plate concept. Our staff meeting approved this idea as did the legislative leadership. We scheduled the meeting with service-station dealers at the fairgrounds.

At the statewide dealers' meeting, where the odd-even voluntary rationing plan was adopted overwhelmingly, I was jeered and hooted for a mild defense of the customer. The outpouring came when I countered criticism with the observation, "I have been governor for seven years and have never found the people of Oregon to be stinkers." The reaction to that inoffensive piety indicated how uptight the dealers—and therefore the driving public—had become. Odd-even cut the lines almost in half, attracting increasing interest as much of the nation followed Oregon into the noose of strangulating gasoline supplies.

With the Federal Energy Office publicizing The Oregon Plan, besieged states would turn to Oregon for the formula. One governor up against it, Tommy Meskill of Connecticut, thought about putting it in as a last resort before coupon rationing.

"Can you guarantee it will work?" he asked me on the telephone.

"What are you doing now?"

"Nothing."

"You're damned right it works a lot better than just wringing your hands and whining."

Connecticut tried it and it seemed to help cut down the hand-to-hand warfare at the gas pumps. Oregon's lead in the energy crisis —hailed by the President, the Federal Energy Office and a variety of dealers and motorists—wrung a whimsical admonition from Wisconsin Governor Pat Lucey. Himself an innovative governor, Lucey wrote me this note in early February of 1974: "Quit doing so much; you're making us all work too hard."

As part of my commitment to conservation, I gave up my official Lincoln Continental in January and leased a German-made Audi compact car from Audi-Porsche Northwest of Beaverton. Since I had criticized gas-guzzling American cars as "Belchfire Eights" and "Gas Glutton Supremes," it seemed only right that I switch to a smaller, less wasteful car. While the Audi was a very nice car, it was ill-suited to a 77-inch governor. It didn't adapt itself for use as a makeshift office. The four-cylinder engine and lightness created vibrations which made paper work difficult. It wasn't commodious enough for spreading out papers or carrying staff members. So it wasn't practical for a governor's car. I considered keeping it as a vehicle for short trips in Salem, but I just couldn't work comfortably in the small car. Also, dealers of Detroit's best were understandably furious at my desertion from American lines. I asked Ron Schmidt how I might gracefully return the car since so much publicity had been given to it as a conservation move.

The assignment was one which required considerable thought. Schmidt, with his quick wit, wrote the following as a press release:

> An Audi I leased for McCall,
> Was fine except he's so tall.
> So we gave the car back,
> Re-confirming our knack
> To be humble, eat crow, and crawl.

Instead of howls of indignation, Ron had left nearly everyone laughing.

There were few light moments, however, during the energy crisis. When the Arab embargo was lifted in the middle of 1974, the supply of oil was again plentiful, but the Organization of Petroleum Exporting Countries (OPEC) had emerged as a new world economic order and we remained as vulnerable as ever to another boycott. Their action should have caused a reordering of some of the basic values of American society. That it did not was a gross failure of national leadership.

Congressman Al Ullman, chairman of the House Ways and Means Committee, has been among the few leaders at the national level to make a genuine attempt to develop a federal energy program. His Democratic colleagues scuttled Ullman's comprehensive 1975 energy plan. But Ullman has kept trying.

"Everybody has talked about conservation but, as Mark Twain said about the weather, nobody has done very much about it. We are going to try to do something about the energy crisis." President Carter's energy chief, James Schlesinger, made this wry comment in early January of 1977.

For the sake of all of us, I hope that the Carter-Schlesinger team succeeds in doing just that.

CHAPTER 16

My Confrontation with Cancer

Oregon's sunshine in September is a benediction of golden warmth, but a shot of chill riveted through it at the University of Oregon Medical School in Portland one afternoon in 1972. The medical school had just pronounced on the physical condition of the nation's tallest governor, and I being that governor suddenly felt that day turn clammy.

Maybe it wasn't cancer—now. Maybe it could be turned back through the intensive ingestion of a powerful antibiotic. Maybe it couldn't, but the suspect area would be watched to see if deterioration might make a biopsy necessary. And if the biopsy indicated it, then the entire prostate with its malignancy would have to be removed.

By the time I got back to the Capitol, 50 miles south of Portland, the medical school's kindly urology department head, Dr. Clarence Hodges, had relayed this word to my chief of staff. I returned to a hushed executive suite—to downcast eyes, quiet tiptoeing and typewriters whose clatter seemed muted.

Two top aides, Bob Davis and Ron Schmidt, marched solemnly into my tiny working office. Davis spoke first.

Then came the orders, all wrapped up in the warning that I stood a chance to avoid a showdown with cancer of the prostate, if I would just listen and mind. I was told it was all arranged: my wife Audrey and her 6-foot, 5-inch husband were to leave that evening for California's lovely Carmel Valley, to remain incommunicado there for two weeks of rest and medication.

For a 60-year-old, I obeyed with lamb-like meekness; and happily, the next few days proved that the allure of Quail Lodge would help assuage the shock of the medical school findings and the fuzzy dreaminess induced by the intake of four massive cap-sules a day. They were the antibiotic erythromycin, and its pur-pose is to reduce prostate infection.

One day, though, after we had been there about a week, I couldn't resist a fierce pull to break out of my trance-like existence. It might have been the last time; who knew for sure? So I played 18 holes of golf and three sets of tennis in a burst of energy that, once expended, left me even more firmly bemused, and stiff in every joint.

But once returned to the medical school and within range of Dr. Hodge's inquisitive hand, I learned that the initial counter-move at Quail had registered progress. He then cut the medication one-fourth and ultimately one-half over a period of months, with examination indicating continued headway. By early spring, Dr. Hodges had cancelled the antibiotic. He told me, on April 20, to come back in about a month.

Busy public figures nearly never put first things first where their health is concerned. Almost as an afterthought, then, I jammed a return visit to the medical school into a schedule of a lot of official appointments in Portland. But that was mid-July, not May 20, and in three months, a solemn Dr. Hodges informed me, a favor-able prospect had reversed itself. He dropped the bleak news on a Wednesday on a governor and first lady who took it with a shudder.

"Was it too late?" we wondered.

"Would an acting governor have to fill in?"

"Would the governor ever get back to work?"

"Would our life style have to change, or would the governor have any life to restyle?"

Later that day, July 18, a news release from my office summed up the immediate scenario:

"Governor Tom McCall will undergo a diagnostic procedure Tuesday to determine whether a swelling of the prostate will require surgery. He will enter the University of Oregon Medical School Hospital Sunday afternoon and will be hospitalized for at least two or three days following the examination on Tuesday.

After his release from the hospital he will recuperate at home until August 6.

"The Governor's physician, Dr. Clarence Hodges, said that if surgery is required it will be performed later Tuesday and a longer period of recuperation will be necessary. Dr. Hodges, head of the medical school's Department of Urology, said the prostate condition was tentatively diagnosed when the governor entered the hospital in September for treatment of a urinary tract infection.

"McCall will adhere to his schedule the rest of the week. He went by helicopter this morning to Rogers Camp in Tillamook County to speak at ceremonies marking reforestation of the Tillamook Burn. He is scheduled for staff meetings and office appointments during the rest of the week."

The announcement elicited an outpouring of cards, letters, telegrams, flowers, calls and prayers. It wasn't a one-shot reaction. It went on for weeks as a welcome bolstering force for which the McCalls will be eternally grateful.

I remember murmuring sleepily on surgery day when they wheeled me out of my bower of roses: "It looks like Babe Ruth's funeral must have looked."

It was proved later that this was "Surgery Day I." Between then and unexpected "Surgery Day II," I underwent a relapse, an apparent bomb threat and an ambulance dash to an unknown hospital under cover of darkness. But the July 24 processing did determine that the glandular tumor was malignant and Dr. Hodges and his team kept right on going until the prostate was removed.

A middle-aged lawyer friend of mine in nearby Washington County wrote to tell me that he had undergone the same operation—"an operation that all men have had or will have."

I asked Dr. Hodges if prostate cancer surgery was that universal and he amended my friend's statement by saying: "It's an operation that all men have had or will have were they to live long enough."

A not uncommon aftermath of such surgery is inflammation of the genito-urinary tract, and that's what sent my temperature soaring five days after my August 5 release to recuperate at the McCall beach cottage at Road's End.

As my driver, my doctor and I raced through the darkness for the medical school, 130 miles away, my fevered mind wasn't so sure but that my personal Road's End was at hand. Back at the medical school, they wheeled me into the same eighth-floor room I had so recently evacuated. The tests and consultations started all over again. The question revolved around whether more surgery was necessary. If so, what kind. . .how much?

At 9 o'clock a night later, I was on wheels again, taking an un-announced, unexplained horizontal dash to a different wing of the hospital. The reason came out when I got there: an apparent nitro-glycerin bomb had just been discovered on top of a locker in a seventh-floor laboratory, approximately, but not exactly, under my room. State and local police used bomb disposal equipment so adroitly that there was no explosion until the device was safely discarded at a detonation center outside Portland's city limits. To this day, no one is quite sure who left the explosive at the hospital or whether I was the intended target—but that hectic night, hospital and police authorities quickly decided they couldn't take any chances.

This time the nocturnal flight was made by ambulance. It rolled to a stop at the admitting section of Salem Memorial Hospital, which became home for the governor and a state police security watch for the next 10 days.

Here, two days later, Dr. Hodges presided over an operation that was even more delicate to talk about than to perform. But that coincided with a course we decided upon the day before the hospitalizations began in July. "We" were medical reporter Ann Sullivan of the *Oregonian*, Ron Schmidt, and the Governor. Sullivan felt keenly that we ought to have full blow-by-blow disclosure because the story was one the people would follow and heed. She saw it, in short, as a potent aid to the American Cancer Society's education program about a widely prevalent but only lightly discussed form of malignancy.

Audrey embraced McCall on his homecoming. "I was never so happy,"
said McCall.

"GOVERNOR, YOU'VE JUST GOT TO PUT THIS LEGISLATIVE WORK ASIDE
AND GET SOME REST. DO YOU REALIZE YOU JUST VETOED TWO GET-WELL CARDS?"

*"The governor's aides gave him the original of this cartoon. It is unique: it says
something nice about somebody."*

Its location, the prostate, is hardly a subject for chitchat over the teacups. The organ provides fluid that is a vehicle for the sperm to live in during its brief transit from male to female. Its removal and celibacy are synonymous.

Related parts also came in for surgical attention, and detailed mention in publicity connected with the operation following the relapses. A few constituents protested the explicitness of the coverage. A North Coast resident complained to the editor of the *Oregonian* that he found "it distasteful to have the Governor's glands with breakfast in a family newspaper."

Among others who felt the same was the Governor himself. Not only was he almost mortally embarrassed by Ann Sullivan's stories—segments of which were too graphic for television—he, after all, was the victim of all the repulsive symptoms, agonizing doubts, and painful stumbles of recuperation.

A wan governor, down 21 pounds from the 230 he weighed in early July, wobbled home on a warm late-August day to begin a life temporarily burdened by diapers, pads and clamps. But Audrey's care and food were great. The sun was bright and there was and is—more than three years later—every sign that this cancer has been wiped out.

And Ann Sullivan was right about the salutary reaction to having descriptions of a leader's cancer travail widely circulated. Enlightened editorialists across the state allowed that the importance of the lesson to be learned justified the candor of the coverage.

As Dr. Hodges observed, "Everyone (urologists) noticed many more men becoming solicitous about symptoms and seeking examinations. The beneficial effects seem widespread."

In the weeks afterward, when I walked to the Capitol, trying to build my strength back, old-timers—and even some men in their twenties and thirties—stopped me to swap prostate surgery experiences. Maybe every man won't have it, but surely enough are threatened that all ought to make sure, before it's too late, that they escape the boom that was lowered on America's tallest governor.

My son, Sam, was actually the first member of the McCall family to go public about an untalked-about affliction. He appeared in 1970 on a nationally televised NBC interview with Sander Vanocur, talking about his drug addiction. It was a remarkable interview, with Sam speaking compellingly and realistically about his ordeal.

It began in 1962 when Sam had two abdominal operations and then went to the medical school hospital for three weeks with grinding lower-GI pains. Exploratory surgery disclosed massive adhesions. It was in this period that he was prescribed darvon and allowed to eat it like candy. Its addictiveness was not known until years later. But that was how Sam became hooked. He has been a state hospital aide and patient. He has given a number of talks to high school groups on the drug problem, including some appearances in Montana.

At the time Sam made his nationally televised appearance, I was running for re-election. Some friends noted that there was some political risk involved in the interview. But Sam wanted to do it—and I felt that was more important than any political consideration. Sam's warmth and candor brought hope to many parents and a more realistic perspective than just trying to hide it when you exploded inside. His message was that something might be done for it, and that people should not be fearful of seeking help and doing something about it.

CHAPTER 17

Passing up the Senate

Three times in six years the public opinion polls gave me wide leads when matched against incumbent United States senators. The Republican National Senatorial Committee wheedled hard to get me to run in 1968. Their polls indicated that I would have been the favorite over Senator Wayne L. Morse. While I thought I could probably win, I was somewhat skeptical about the poll. The Tiger of the Senate had always overcome adversity in the past and had handily carried the state four times. A more compelling factor, however, was that I had just begun my governorship and felt it was important to serve out my term.

It often occurred to me over the next six years that I ought to improve on the record of my illustrious Massachusetts grandfathers, both of whom were beaten by the same politician running for the U.S. Senate in the same year. This was in 1918 when Sam McCall turned over the Massachusetts governorship to Calvin Coolidge, declared for the senate and then unexpectedly withdrew because he felt his candidacy against incumbent John W. Weeks would weaken the war effort. Grandfather Lawson then entered the race as an independent—and, though he ran behind Weeks, received enough votes to throw the election to Democrat David Walsh.

Five years earlier, Grandfather McCall had lost to the conservative Weeks in a bitter contest. After retiring from congress, where he had served for 20 years, McCall expressed "an ambition to serve in another capacity." The Massachusetts Legislature was to elect a successor to retiring Senator Winthrop Murray Crane. The *New York Times* endorsed McCall in an editorial, saying, "He has the gifts and acquirements that fit him for public life, for the senatorial career. He is a man of matured opinions and strong convictions." Charles William Eliot, president of Harvard University, was among the progressive leaders supporting McCall's election.

When the Massachusetts Legislature convened, McCall led in the balloting. A two-thirds majority was needed to win the senate seat. For three days, Sam McCall continued to lead. But, on the fourth day of the caucus—and 31st ballot—he was defeated by John W. Weeks, a conservative congressman. Sam McCall rebounded to become the first three-term governor of the Bay State, but there was always a disappointment that he had not realized his senatorial ambition.

There was always a subconscious influence, during my years in public office, of wanting to emulate Sam McCall. This influence grew as I learned what a superb, sensitive, visionary and yet sound public official he had been. I thought of myself as a very pale carbon copy of Grandfather McCall and looked upon the senate as an opportunity to succeed at the one level he had failed.

The most favorable circumstances for a senate race were in 1972 when Mark Hatfield faced re-election. Hatfield, once the golden boy of Oregon politics, had been a contender for the vice presidential nomination in 1968 and had talked about running for the presidency in 1972. The impression was widespread that Hatfield was much more interested in advancing his own career than in taking care of our state. His activity on the lecture circuit drew much criticism. I noted in an interview at the time, "If a senator lives 2,500 miles from his state, most of his traveling should be to the state and not to Ivy League campuses."

Hatfield's political stock hit rock bottom in the summer of 1971. The Portland Young Republican Club commissioned a poll by J.R. Weber and Associates, released in June, which showed me leading Hatfield 60 percent to 30 percent. Since the Weber poll was not widely known, there were some doubts about the sampling. But, on July 1, *Oregon Journal* Political Editor Doug McKean dropped a bombshell. It was a poll by Bardsley and Haslacher, the most reliable public opinion analysts in the Pacific Northwest. McCall received 62 percent against Hatfield's 24. Hatfield also trailed two prospective Democratic candidates, Congresswoman Edith Green and former Congressman Bob Duncan. The same poll showed me well ahead of all prospective Democratic candidates.

Hatfield admitted he was on the ropes. "There is no question," Hatfield said, "that I'm in serious political trouble in Oregon. . . . My main problem has been, and continues to be, communications. Somehow, in the last four and a half years, I have failed to bridge the 3,000-mile communications gap between Washington, D.C., and Oregon."

The press took advantage of me from time to time. They knew they could always get a direct answer. Floyd McKay, who had my old job as the KGW political analyst, set me up in early July when he asked me, "Do you think Senator Hatfield is doing an adequate job?" Floyd knew perfectly well what I would say, but the media relished the prospect of a Republican donnybrook.

"He just hasn't done a very good job," I told Floyd. "And it might be provident for the State of Oregon to replace him."

Hatfield returned to Oregon for some fence-mending in August. Although he had talked of stepping down voluntarily, he began running hard.

On November 13, another statewide poll was published. This time it was the Oregon Poll, conducted by Richard L. Kennedy and Associates of Eugene. His poll was a regular feature in several newspapers and commanded wide respect in political circles. McCall held a 55.8 percent to 34.8 margin over Hatfield. I led all Democratic candidates, as had been the case in previous polls. Hatfield trailed two Democrats and held a slender margin over former Senator Morse, whom I led by 23 percentage points.

Some people have said that Hatfield and I have had a running feud for years. I don't think this is the case. We always enjoy seeing each other—it's just that we have a completely different kind of chemistry. He's like a cat and I'm like a dog. I'm open and forthright and Mark is distant and tremendously politically oriented. Still, I have always thought of Mark as one of the most capable people in public life in terms of brain power and ability. His religious convictions are deep and genuine and he is kind to persons under duress.

By January, another poll showed Hatfield within 10 points of me. He had been campaigning extensively in the state and I had yet to lift a finger. Hatfield announced his bid for re-election on January 24. He boasted two powerful conservative endorsements at his news conference: former Secretary of State Howell Appling and Bob Hazen, who had been Ronald Reagan's state chairman in 1968.

Hatfield had been a vocal critic of the Nixon Administration's war policy in Indo-China. However, with the election approaching, he seemed to be renewing his ties with President Nixon. Hatfield reminded Nixon's associates that he had given Nixon a timely endorsement in 1968 and had delivered his nominating speech in 1960. Hatfield wanted to cash those chips in, and the administration reciprocated. The efforts of the Nixon Administration to avoid a party-splitting primary were fervid. Senator Bob Dole of Kansas, the Republican national chairman and Nixon's hatchet man, advised me that President Nixon would prefer Hatfield's re-election to a party-splitting primary. I told Dole it was unlikely that I would run—but made no commitment.

I resented outsiders trying to influence an Oregon election. Anne Armstrong, the striking and beautiful politician from Texas who was later to become the first woman ambassador to Great Britain, was vice chairman of the Republican National Committee in 1972. She made an appearance at the Jantzen Beach Thunderbird and said, "Mark Hatfield is a great senator, a great Republican and a great American."

I stood up in the back of the room and said, "Just a minute, Ann, and fellows, I want equal time on that." My wry remark produced a good bit of laughter. I didn't enter a debate with our charming visitor, although I did feel the Nixon Administration was intruding.

Congressman Wendell Wyatt, an old friend of Nixon's with close ties to both me and Hatfield, called me aside after we dedicated a fish ladder at West Linn. We withdrew to a room at the West Linn Inn and Wendell said, "The President is worried that you and Mark will have a primary race and spend half a million dollars and tear up the Republican Party. He thinks this could cost him Oregon and, quite possibly, the presidency."

Nixon was trailing Democratic front-runner Ed Muskie of Maine in several Oregon polls at the time. So Wendell's argument had a ring of authenticity.

"I probably won't do it," I told Wendell. "But I'm still undecided. The minute I know, I'll let you know so that the President will be aware."

Hatfield's detente with Nixon became even more clear when Attorney General John Mitchell and his outspoken wife, Martha, gave a fund-raiser for Hatfield. In the fall campaign, Wayne Morse would make an issue out of the Hatfield-Mitchell connection with unmistakable pejorative connotations.

The Nixon Administration may have concluded that McCall was too much of a maverick to hold a Republican senate seat. I had been sharply critical of their antiquated economic policies. For months I had called for adoption of wage and price controls. In September of 1970 on CBS national news, I blamed old-fashioned economic policies for the recession and urged controls. When I went to the White House to take up my case with administration officials, Federal Reserve Chairman Arthur Burns peered at me through his pince-nez as if he were discovering a grub on the table of the Oval office.

"I'll tell you, Governor," he scolded, "if we ever adopt the blanket wage and price controls you advocate, we'll be well on our way to being a full-fledged socialist state."

My advocacy of them and the White House disenchantment with them see-sawed for months. I won a point or two but the careening balloon of inflation still soared.

Another encounter with the Nixon White House came after my toughest veto decision—turning down a farm labor bill in July of 1971. Chicanoes prayed at an altar on the front steps of the Capitol at Salem while I was making up my mind. Their threat of a boycott against Oregon farm products almost made me sign the bill, but I vetoed it and was joyfully swarmed by migrant workers who had been praying day and night for a veto.

I was upbraided by Oregon's Establishment for the veto—followed by Under Secretary of Labor Larry Silberman rebuking me at the White House for rejecting the measure. The White House had intended to key national farm labor legislation off the Oregon bill when it became law. I pulled out the rug. All this and the nerve gas episode, and my verbal duel with Agnew hardly made me fit the Nixon Administration mold.

Senator Bob Packwood thought I should take on Hatfield. Packwood and Hatfield had never made any secret of their distaste for each other. As Senator Paul Douglas of Illinois said, "It is a rarity when two senators of the same party and state get along well together. Conflicts are inevitable." Packwood had been a student at Willamette University when Hatfield was on the faculty —and they had some friction even then. Packwood and I had been fairly close. I had been the only statewide Republican elective official to help Packwood found the Dorchester Conference in 1965. I was their principal speaker. Hatfield had nothing to do with it. Most Republican officials thought we were organizing a Trotskyite cell over on the coast. It was a very important meeting and was a ground-breaking effort at getting Republicans to inject common sense and humanity into the discussion of issues.

Packwood's motives in trying to get me to run against Hatfield weren't entirely altruistic. He recognized that I would have no alternative but to leave public life in 1974, unless I ran for the senate against him. So self-preservation was undoubtedly a factor, as was the chance to become senior senator.

The junior senator came to my house at Road's End on February 26, 1972, and urged me to run. He promised all the covert help he could muster, including all his troops, statewide. He told me that Hatfield would be able to raise $750,000 for the primary alone. "If I ran," I said later, "I'd limit that to $50,000. Any more money than that and a candidate gets bought."

Packwood's closing remark was, "Tom, if you wait and run against me, then you'll be the junior senator to Mark Hatfield—and let me tell you, that's no fun."

An embattled Richard Nixon asked McCall about the "Third Force" during the 1974 Mid-Winter Governors' Conference. A week earlier, McCall had been the first Republican governor to call for Nixon's resignation.

Mark Hatfield hosted a reception for McCall and Bob Packwood in January of 1969. McCall's opinions of the two senators were often salty. He later considered running against both men.

william sanderson 1973

"THIS ONE'S SAME AS THE OTHERS, GOVERNOR.
TREAD'S ALL SHOT. GOOD THING YOU'RE CARRYING A SPARE."

"Bill Sanderson and other pundits had a field day when McCall considered
switching parties in 1973."

Other Republican leaders, however, protested that I would literally be giving the governorship to the Democrats. At that time, the president of the state senate was first in succession to the governorship. Then Senate President John Burns was only 36 and, although dedicated, lacked the stature to be an effective governor. He was also a Democrat and had never run for office outside of his legislative district.

The Republicans had a rare opportunity to win control of the state senate in 1970. A special committee on insurance, headed by Salem *Capital Journal* Managing Editor Jim Welch, advised me on filling insurance commissioner vacancies. The committee unanimously recommended the appointment of Democratic Senator Cornelius C. Bateson of Marion County. This removed an unbeatable Democrat from the senate makeup—opening the seat up for Republican State Representative Wally Carson.

All the Republicans had to do to win control of the senate for the first time in two decades was to hold their "safe" seats. State Senator Robert L. Elfstrom of Salem, and 18-year legislative veteran and former Salem mayor, had always seemed invincible. A poll by Richard Kennedy, the Democratic legislator from Eugene and usually reliable pollster, indicated that Elfstrom had a wide lead over Democratic challenger Keith Burbridge, a railroad engineer. A confident Elfstrom let up and Burbridge pulled the biggest upset in the state that year. This meant that Democrats retained the senate.

Had Elfstrom won, Senator Anthony Yturri would have been senate president, and I would have had no inhibitions about having Yturri succeed me. He would have been a sound and able governor, a conservative pragmatist.

So party loyalty—because the Republicans had twice nominated me for the governorship—was the greatest deterrent to my going against Hatfield.

On March 7, 1972, I said, at a press conference in the Ceremonial Office, "I will not be a candidate for the United States Senate. . . . My prime commitment is to Oregon and the Oregon family. I feel I can do the most effective job for Oregon by finishing what the Oregon family re-elected me to finish two years ago."

Former State Senate President Ben Musa called me from The Dalles when I withdrew from the senate race and soothed me, "Remember, sir, there is no higher honor in political life than to have your neighbors elect you as governor."

Hatfield, with only token opposition in the May primary, was renominated with ease. His political resurrection became complete when he defeated former Senator Morse, the Democratic candidate, in November. Polls indicated that Edith Green or Bob Duncan would have probably beaten Hatfield.

I supported Hatfield without speaking ill of Morse, whom I considered a friend. Hatfield has gained strength in the state since then. He seems to be maturing as a senator. I was impressed when he opted for a seat on the Appropriations Committee instead of the more glamorous Foreign Relations Committee. The academic community lost a fine lecturer when Hatfield went into politics. People still talk about his political science lectures at Willamette University on the 1952 Republican convention. After my experience in the classroom at Oregon State, I decided that Mark would have been a lot better as a professor than he was as a senator, and I would have been a lot better in the senate than I was in the classroom.

In the spring of 1973, I almost changed parties to mount a Democratic senate campaign against Packwood. The Democratic legislature had been the most cooperative and innovative of any I had worked with. I was becoming increasingly disillusioned with the national leadership of the Republicans. By contrast, the Democrats seemed to be pulling themselves together in a manner reminiscent of the early New Deal period. Democratic National Chairman Bob Strauss said he welcomed the prospect of a McCall switch and senate candidacy.

Strauss and Senator Lloyd Bentsen of Texas, who was then chairman of the Democratic Senatorial Campaign Committee, both called me within a span of two days. Their message was essentially the same: whether I became a Democrat at midnight, in rain, sleet, snow or hail, regardless of the weather or the time of day, they would fly to Oregon to be at my side for the announcement and cheer me on as a strong addition to the Democratic party and the senate. University of Oregon political science professor, Jim Klonoski, at that time chairman of the Lane County Democratic Central Committee, was all for it. So was the Democratic chairman in Benton County. House speaker Dick Eymann and Congresswoman Edith Green suggested I change parties for a 1974 senate race. Leading figures in Oregon's AFL-CIO did the same. Several polls were taken with McCall, as the Democrat, facing Packwood. I led Packwood in the first survey and, in a later poll, had widened my margin by 10 points.

An item in the June 4 issue of *Newsweek* said that I was on the verge of switching. *Newsweek* made its report on the eve of the National Governors' Conference at Stateline, Nevada. I told some 50 reporters at Lake Tahoe that the Democrats were "not pushing, just darn friendly." The *Oregonian* gave it a banner headline, "Democrats woo McCall to change party affiliation."

On June 9, I was in Portland to ride in the Rose Festival Parade. Along the parade route, people in every block called out, "Switch, Tom switch!"

It was all very flattering and politically enticing. But something happened.

Democratic National Committeeman Blaine Whipple, who has long had designs on public office during his years of incompetence as a party leader, sent me an insulting letter saying that I should start out as a Democratic precinct committeeman. It was not unlike telling Hank Aaron that you can come to our baseball team, but you are going to have to engage in batting practice two hours before each game. The letter was co-signed by National Committeewoman Alice Corbett—but it was Whipple's connivance, written on his real estate business letterhead.

That letter cost the Democratic Party a new senate seat. Until then, the Democratic leaders had recruited me as a political leader who was progressive and almost nonpartisan. I viewed the switch as a means of serving out the governorship well and having a short, inexpensive run for the senate. The letter revealed the cheap political trickery I would be subjected to if I changed parties.

On June 13, I responded to Whipple and Alice Corbett:

"It was good of you to write to delve into the 'press speculation' about my possible change of parties. And that's what it's been, more speculation than substance. . . . The speculation arose out of seemingly local assumptions that I ought to change parties in light of majority Democratic support for my tax program in the 1973 Legislature. Many Republicans supported it, but even more did not. Since I characterized the loss of that measure as the bitterest blow of my public career, there were some who thought that in my disappointment I might want to abandon my party.

"Indeed, I am grateful to the visionary manner in which most Democratic candidates and legislators pushed for that program of tax-educational finance reform. I'm grateful, too, for the friendly beckonings of many Democratic governors, National Democratic Chairman Robert Strauss, Senator Lloyd Bentsen, who is chairman of the Senatorial Election Committee; Congresswoman Edith Green, Oregon House Speaker Richard Eymann, and four of the top Oregon figures in organized labor. . . .

'I have had contrary advice from Republican Governors Reagan, Evans and Rockefeller, Senator Charles Percy and many other friends in my party.

"All of this is pretty heady stuff, rather in contrast to your pointed lecture on party orthodoxy. I recognize your duty as party officials to toe the party line, but it seems to me in the past that it has been the Democrats who often expressed open discomfiture with the strong party discipline exercised by Republicans in the Oregon Legislature.

"Nobody wants to be a blind party hack. I think the issue is more one of leadership, of going down the line for what you believe in to be right than consistently for what someone else believes is right. Oregonians seem to expect that of their elected officials.

"But enough is enough. Last Saturday I intemperately snapped at a reporter who again raised the old question, and said there ought to be a moratorium on the speculation. Obviously, though, it's only I who can apply the moratorium; and I herewith do.

"It's unthinkable that I should be in the position of subjecting Senator Packwood, my family (and even myself) to the conjecture for a moment longer. I intend to remain in my party, to endorse Senator Packwood and to work vigorously for his return to the United States Senate. The fact that Senator Packwood is often provocative is not justification for trying selfishly to terminate his promising career in national politics.

"One of the principal reasons that I'm remaining in the party of my ancestors is to help in any way I can to restore a fully progressive outlook to the Republican image in any way I can. But at the same time I pledge to honor and reward the most gifted and loyal public servants regardless of political registration. I will continue, like most Oregonians, to split my ticket and give aid and comfort to true statesmen and stateswomen. . . .

"It is hard to arrive at the conclusion that one's life in elective politics is just about over—and harder still to accept that conclusion with equanimity. The difficulty in facing it, coupled with the tax program defeat, may have made me more restless than usual, politically.

"As a maverick soul, tuned only to public need and to enhancing Oregon's natural loveliness, it really makes little practical difference which party I claim as my own. Each has its quota of heroes, anti-heroes and plain, decent people. The McCalls have been in the Republican Party for generations, and it has worked out fairly well; so I think I'll just stay put."

I received many letters and comments about the decision to remain a Republican. One of the most generous assessments came from Congressman Les AuCoin, who was then majority leader of the Oregon House of Representatives:

"The Republican Party is a better party today that Tom McCall has chosen to remain with it. For the Democratic Party, it has lost a special opportunity for greatness. As a Democrat, this saddens me a great deal. But we desperately need men and women in both parties who dare to dream; to reach; to try what has not been

tried before. Your decision to remain in the GOP will help it meet
this challenge and responsibility.

"Greatness. How does one measure it? I'm not quite sure, but it
does seem to come in small doses today. The special tax election
last spring revealed a dearth of it and, frankly, how downright
self-serving some politicians can be.

"But in your defeat, you may have scored your greatest victory.
Spurned by members of your own party in the Legislature,
battered by some of the biggest moneyed interests in the state,
misunderstood by many of the people in a climate of political distrust, attacked by some of the sheerest political demagogery I've
seen, you had the courage to work relentlessly for a cause that
was just. In this, you triumphed. And for this, you will be
remembered, Tom. It will be remembered that you didn't flinch
once. And, years from now, it will be discovered that you were
right.

"Last Thursday came your decision, and beyond my party's loss
was the loss it meant to the public. This saddens me most of all. It
is difficult for me to accept the idea of Tom McCall not being in
public office. In these times, whatever registration you might
choose, your steady hand is needed.

"I say these things not because you and I have always been on a
political honeymoon. I remember, for instance, losing your
endorsement in the 1972 campaign. But I also remember, as news
editor of the *Redmond Spokesman,* sitting on a bale of hay at the
Deschutes County Fair and interviewing you when you ran for
statewide office for the first time. And I have followed with
admiration the public career of Tom McCall ever since.

"As governor, you've written a record that others will be
challenged to match for years to come. I wanted you in my party.
But I respect your decision and hope to enjoy, always, the
friendly relationship we have had."

I wrote Les that his letter meant "more to me than just about
any I have ever received." Then, I confided how close the decision
had been:

"I was really quite serious in my recent contemplation of the virtues and drawbacks of the two parties. It was so close a thing that I was almost waiting for a tie-breaking sign. It came from those paragons of pygmyism, Ivancie and Whipple, who spoke not without ulterior (and I believe) selfish motive. And that reminded me that Cook was also over there and others of a stripe that didn't make my neanderthals seem so God-awful."

My cancer operations in the summer of 1973 seemed to make my decision about leaving politics all the more definite, but my recovery and the national leadership role which Oregon played in the energy crisis gave me ample reason to reconsider; so did heavy pressure from state Republican leaders. Congressman Wendell Wyatt, who had helped talk me out of running against Mark, urged me to confront Packwood. So did Democratic Congresswoman Edith Green, who described Packwood as a "lightweight."

Actually, I could have succeeded Wendell as First District congressman in 1974. That spring Audrey and I went to a reception with Wendell and Fay. We were having a drink in a little side room when Wendell told me he was not going to run. He told me first, outside of his immediate family, because he wanted me to consider running to replace him.

"It would be a tremendous honor," I told Wendell. "But, on the other hand, why should I be a freshman congressman and Bob Packwood be a United States Senator?"

After eight years as governor, I didn't want to deal as a junior associate with Hatfield and Packwood. But I probably should have taken up Wendell's offer. Even though a freshman congressman is the lowest thing in Washington, it would have given me an opportunity to have a national forum, serve the state as a member of a body that my grandfather, Sam McCall, had served in for 20 years. I should have at least discussed it with Audrey and pondered it more. I don't think there would have been any serious opposition if I had come out early and with Wendell's blessing.

The option of being certain I would live gave me a sort of new-found freedom. A health report I received in early March before departing from the Mid-Winter Governors' Conference at Washington, D.C., showed no recurrence of the prostate malignancy. I was buoyed by a public-opinion survey which showed me clobbering Packwood in the Republican primary.

Packwood would have been a formidable opponent. He can conceive campaigns and strategies better than anyone I know. When he was a legislator, he got a lot of money for recruiting Republican legislative candidates. His "black book," a campaign handbook, was a tour de force. The Dorchester Conference was a remarkable achievement. But the strategist and organizer is generally not a statesman. I always viewed Packwood as someone who would have made a marvelous chairman of the Republican National Committee. Bob has never been issue-oriented or moved by great causes.

There was no acrimony or personal enmity. I liked Packwood. The Packwoods threw a beautiful dinner for Audrey and me at his house, with an illustrious group of cabinet members. I said, "Bob, I just can't come into your house and accept your food and drink until I let you know that I'm about to decide whether to announce for the senate, for your job."

This made a mess of the evening, but it was better than being hypocritical. Packwood's dinner, however, was his campaign kickoff. Energy czar William Simon was there, as was Office of Management and Budget Director Jim Lynn. They were all set to argue me out of running against Packwood.

Simon had been advancing Packwood's candidacy all spring by leaking him any positive news on the energy front—while sticking me with anything that was bad news. That night Simon told me that Packwood was one of the leaders discerning the scope of the problem on energy and in leading Oregon and the nation to answers. Yet when Packwood was asked about Oregon's odd-even rationing plan, he had been out in the boondocks of the Virgin Islands vacationing with his family. He confessed, to his credit, he hadn't heard about it.

Nevertheless, Simon was pushing him as a great leader. Simon's comment, "Packwood, not McCall was responsible for Oregon's energy leadership," was widely reported in the Oregon press.

Simon was, in a sense, discrediting the entire Oregon effort. He already had destroyed his predecessor as energy czar, former Governor John Love of Colorado. It was really a good break for America when, in 1977, Snob Simon headed back to Wall Street where he belongs.

Packwood pleaded with, cajoled and threatened party leaders back in Oregon. When the Teamsters Union endorsed me for the senate, Packwood angrily called L. B. Day: "I won't forget this," Packwood snapped.

"Neither will I," L. B. shot back.

During my week in Washington for the Governors' Conference, I had pretty much decided to run. At one point, old friends Dale and Maxine Mallicoat toasted my decision over dinner with Audrey and me. If I had been elected, I would have asked Dale to organize my senate office. I don't know if I could have persuaded him to stay in Washington much longer—but he would have been able to make an incredibly large contribution.

Upon my return to Oregon, I asked Ron Schmidt to prepare a confidential report on the senate race. Ron had never been one to pull his punches. I knew that his assessment would be realistic.

Schmidt wrote a long memorandum outlining the reasons for and against my candidacy. He said I could probably win the primary and general elections. "Service in the Senate would culminate 10 continuous years of public service," he wrote. "It would probably close the circle on your own view of what your personal history should be. Realistically, the presidency is out of reach for you. But capturing the vice presidency is a realistic thought, made more realistic by service in the United States Senate where you would fill whatever foreign-policy knowledge gap that you have."

"Packwood has an image of not having performed," Ron wrote. His campaign organization, however, was well-geared. Schmidt said Packwood would probably have more money. He also had "firm commitments" from Vice President Gerald Ford and Senators Barry Goldwater, Howard Baker, and Charles Percy to campaign for him. Schmidt thought the Nixon Administration help might work against Packwood.

Schmidt reported there was strong labor support for a McCall candidacy. Walter Gray of the National COPE told Schmidt, "Put us down for McCall." Wendell Wyatt offered to "help behind the scenes," but declined to be chairman of a McCall campaign. Packwood had already recruited a number of past McCall supporters for his finance committee. Schmidt said some would feel alienated by me because of my previous statements that I would not run.

These statements posed a credibility problem, Schmidt said. "Going back on your word to Packwood subjects you to the charge of 'politics as usual,' " he wrote. "This would be the roughest primary campaign in the nation." Packwood would "come down hard on the issues of health, age and integrity."

Schmidt was concerned about the physical and mental toll of a senate campaign. "I'm not sure you can stand the pressure of an exhaustive, two-month, bitterly contested primary campaign. The moment you enter the Senate race you would no longer receive the kind of publicity you're getting, or the kind of understanding you have from the Oregon press. . . . A loss would hurt you much more than it would Packwood. Based on your reaction to the school tax defeat, you would interpret a loss in this race as a personal rejection. It would not be that, but I'm afraid you would take it that way.

"There is much to do as Governor in these last months, and it would be questionable that you could oversee the work. Instead, every day from now to November would be spent campaigning, leaving you much less time for yourself and your family. I gather you've been trying to protect that time, and it would be unprotected if you run."

On Tuesday night, Ron brought this report over to my house. For more than three hours, we discussed it. Andrey, who had twice before vetoed a senate candidacy, seemed more receptive this time. On the basis of our discussion, I was still leaning toward running. The next day, I had some second thoughts. Audrey wanted me to make a decision. She told me, "I'm going to the beach for the night—I just have to get away." When she left for Road's End, she thought I was going to challenge Packwood. I called her that night and said I was going to do it. Audrey was favorable. "Great," she said, "that's fine."

But on Tuesday morning, I just came to the conclusion that finishing my governorship with a flourish and taking on the agile Packwood were competing burdens to which I couldn't do justice at the same time.

That I would never be in the senate made this last decision the toughest, especially because it meant my career in elective office was probably drawing to a close. Another determinant was my desire to live in Oregon—which outweighed the comparative unattractiveness of Washington life and transcontinental commuting between job and constituency.

I called Audrey to break the news. It came as a surprise to her since I had been so enthusiastic about a senate campaign. She enjoyed politics and was always my partner and confidante in fact as well as in name. After telling Audrey, I called Packwood and told him. He seemed relieved and was extremely gracious in his comments about my years of public service.

At an afternoon news conference, I asked reporters to forgive me for imposing on their indulgence on the same subject for so many times. I explained, "Engaging in completely sincere inner searching and deliberation is a process I go through publicly. . . . I'm frank about my considerations where most politicians deliberate in secret. I enjoy talking with people to get their help with the answers to great questions, and in talking with them my own thoughts must come out."

It was an emotional session with my staff and the Capitol press corps, most of whom I had known for years. I doubt if many politicians could have resisted the margin I had over Packwood or the two earlier opportunities I had passed up, but it enabled me to wind up my second term most productively and effectively. Being governor was "tops" as far as I was concerned.

CHAPTER 18

The Third Force

After telling "The Oregon Story" at the Center for the Study of Democratic Institutions in Santa Barbara on a spring morning in 1974, I came away both inspired and puzzled. A three-hour exchange, with some of the world's pre-eminent scholars, about population, energy, the environment and the political process ended up as something of an admiration society. Rexford Guy Tugwell, the systematic thinker who had shaped much of the New Deal for Franklin D. Roosevelt, was there. So was Robert Maynard Hutchins, founder of the center and longtime president of the University of Chicago. Finally, two or three of them said, "Governor, why can't you be President of the United States?"

My reply was: "The messenger is far less important than the message." With my cancer operations, I told them I might not run for anything except a mortuary.

I pondered their questions further on the flight home. I wondered why they thought about Tom McCall as a potential President. Some special qualities were there serving as a catalyst. Were they special, or was it that in the Watergate trough they just seemed that way? Perhaps I seemed to be a welcome contrast. Maybe they hadn't seen a political leader who simply talked about the issues with compassion and understanding. As I reviewed the morning, it really hadn't been all that spectacular as far as the making of the next president was concerned. But it had been very stimulating.

A television reporter and cameraman hit me on the airport strip and I told them: "There has got to be a better way than this two-party system which is not getting to anything. You've got to have the spirit of life in America and an existence that preserves what you have. You've got to have a spirit that doesn't worry about politics to lead America."

There was a great surge of interest after that interview. It was funny, heart-warming and very humbling to learn how so many people agreed with this miniature Bigfoot about the need for a Third Force. In covering more than 50,000 miles during 1974, there wasn't a stop where I didn't find admiration and enthusiasm for the Oregon Story. It was a beacon that lighted up countenances everywhere. The Oregon Story is the story of a can-do state with the push and courage and thinking apparatus to risk innovation wall-to-wall. I'd get hammered at home for making Oregon sound so good! Oregonians couldn't figure out how this jibed with my "Visit, Don't Stay" doctrine.

The answer, of course, is that the Oregon Story is about a formula that is exportable, hopeful and regenerative. Everybody likes to hear it because it is the antithesis of air, water and political scum and pollution.

It became downright alarming because it was so pervasive and because this relatively unknown politician from a lightly populated state—far from the center of the power structure—was so consistently seen as an answer to America's Watergate malaise. An informal spring poll in the *Christian Science Monitor* showed me leading such major presidential contenders as Edward Kennedy, John Connally, Walter Mondale, George Wallace and Edmund Muskie. (Jimmy Carter was not mentioned in the poll. Senator Charles Percy won the poll, with Common Cause Chairman John Gardner second.)

Several months after he had interviewed me for his public television "Journal," Bill Moyers said, "McCall is my candidate for President in 1976—irrespective of his party."

Long articles analyzing a McCall candidacy appeared in such major publications as *Time, The New Yorker, New Times,* the *Washington Post,* the *Los Angeles Times, Newsday,* the *Philadelphia Inquirer,* and the *Miami Herald.* In his column, Nicholas von Hoffman of the *Post* wrote: "As governor he's done what we say we want our politicians to do, although when they do it we usually don't vote for them. He has been unmistakably forthright about every public issue. . . . That President McCall would spin us around and send us off in marvelously new directions is more than history teaches we should expect. But what we would get from him is the example of modesty, simplicity and openness we are so desperate for that we imagine we can even see it in the actions and character of a man appointed by Richard Nixon to replace Spiro Agnew."

Such national publicity has often hurt political figures in their home states. The feeling is that he has grown too big for his britches and has gone highhat on his friends and neighbors. Oregonians have never taken kindly to "favorite son" presidential candidacies. And there was some snickering about my "Third Farce" and jokes about who would serve in a McCall Cabinet. However, there was also some encouragement.

An *Oregon Journal* editorial noted: "The McCall style, extended to a national base, would be a welcome, if shocking, change from the White House isolation the country has known. Regardless of his chances operating either within or outside the traditional party structure, one observation should be made: We'd rather have Tom McCall in the White House than a lot of persons who come to mind, including the one elected a little more than a year ago."

The *Oregonian's* editorial page commented: "McCall's first problem is to 'get off the ground' as a serious presidential candidate. It may be that many campaign contributors, weary of seeing their money wasted in Watergate fiascos, will rally around the Oregon governor. He is obviously the tallest and most exciting lightning rod on the American political scene."

In the early spring, we had $150 in small checks from Third Force converts. A Lake Oswego woman sent me a poster urging a 1976 presidential ticket of Tom McCall and Ralph Nader, whom she described as "the breathing person's choice." Somebody else came up with a "McCall for President" bumper sticker—only this one had space on it where you could vote yes or no.

As I discussed the Third Force across the land, I expressed hope that we could reach the point where $100 million campaigns were shamed out of existence and politicians were forced to conjure with the idealistically relevant.

Dr. George Gallup, the dean of public opinion polling, said the post-Watergate Republican party was little more than a splinter group. Gallup said the time might indeed be ripe for a Third Force. He noted that his polls showed a profound dissatisfaction with party mechanisms, persiflage and rote—and with most of the product rolling off the assembly line every other November. His polls also revealed an innate faith that the basic system will work, given the right operatives and approaches.

No less a politically astute Democrat than Frank Mankiewicz—erstwhile righthand man for Robert F. Kennedy and architect of George McGovern's 1972 presidential campaign—said that I was onto something. "McCall, the independent, could bust down the middle and win it in '76," he said. Mankiewicz explained the unlikely scenario this way: "McCall is something different. McCall is genuinely independent. . . . I think somebody is going to win the presidency soon, not on a third party platform, but independent. In other words, somebody is going to come along and he's going to say 'Screw your party. I'm not going to your conventions and make your deals. I'm not Republican or Democrat. I'm not going to run in the primary. I am me and I'm running for President. Don't tell me in the United States of America a man can't run for President.' And he's going to do all right. I think a man like McCall could do that. I think this country is fed up to the teeth with parties."

Richardson, the cool, clipped Brahmin and hero of the Saturday Night Massacre, was interested in the Third Force. After resigning as Attorney General, he had become a Woodrow Wilson Fellow studying state and local government at the Smithsonian Institution. Richardson invited me to join him as a Wilson Fellow at the conclusion of my term in January of 1975. My impression was that Richardson saw himself as a likely Republican candidate for the presidency. Many idealists fell out of love with Elliot in the fall of 1974 when, offering himself as parsley on the chicken-and-

The guests of honor arrive at a governor's farewell dinner.

McCall gets a kiss and an ovation.

pea circuit, he barnstormed for some of the most reactionary mountebanks in American politics.

Unlike Richardson, I had drawn the line at such indiscriminate barnstorming. Governor Winfield Dunn of Tennessee, chairman of the Republican Governors' Association, had asked me to serve on their campaign committee. I declined for a number of reasons. In a letter to Governor Dunn, I said:

"For some time, I have enunciated the thesis that issues are more significant than party labels. Therefore, I might prove to be more of an impediment than an asset in the case of Vermont, say —but I very conceivably could help out if Houston Flournoy were our nominee in California, and help, too, other states where the party nominated other progressive Republicans who generally reflect my well-known views on the environment-energy issues.

"So you see, then, Win, I couldn't subscribe to a committee effort that, in certain instances, would turn out to be anathema to my conscience. Not that my RGA colleagues are without conscience; it's my unusual order of election priorities and candidate requirements that make *me* difficult, not my fellow Republican governors.

"But since that's the way I am, I don't want to be privy to the committee's strategy from the advantage of holding an inside position. It wouldn't be right from any point of view when you realize that I sometimes feel compelled to judge candidates by how and what they think, in preference to buying them solely on party label.

"All this, to summarize, doesn't mean I wouldn't try to go to town at the hustings, time permitting, for a Republican gem who thought I might be helpful. So just let me free-lance on sort of an on-call basis—and give me such committee briefings as you think you can safely share with this intolerable maverick."

Several months later, at the 1974 Mid-Winter Governors' Conference, Dunn sad-eyed me in the cavernous lobby of the Washington Hilton. I had been castigated by some of my Republican colleagues for endorsing Idaho's Democratic governor, Cecil Andrus, for re-election.

"Why do you look at me so despondently?" I asked Dunn. "Is it because of Cecil?" Dunn nodded his head.

"Isn't he a great guy?" I asked. "Isn't he a fine governor? Doesn't he work well at Governors' Conferences?" To each of these questions, Dunn responded in the affirmative.

"Well, then," I said, "is it because he's a Democrat?"

"Yes," said the chairman of the Republican Governors' Association.

This, to me, was an indictment of partisan politics. When you have a superb public administrator and political leader, you should never try to gut him simply because you happen to belong to another party. In speaking at the kickoff rally for Cecil's campaign, I told the people of Idaho: "You'd be crazy to throw him out." (He won re-election and went on to win the chairmanship of the National Governors' Conference and appointment as Secretary of the Interior.)

I saw the Third Force not as a third or fourth party, but as a train of thought that might pierce the leathered hides and stultified thinking of the political professionals running the major parties, and as a mass of voters that would selectively choose our leaders without regard to party label. It was, and is, a nonpartisan alliance of reform-minded citizens.

One of the incredible phenomenons spinning off the Watergate trauma was the think-one-thing-say-another syndrome. Nelson Rockefeller made a compassionate plea for fairness to President Nixon at the Dorchester Conference. A few minutes later, he told me: "Dick is without roots. So what could you expect?"

It was at the same Dorchester Conference that I became the first Republican governor to call for Nixon's resignation.

"The President should not put us through the agony of impeachment and trial," I said. "If he is not going to open up, he should resign. The President is almost certain to be impeached and tried. This is a trial the country does not need. The nation will survive, no matter what happens. But it deserves not just to survive but to go forward. The President must let it go."

After my speech, the Dorchester delegates voted 286 to 119 in favor of a resolution calling for Nixon's impeachment.

Our national government was beyond the crisis state. Watergate had already left wounds which would take years to heal. Nixon's resignation just seemed to be the least painful of alternatives. Nixon looked pale and haggard when I saw him the following week at a State Dinner for the nation's governors. I wondered how much longer he could physically and mentally persevere—how much longer his yearning to cling to power would paralyze the nation.

Several Republicans of stature, fighting the straitjacket of Watergate, became quite taken with the Third Force. In Honolulu, Clare Boothe Luce, whom *Esquire* magazine described on its cover as the "Woman of the Century," counseled me after a long dinner discussion, "Governor, go back to the mainland and announce you're starting a new party."

Former Michigan Governor George Romney was in Florida when he read a newspaper article about the Third Force and telephoned me.

"Tom," Romney said, "the Republican and Democratic parties ought to take a sabbatical to get their houses in order." The square-jawed, straight-shooting Romney went from there to rough-sketch emergency action. He proposed a meeting of leaders who put the country above self and party. This "interim influence" might bring about the election of a nonpartisan president in 1976, committed to a single term and dedicated unremittingly to getting a sorely perplexed America back on the track.

I expressed doubts about "holding a convention" because "political convention" seemed just about as opprobrious a term as Watergate. But I thought the idea of convening a "council" had a lot of grab to it, bringing together the Romneys, the Gardners, the Naders, the Proxmires, the Richardsons, the McCarthys, the Evanses, and, yes, even the McCalls, along with frisky educators, businessmen, labor seers and whoever else packed some punch and wanted to sacrifice to restore America's equilibrium.

John Gardner said that my emergence on the national scene made me an ideal standard bearer for the Third Force. As Gardner viewed it, my lack of ties to the Washington establishment and to the special interests made me "a very constructive person to build around." Gardner, a former Secretary of Health, Education and Welfare, was deeply troubled by his country's plight.

Just as troubled was former Minnesota Senator Eugene J. McCarthy when he called me in Washington and suggested that we team up as independents in 1976. "Why, I'd even take second spot," McCarthy said.

The Third Force came on stronger and stronger as I stepped up my travels. From nearly every perspective I could find, the country was more desperate and sullen and despairing and disappointed than anyone had ever discovered it to be, officially or scientifically. It was depressing, stop after stop, to hear the same voice with the same knee-jerk Watergate comment: "Anyhow, everybody does it."

Everybody does it—like hell—I'd flare back. And the retelling of the Oregon Story was on.

Eight hundred students at Stanford University packed the main campus auditorium for my appearance. They were literally sitting in the aisles. One student rose during the question-and-answer period and said, "Perhaps you would consider running for president. . . . If you've considered it but decided not to, perhaps you'd reconsider. Of the governors that have expressed that desire, you're probably the best that I've seen so far."

They gave me a rousing ovation when I said, "If I have to run for president to keep on spreading this message, that would be a twist of fate I would not welcome, but I would accept it."

There were some ego-trimmers, too, such as a reporter at a May news conference in Tucson who wondered, "How can you entertain such ambitions when about the only thing you and Oregon have done is pass a returnable can and bottle bill?" I replied that the spirit giving rise to the Bottle Bill and a swarm of innovative things in Oregon ranging from better police training in villages to a Pacific Rim cultural center—that spirit is what makes people hopeful about Oregon and its messenger.

The Third Force and its chief spokesman were getting so much national attention that the CBS news program, "60 Minutes," decided to cover it. For more than a week in June, a special camera crew with and without Mike Wallace recorded conversations between John Gardner, Ralph Nader and Elliot Richardson and me. They shot a mile of film in Seattle, Salem, San Francisco and at the old family ranch in Central Oregon that my mother wrote about in *Ranch Under the Rimrock*. Now, in her late eighties, she rose to the occasion and staged a lively battle of wits with the vaunted griller, Wallace himself.

CBS was ready to go with the Third Force segment early in July. Wallace reported the film was in the can in excellent form, but he chose to postpone it rather than edit it to fit the time available for the July date. It was rescheduled for "a sure showing" August 14. Then came President Nixon's resignation and the CBS management decision that the Third Force had overnight lost its timeliness.

Twenty-five million people would have learned about the Third Force had the CBS program been aired. There's little doubt that it would have been well launched had President Nixon somehow stuck it out. The Third Force eludes definition. Its genesis was the Oregon Story with the story's emphasis on problem-solving in a climate of openness and probity, reverence for nature, and sometimes daring innovation—free from conniving, coercion and partisan gamesmanship.

I think the Third Force should continue to be an influence on both parties, like a neon sign that comes on saying, "These are the Ten Commandments, no matter what party you belong to." These commandments would include protecting the environment, stressing energy conservation, developing a new openness in government, creating a national presidential primary and national initiatives, eliminating the seniority system in Congress and protecting consumers. The Gardners, the Naders, the McCarthys and the McCalls had these basics in common. Just their standing together with their selfless goals and immense credibility constituted a Third Force in itself.

President Ford's honesty and openness made him a perfect personality to lead us back toward the light of national self-respect. History will remember him kindly, not for any great social advances but for his heart-and-soul commitment to leadership. I was amused by a Eugene *Register-Guard* editorial about why Ford didn't consider me for the vice presidency. Under the heading, "Not Ready Yet," the editorial writer said: "Pleased as this newspaper is over the selection of Nelson Rockefeller as vice president designate, a certain sorrow persists because the nod didn't go to Oregon's Governor Tom McCall. Yet, it's understandable. Oregon was ready for McCall. It may be a few years before the rest of the country can cope."

Gerry Lewin

The outgoing governor enters the House of Representatives to deliver a farewell speech. House Minority Leader Roger Martin and Senate Minority Leader Victor Atiyeh escorted fellow Republican McCall.

CHAPTER 19

Beyond the Governorship

January 9, 1975. Nearly 1,300 people crowded into the Grand Ballroom of the Portland Hilton for a "Toast and Roast" of Oregon's outgoing governor. They came despite miserable weather—rain, snow and sleet. Among those braving the elements to attend were five neighboring governors—Dan Evans of Washington, Cecil Andrus of Idaho, Mike O'Callaghan of Nevada, Cal Rampton of Utah, and Stanley Hathaway of Wyoming. Evans said, "Oregon is the fastest-growing state in the West because McCall has asked people not to move to Oregon. . . . We always looked upon Oregon as our Gaza Strip."

Angus Bowmer, director of the Oregon Shakespearean Festival, said, "Can't you just see Tom McCall as Hamlet? 'To be, or not to be. . .a U.S. Senator.' Barrymore never played that indecision scene better or as often."

Mayor Neil Goldschmidt of Portland said, "Tom McCall has made an impact on Oregon. So did the Columbus Day Storm."

It was a marvelous evening of nostalgia and good humor. When you get those kinds of accolades on your departure, you shouldn't ever show your face publicly again. I recalled my eulogy to former Governor Charles Sprague and said I hoped to be worthy of it: "He tried, oh Lord he tried. There was no final victory. But did he not point the way?"

Four days later, I went out of office having served longer than any of Oregon's 29 previous governors. I would have enjoyed continuing on the job, but the Oregon Constitution prohibits three consecutive terms. My redoubtable mother, Dorothy Lawson McCall, announced her candidacy to succeed me, pledging to carry out my policies but without "his foot in the mouth." I was greatly relieved when she cancelled her race because she "didn't want to get into the muck of politics." A Salem *Capital Journal* poll reported that when people learned "there are no McCalls on the ballot, they say they don't think they'll bother to vote." A subsequent editorial pointed out, "Refusing to vote won't keep McCall in office."

In my farewell statement to the legislature, I said: "This chamber has been the scene of many battles for the Oregon cause. At the same time, working in this building is a delicate responsibility and keen honor for all of us who have had the opportunity.

"In all honesty, though, I must say the entrance is more invigorating and pleasant than is the exit. But it is not in the Oregon style to dwell on goodbyes. Though we fully understand that the past gives us our foundation and our generating guidance, we are more ardently concerned with the future and how to get there.

"I am not here for purposes of saying goodbye, nor for probing the file cabinets of the past. Let me leave this assembly today the way I entered it: Full of hope for tomorrow and actively at work helping to realize the hope."

The winding-down process is terribly difficult. John F. Kennedy once observed that no matter how one viewed public office, he was bound to find leaving office a wrenching affair. Except for a very few people, there is never a real satisfaction in being a private citizen when you have held a public office. You lose your staff and your ability to do things for people. You also lose your challenge, at least temporarily. You still get the huge volume of mail you did as governor, but, without a staff, you cannot answer everyone. It is frustrating.

I am more fortunate than most retired governors in that I do have a very stimulating profession. I've been in journalism since 1936 except for my departures for politics—and even then I continued to write whenever I could. I asked Governor Sprague once when he was working for his paper, the *Oregon Statesman*, if he missed public life.

"No," Sprague said, "I'm in public life in the most interesting way I've ever been." He wrote his column, "It Seems to Me." And with his great mind and unique understanding of public issues, he became the conscience of the Pacific Northwest.

In my earlier years as a reporter, I always dropped by the Governor's Office, the most important center of news in the state. Yet, I now found that I really couldn't come back to the State Capitol and peer over the shoulder of the new governor.

I had a nice new press card, signed by the Senate President and House Speaker, identifying me as a representative of the *Oregonian*. Since I had a radio commentary six times a week on 13 Oregon stations, and I had been close to the legislature as newsman and public official since 1949, I thought about going back. But just how could you get back in, except by telephone, when you were given such a touching farewell by the legislature as that tendered me my last day as governor?

Needless fear, perhaps. Except I have such a respect for the governorship—which I and 30 others have held—that it's difficult to believe that an occasional visit to the Capitol won't give rise to a ceremonial greeting. Bob Holmes, for instance, a two-year governor, defeated in a bid for re-election, was always treated with the utmost respect and even deference when he showed up on the house or senate floor. Bob was treated with respect because he was a good, bright, decent human being. The deference came because he was an ex-governor, and only an occasional visitor, and he accepted the ceremonial trappings with great grace.

In my 10 years in office, every time I entered the senate and house chamber I was under escort, laden with trappings. A gavel rapped, and all stood at attention. And every time I attended a legislative committee hearing, I was ushered to the witness table and expected to testify. I hoped some of this respect and deference was for me, but I have to accept that it was mostly for the office to which I was elected.

So I couldn't go back to the Capitol that winter. I circled the beloved edifice hungrily a couple of times, but then I would walk all over Salem—like the little match girl—and try to wind down and try to say, "You're not governor anymore."

There were numerous intriguing job offers ranging from being a bartender in Eugene, to serving as political adviser for an international order of nuns, to becoming a Woodrow Wilson Fellow at the Smithsonian Institution. I had been approached about the presidency of the University of Oregon, but their presidential search committee decided that the age of the new president would be "not over 58 as of July 1, 1974."

I wasn't bitter about their decision, although it struck me as a little arbitrary. I discussed my thoughts in a note to university student Gary Dickson, who had supported me for the job: "I was a little teed by the U of O Presidential Selection Committee's ruling me out with a provision of arguable legality. I had been approached in the fall of 1972 about succeeding Bob Clark upon his retirement in 1975 and was immediately interested (and very proud that I might be wanted back), but as I deliberated on it, I wasn't sure I could shoulder another heavy administrative load after ten years in statewide elective office.

"Whatever my interest amounted to, though, it became academic with the selectors' adoption of a prohibition against considering anyone born prior to 1916. I can see why, in a way, because of the turnover problem, but you can debate whether a president ought, on the other hand, to serve an eternity. And three or four years out of a gent who loved the school and had a wide public following—well, those might be golden years for the dear old U."

If it was hard to be told I was too damn old, it was reassuring to get feelers about college presidencies from three states in the Pacific Northwest and a teaching offer from the University of Vermont. I very seriously considered going to Linfield College in McMinnville. I went over and walked across that green campus after a football game. It would have been a very comfortable but challenging job. I finally decided it would be too comfortable and declined.

At Oregon State University, a Tom McCall chair of communications and public affairs was established. I thought teaching and the contact with young people would be very stimulating. We liked Corvallis and were supposed to have a nice house in that tranquil college community, but university officials and friends just couldn't seem to find us a new place to live. So I was commuting from Salem. It wasn't easy—commuting 90 miles a day and sitting up writing longhand until 11 p.m. Most 62-year-old professors would have a file of 600 lectures and could update them by typing inserts for 15 or 20 minutes. My two classes took no less than 50 hours a week.

I had to write from the bare paper up. And I had long classes, more than 50 minutes for my morning lectures and two hours for my afternoon seminars. I was accustomed to writing television and radio commentaries—from a minute and a half to three minutes. So I was experienced at sprints but not the marathon. There was a lot of outside advice. One college professor wrote that my position on the Oregon State faculty should be called a stool since I wouldn't dignify it enough to designate it a chair. A Southern Oregon newspaper editor claimed that I didn't have enough experience as a newsman to teach journalism. Perhaps he considered my 40 years in journalism as an apprenticeship.

At any rate, the students seemed to find my courses interesting. There was a great two-way dialogue. And they gave me a fairly good rating.

On May 20, I told OSU President Robert MacVicar and Dean Gordon Gilkey of the College of Liberal Arts that I was leaving at the end of the term. They had been pressing me about my future plans and gave me very little time to make a decision. I just couldn't continue the punishing schedule of commuting every other day and keeping up with my outside interests. If we could have found a good house in Corvallis, I wouldn't have budged. I think I might have settled into the academic routine. The lectures were coming easier, but the term wasn't even over and they were calling my hand.

I told my students that I could use my time advancing the principles of the Third Force. "Students will be sorry to see him leave," said the Oregon State *Barometer.* "But those who are interested in getting the most that McCall has to offer will agree he made the right decision."

Briefly, it appeared that the Ford Administration might want my services. The *Wall Street Journal* reported that I was under consideration for Secretary of Housing and Urban Development. That came as news to me and didn't have the attraction that another post, such as Secretary of the Interior, would have had. President Ford had once asked me if there was anything I wanted. I told him, "I've been able to resist moving to Washington all my life. Maybe you have a board or something that would be connected with some issues I have some familiarity with." I was later appointed to the Coastal Zone Management Advisory Council and the Environmental Health Sciences Council.

Vice President Rockefeller, Energy czar Frank Zarb and Interior Secretary Rogers Morton wanted me to revive a national energy conservation campaign. Consumer advocate Sylvia Porter, who had been head of the Citizens Action Committee, called me and promised to be an energetic worker on the committee if I would take over the chairmanship. I told Ms. Porter that I'd do it part-time on the condition that I could continue to live in Oregon—and President Ford gave our effort his full support.

Rockefeller said, "We'll get this taken care of in no time."

A curtain of silence then fell. Jerry terHorst, the syndicated columnist and former White House press secretary, reported that Chief of Staff Donald Rumsfeld spiked my appointment. Rumsfeld was already undercutting Rockefeller in an effort to gain the vice presidency for himself, and he probably saw me as a dangerous liberal. In any event, I never heard anything of it again. TerHorst, in his column, had endorsed my appointment as "a natural."

Rumsfeld also spiked the suggestion of McCall for Interior Secretary. The vacancy came up in July when former Wyoming Governor Stan Hathaway was broken on the Washington, D.C., rack. Environmental activists tore Stan up and down in a searing six weeks of confirmation hearings. They were merciless because his record, as they saw it, made him a threat to the sanctity of what's left of America the beautiful. I refused to join the wolfpack because I knew Stan Hathaway and had heard Stan tell his fellow governors about stripmining: "If it costs $5,000 an acre to restore the land, it has to be done."

The White House should have been more sensitive in projecting what might happen to Hathaway after the bruising confirmation battle. But White House string-pullers added some tensions themselves in pressuring Stan to switch on stripmining and accept an impossible, unqualified undersecretary. Hathaway finally checked into a Bethesda, Maryland, hospital, slumped in depression—and resigned.

A McCall boomlet developed within the prestigious Board of Governors of the Nature Conservancy. They weren't getting into politics as they are a nonpartisan group. The board just had a show of hands and voted 100 percent that they wanted Tom McCall as the next Secretary of the Interior. Laurance Rockefeller, intrepid conservationist, went to the White House and proposed my appointment to Rumsfeld. He had no better luck than Brother Nelson did on the earlier nomination. Laurance said, "Well, why don't we take this up with the President's environmental adviser?"

"We don't have one," Rumsfeld said. But he immediately designated one, a handy White House staffer with no environmental background.

The Third Force seemed to be coming back in the summer of 1975. I was getting more speaking invitations than I could handle, from all parts of the country. Ronald Reagan was overtaking President Ford in the Gallup poll and George Wallace led the Democratic field. That lamentable possibility—Reagan v.s. Wallace—would have left perhaps 65 to 70 percent of the electorate alienated and looking for a rational progressive. I got many letters saying, "What a wonderful system you've got in Oregon! You've got to lead the country out of the wilderness." E. Palmer Hoyt, the longtime publisher of the *Denver Post* and a confidant of Presidents Eisenhower and Johnson, was in favor of my candidacy. Cleveland industrialist Dick Sklar, a selfless ex-McGovernite, liked the idea, too.

But going up against a sitting President—even an unpopular President—seemed like too much of a long shot. If there hadn't been a Republican chief executive, my chances would have been considerably better. Ronald Reagan had great courage in putting up the fight he did. I decided that my best contribution would be talking the issues and providing commentary on the American political scene.

I was doing a column for the *Oregonian* and syndicating it to a group of newspapers. I did some pretty good work and it was well displayed. Yet they unceremoniously booted me off the *Oregonian* when I joined Channel 2 as a full-time commentator. The reason the newspaper gave me was "the Gerry Pratt law." Pratt had been an enterprising business columnist for them. He was a little hard to handle. So when he started doing equal time on television, they used that as a pretense for getting rid of him. I felt it was a false standard when they applied it to me. They claimed it was a rule that applied to everyone. I felt it was a phoney policy. Any syndicated columnist worth his salt—a Bill Buckley or a Nick von Hoffman—is in demand as a television commentator. To deny someone that kind of outlet seemed unfair.

When I went to work at KATU—where I was working for my old KGW boss, Tom Dargan, and with former KGW anchorman Dick Ross—we moved back to Portland. Audrey and I were very insistent on buying a house inside the city because cities are the best places to live. It's ill advised and thoughtless for people to go tearing out to create suburbs around a great city like Portland.

Suburban developers are ripping out some of the finest farmland in all the world. If you buy a home in the suburbs, you have to drive a long way to work. This wastes a lot of energy. It's a tragic example, for our children, of poor land-use planning. I talked with someone about this recently and he said, "Why should we care about 1990? You and I will be worms then—nothing but worms!"

"It's important to think of future generations," I coaxed. He snorted, "What have our kids ever done for us?"

I'm not looking for flowers or a monument, but we've got to save what we have now before it's too late.

Our house on Southwest Broadway Drive is very convenient. We're only a few minutes from downtown Portland. The television station and KEX radio, where I do commentaries, are at the bottom of the hill. It is a very comfortable house. Audrey has a marvelous garden and has spent a lot of time making the house prettier. I have a basement study where I can write. Whenever possible, we like to get down to Road's End for a weekend. Some day we may retire to that tranquil harbor, though I will never be content with the role of disinterested elder statesman. I hope to stay creative as a writer and as a political theorist. I really don't know the meaning of the word "retirement."

KATU photo

McCall returned to television news in 1975, joining Portland's KATU as commentator and news analyst.

CHAPTER 20

Winding up Again

Like some gangling farm boy who's having his picture taken, you hardly know what to do with your hands. Strangely, how applicable this is to older politicians winding down. They can fake the contented life pretty well until the stretch drive of a presidential year. Then, though, the home pasture has to be awfully green and far removed from the excitement for the retired fire horses not to snort and start galloping.

Edith Green, 66, folded her busy alter-political regimen when the Ford camp beckoned. She had the time of her life campaigning with the President in the closing days of his vote drive. In the rain at Portland that last full week of it all, the former Democratic congresswoman was jubilant as a Ford introducer and testimonial-giver—a lively little bug under a huge baseball cap that Dom DiMaggio had presented to her.

At 88, Mother McCall also was firehorsing at the hustings—a venerable Republican-turned-Carter supporter and designated honorary chairman of the Georgia Democrat's Oregon campaign. As in her second book, *Copper King's Daughter*—with her, action is still the name of the game.

She has been registered as a Republican since women got the franchise. But she has always been politically independent and would let you know she had cast her first vote for Democrat Woodrow Wilson. Her staunchly Republican husband, who drove her some 30 miles from ranch to polling place, nearly pushed her out of the car when he heard of her decision.

It wasn't hard for me to figure out the process that brought her to Carter's side. She hasn't missed a network interview program in a decade, and she watched the Democratic National Convention from gavel to gavel. She began to be clinched by Carter's hour-long "Meet the Press" program the day before things got rolling at Madison Square Garden. She also liked Jimmy Carter's acceptance speech. But, most of all, she empathized with Lillian Carter. Our matriarch also had raised young men on the farm, including one governor—and a Walter Cronkite interview brought our matriarch closer to Jimmy's matriarch and the Carter family, so close that Dorothy sent Lillian, 10 years her junior, a copy of *Ranch Under the Rimrock,* autographed with the words, "From one governor's mother to another."

She also knew of the warm friendship of her second son and Jimmy Carter. But I didn't try to influence her either way, not knowing, for sure, what my own personal decision on the presidency would be.

When Jimmy Carter learned of Edith Green's defection, he is said to have remarked, "I'd rather have Dorothy Lawson McCall any day!"

I got politics out of my system via my radio and television commentaries and a preoccupation with Bottle Bill initiatives in four states. At least I thought this regimen would keep me out of the partisan fray, and it did, although I was sorely tempted the last months of the presidential race.

Then, one early September morning, there he was on the other end of my home telephone saying, "Hello, Tom, this is Jimmy. I need your help."

"What kind of help, Jimmy?"

"One of three kinds—an endorsement, an endorsement and a few speeches, or your campaigning for me full time."

The third week in September, the telephone in my kitchen rang in the evening.

"Hello, Tom, this is Jerry. You're an old pro at this sort of thing. Have you any thoughts on how I'll do in tomorrow night's debate?"

"Well, Mr. President, you'll do all right because you're an old football player. You've had to be 'up' on a Saturday afternoon, performing sometimes before 100,000 people. So you'll get over your butterflies sooner than Jimmy will—and that could be the difference."

It was early in October when Gene McCarthy called, only a couple of days before his Independent Party Convention in Madison, Wisconsin. He said flat out he wouldn't offer me the vice presidential spot on his ticket. But he would trace a scenario.

It went something like this: he'd be talking about his cabinet and laying on an inspirational message. None of the maybe 2,000 people there would know he had picked his running mate until McCarthy beckoned toward the wings. Out would come Tom McCall—and they'd tear the place down. Gene didn't say whether they would be motivated by rage or approbation, but I took it as quite a compliment.

I heard reports of political polls that showed me with a high confidence rating with the people of Oregon. Not long before I left office, the Salem *Capital Journal's* poll showed a 78 percent approval rating. However, I never saw any of the 1976 polls. I had to assume they existed when in May both Idaho Senator Frank Church's forces and those of California Governor Jerry Brown urged that I moderate their Oregon primary telethons. Brown had called me to seek advice on his write-in campaign before entering Oregon. And a friend of mine overheard the California governor happily telling a campaign aide, "I feel that Governor McCall is going to endorse me."

A news commentator has license to make endorsements, I suppose. But, over the years, I have tried to maintain a policy of refraining unless an able public servant were threatened by an abominable creep. As governor, of course, I had more leeway and utilized it, regardless of party, to reward competent legislators and other state officials who had gone to bat for my major programs.

Efforts to involve me—or, more precisely, my Oregon coattails —became less avoidable as the year wore on.

President Ford had me over to the Oval Office when I was in Washington, for a meeting of his Citizens Committee for Environmental Quality. We had a most amiable visit. It opened with my giving him my wife Audrey's critique of his first presidential debate performance.

"She thought you were magnificent, Mr. President," I said. "But she ended up asking why it was that Republicans always talked about inflation and unemployment so impersonally—why they always seemed to talk more about dollars and things than people."

The President smiled and told me that Audrey might have been on target. He cited his polls as showing him ahead of Jimmy Carter in experience and presidential image but that Governor Carter topped him 60-40 on the question, "Which of the two candidates seems to you to be the more compassionate?"

I made a pitch to the President of his designation of 400,000-acre Chamberlain Basin in Idaho as a part of the national Wilderness system. Governor Cecil Andrus of Idaho had asked me to approach the White House on the subject, and he planned a follow-up the next week when he would be in Washington.

At the mention of Andrus's name, the President brightened and said, "He strikes me as being a very fine governor." Which, indeed, was true but I reminded Mr. Ford there was a risk in saying kind things about Democrats. My endorsement of Democrat Andrus for a second term against mediocre Republican competition had earned me an even more remote station in the wilderness reserved for Republican outcasts.

Whether I would seek a third term as governor in 1978 colored my judgment probably more than anything else during this wooing of Tom McCall. This consideration lay behind a provisional "no" I had given the Carter camp on Governor Carter's invitation to join his campaign.

In late September, I was paged at Portland International Airport. Ron Schmidt, now working in the Carter campaign, relayed a request that I reconsider. He said there would be a news conference in Atlanta the following Saturday. Jimmy Carter and I would be there together, and my pledge of allegiance to the Georgian would give his campagin a shot in the arm, at a time when his lead was diminishing in the polls.

Gerry Lewin

David Falconer

McCall found himself in the middle of this triangle of 1976 presidential contenders. As a television newsman, he didn't have to make his choice public.

Two old warriors refought their political battles when McCall interviewed Vice President Rockefeller on Portland television.

Schmidt said, "If you'll do it, you can write your own ticket later on." I personally believed Jimmy Carter's repeated claims that he had promised no appointment to a single soul at any time in his long pull toward the presidency; nor did I specify any *quid pro quo* I wanted. Ron was just making a sole try at putting on the heat.

To place this courtship in context, it must be remembered that Jimmy Carter and I had been friends during his entire governorship, that I admired his progressiveness in an unmodern state and that I had yearned for years to see one of my fellow governors in the White House. In a September, 1974, speech on the "Crisis of the Contemporary Presidency," I had listed Jimmy first on my list of possible Democratic candidates. Most of the country didn't know who he was at the time. I was impressed by his concept of zero-based budgeting, his concern for the environment and his humane approach to corrections.

Most governors considered Jimmy cool and aloof. He wasn't popular at Governors' Conferences. But I liked him. We were on a number of panels together, including a nationally televised "Meet the Press." Segregationist Lester Maddox, Carter's arch-enemy, tried to regain the governorship in 1970. When Jimmy helped defeat him in the primary, I sent him a telegram, "Congratulations, Jimmy, on the emancipation of Georgia!"

My respect for Gerald Ford was boundless—"a man of innocence and fidelity"—I said in my November, 1976, talk to the Republican governors—"who did more for his country in a relatively short time than perhaps any other president!"

To have come out for Jimmy Carter in September would have foreclosed my decision on the Oregon governorship a full year before that decision had to be made. I mentioned that to Ron as we discussed the Carter invitation to come aboard—and how, if I did, it would alienate my Oregon Republican base of support beyond any hope of reconciliation.

Ron's rejoinder was that the Oregon GOP Establishment was likely, anyhow, to favor a faithful party wheelhorse—State Senator Victor Atiyeh of Washington County—for governor in 1978. They felt, Ron said, that Atiyeh had earned another shot at the Statehouse (which he had missed in 1974) for his earnest loyalty to the party and its causes. Besides, Ron was certain I would enjoy Washington service under my friend from Georgia much more than beating my brains out searching for votes in this 96,000-square-mile state at the age of 64. Another of my former top aides at Salem, tough Ed Westerdahl, was even more emphatic on that point than Ron, and utilities entrepreneur Glenn Jackson, deemed by the 1976 DemoForum to be the most powerful figure in Oregon, seemed inclined to agree.

Still, cutting the Oregon umbilical so swiftly while discarding my last promising shot at the governorship was a mountainous decision to make on a moment's notice. And, frankly, it was scary, leaving this friendly enclave and plopping oneself right into the middle of a national campaign. It was just too Big League for me to contemplate without shivering.

So I shivered right out of the picture, and probably out of Jimmy Carter's presidential life, although I understand my name appeared on three of those famous lists of potential Carter appointees. In fact, environmental writer Bob Cahn, a leader on the Carter conservation committee, asked me if I would mind appearing on the Secretary of the Interior roster. Not at all, I said, as long as you put me second to Governor Andrus. Cahn liked Andrus just fine but pointed out, "He's not nearly so well known nationally as you are."

Post-election contacts from the Carter camp indicated my name was also on lists for administrator of the Environmental Protection Agency and chairman of the President's Council on Environmental Quality.

In the final boildown, my choice was to accept the Interior secretaryship. . .period. My hopes that it would be offered were zero, but if you're going to pull up your Oregon roots and put them down in a Washington you had shunned for years, you might as well say, "The Cabinet or nothing."

In their formal recommendations to the president-elect for Interior, a coalition of environmental groups included at least three Republicans—Governor Dan Evans of Washington and former Governors Russell Peterson of Delaware and Tom McCall. *New York Times* columnist William Shannon wrote in December that if Carter were to pick a Republican for Interior, either Peterson or McCall would be conservationists "in the great Bull Moose tradition of Theodore Roosevelt and Harold Ickes." But Carter never swerved from Cecil Andrus—and he couldn't have made a better choice.

Republican stalwarts were disturbed not only because Matriarch McCall had endorsed Jimmy Carter but because she seemed to be enjoying her apostasy so hugely. She became a front-line fixture for Carter and Mondale arrivals at Portland International Airport.

Oregon Secretary of State Clay Myers, a Republican since early puberty, fretted over this on two scores: Jerry Ford might lose Oregon, and Tom McCall might lose many a miffed Republican backer. Myers insisted that since my news duties precluded my siding with the President, Audrey ought to make a public endorsement.

Meanwhile, a onetime McCall gubernatorial executive assistant, Robert G. Davis, was trying to patch me into the Ford campaign full time. Like the Carter campaign opening, this would have required my taking about a 40-day leave of absence from my television work, which was a sort of security blanket I was loath to leave.

The Monday prior to the last week of the campaign, Davis did prevail on Audrey to meet the President at Portland International Airport that afternoon and tell the world why she thought he deserved election. This she did and they exchanged hugs. I joined broadcasters at the Sheraton-Portland an hour later in welcoming the President to a regional meeting of the National Association of Broadcasters. It was a familiar greeting:

"Welcome, Mr. President, to this state of enchantment. Visit us again and again. But, for heaven's sake, don't move here to live. Anyhow, we infer from all your activities this month you prefer the house where your family is staying now. . . . You'll be relieved to know we have another governor and a different welcome: 'Oregon, open under new management,'—but I am not so sure that this motto will stay official for too very long."

One television reporter at the NAB meeting snapped at his cameraman, "Why, there was McCall announcing for governor, and we didn't even get it on film!" It's a far cry, however, from those words to declaring for governor—a decision still unreached by me as 1977 moved along. For all the importuning by national political brass, the most moving phenomenon of 1976 for me personally was the hundreds of Oregonians coming up to me and urging, "You've got to run again."

This repeated occurrence has reached virtually boom proportions. My replies have run from "Let's give him a chance to prove himself" through "Why go back into the lion's den, once you've escaped in good shape?" to "Why try to repaint a good picture?"

During an October Portland rally sparked by Vice President Rockefeller, I chatted with a kingpin of the Oregon Republican establishment, Alan, "Punch" Green, Jr. He denied that he and others of the party hierarchy were locked in on Atiyeh. He warned, though, that any open-mindedness on their part would end in my total disfavor if I even dared to endorse Jimmy Carter, much less openly work for his victory.

For a maverick Republican to hinge his fate on approval of the party string-pullers is an anomaly needing explanation. Perhaps this passage from my Republican Governors' Conference speech will clarify it:

"Oregon and Washington are as diverse from ultra-conservative Idaho, Montana, Nevada and Utah (in their brand of Republicanism) as diverse can be. I do counsel you to look to our Northwest corner of this vast land for a clue as to what Republican government can really mean. In 1911, Governor Woodrow Wilson of New Jersey stood on a Portland platform and conceded, "I count myself intensely progressive when I am in the East. But now that I am in Oregon, I am not so sure."

I went on to cite examples supporting the can-do image of these two states where Dorchester-type Republicans are in the majority. This label derives from annual platform sessions which progressive Republicans hold on the Oregon Coast, the first of them being staged at the Dorchester House at Lincoln City, in an effort to divorce Oregon Republicans from identification with reactionary leadership.

Dorchester Republicanism was most aptly described by *New York Times* columnist Tom Wicker when he did a sketch of Dan Evans in 1966, designating him as a "new breed" of Republican:

"If they have a philosophy, it is probably pragmatism, and if they have a clear goal, it is solving the problems of society, the economy and government in a logical, factual manner." I used this quote from Wicker, the day after my RGA talk, at a civic farewell to Dan and Nancy Evans, attended by nearly 1,700 Washingtonians in Seattle:

"He has given so much to state, region and nation," I said of the retiring three-term governor, "and has so much in spirit, commitment and perception of true leadership *left* to give, he must not be allowed away from the public service mainstream for very long. Something with sense to it would be to give low priority to fighting over the party label. . .to begin by asking Jerry Ford, Nelson Rockefeller and retiring Governor Evans to head up a new grouping. . .inviting our best minds in and out of office to organize it . . .and mandating them to pound full-speed ahead on setting up research and planning for programs in all signal areas of public concern."

National Chairman Mary Louise Smith and others who later addressed the governors advanced this concept, but in a more partisan framework, when they proposed revival of the defunct Republican Coordinating Committee. This committee functioned outside the narrower Republican National Committee and sought to heighten the party's attractiveness to a broader sector of Americans.

It will fail, though, if it operates on The-Republican-Tent-Is-Big-Enough-for-Everyone concept. This has proved to be an empty premise because trying to reconcile Right and Left under the same Big Top can only result in a paralysis of actions and ideas. Issue conflicts simply are too diametric to allow healthy, modern consensus or compromise, and history shows that when a stand *is* taken it mostly hews to negativism reflecting control of things by the Old Guard.

Oddly enough, this was true most recently of a decision by Republican governors at the Washington conference. Even though governors generally are pragmatists and movers, the conference adopted with slight amendment a resolution proposed by its most Right-leaning member, Governor Meldrim Thomson of New Hampshire. In effect, they approved the Kansas City platform—a millstone of the Ford campaign—as representing the principles of the Republican Party. It was a surefire way to ensure continuation of the narrowing of the party's base.

Even the wild creatures of the forest know better than to go back to a trap from which they've escaped. But not what the *Los Angeles Times* calls the Elephantus Republicanus. This political beast catches itself again and again in its own right-wing snare. Whatever the fate of the party nationally, it is worth perpetuating and belonging to in Oregon and Washington, as long as it is controlled by the Dorchester breed of Republican. Still, the temptation to register as an Independent occasionally settles in on the New Breed—and not just in the Pacific Northwest.

The thought of Independent status occurred to me most alluringly in the framework of running for the U.S. Senate. I could never stomach the prospect of going into so many pockets for the money to win a Republican primary and then, if nominated, going right back for more. Nor, as governor, could I, in good conscience, have sublimated my responsibilities at the Capitol for a year-long race for the senate. As a broadcaster, of course, the mere announcement of my candidacy would bar me from my livelihood.

So in a mechanical sense, the idea of announcing in August as an Independent—and being nominated by convention in late summer—was appealing. It was attractive in a philosophical sense too. Such a course really would represent a betrayal to neither party because hundreds of thousands of Oregon voters are independent at heart, if not by the party label which is so undemocratically crammed down their necks.

There is something enviable about an independent politician. Perhaps it's his freedom from the rote and persiflage of hidebound partisanship. The sole Independent elected to the Oregon Senate in a long time, Charles Hannon of Washington County, used to chide Republicans and Democrats for "playing that old, silly game of elephants and donkeys."

And Gene McCarthy packed a lot of charisma. Except for the whiplash of his tongue, he reminded you quite a bit of Governor Adlai Stevenson. Certainly, McCarthy's intellect dwarfed that of all contenders in the presidential races in which he was entered. Had his independent candidacy in 1976 been allowed to carry him into the televised national debates, chances are he would have danced circles around Ford and Carter while drawing off enough Carter votes to hand Mr. Ford the election. McCarthy's first approach to me was in March of 1974 when I was attending a National Governors' Conference in Washington, D.C.

"Governor," came the voice on the other end of the telephone, "let's go out and rip ourselves off a couple of primaries. . .and I don't care who's number one on the ticket."

In 1975, we held a joint news conference at the Oregon Capitol. We endorsed an Oregon initiative proposal—later unsuccessful— to permit registered Independents to vote for candidates of either major party in the state's May primary. We then adjourned to the Oregon State University campus where I was a professor of communications and public affairs for spring term, 1975. I introduced McCarthy to a packed and enthusiastic audience in the Home Economics auditorium. The high-noise point of his reception came when he acknowledged the crowd's warmth, saying, "This shows that the Governor and I really ought to be on the road together!"

That constituency, at least, acclaimed the idea and, indeed, I *had* tinkered with the prospect of setting forth nationally to seek my own political fortune.

Jimmy Carter later proved that tenacity, self-faith, love, patriotism and a big smile can beat the Establishment, even for a prize as glittering as the White House, but he had the advantage of belonging to a party which had no president. I doubt he could have gotten off the ground with a Democratic incumbent at 1600 Pennsylvania Avenue. The fact of Republican incumbency there militated against a solo McCall candidacy. It would, in actuality, have seemed so preposterous that I imagined I could never have stood the gales of derision, had I taken to the open road in 1975.

There was nothing nationally for me in the Republican Party. The White House was so afraid of the Reagan conservatives it dared not flash the faintest pre-convention smile of recognition to a moderate liberal, especially one associated with the environmental movement. A McCarthy tie-up, though, would likely have extended both our small yet devoted constituencies. They overlapped, of course, but not completely, and we would have broadened and deepened our base through our complementary candidacies.

McCarthy was talking more frequently and eloquently than the major party candidates about things that bore on the future, as well as the present. He boosted the four-day work week, the "Small is Beautiful" concepts of E. F. Schumacher, the removal of the two-party straitjacket from our political system and the shrinking of the Imperial Presidency down to realistic dimensions. Always, there was the same McCarthy framework of how America should strive to shape its image before mankind: "by demonstrating that all of those things we claim for ourselves—the right to life, liberty, and the pursuit of happiness and a basic belief in the dignity and worth of the individual—are the real strengths of America and the best gifts we can offer the rest of the world."

My esteem for McCarthy remains high. If you hear him exercising his rapier mind, or read his poems or his 1975 look at contemporary America, *The Hard Years*, you have to recognize him as an exceptional American. And you have to acknowledge him as the most unplatitudinous of all politicians—quiet, sardonic, disdainful of sham and artifice. Ingenious, too, judging by the ploy with which he kept communication lines open with this former governor of the state that pioneered in legislation requiring a deposit on returnable beer and pop containers. Even in the heat of the 1976 campaign, McCarthy found time to write and send me a poem, "On the Bottle of No Return."

I do not know what "Act Two" will be. I have no present plans to run for the governorship or the senate. As long ago as 1970, I expressed doubt that I would run again for public office. As much as I like to be with people, campaigning for myself is distasteful. It has to involve a certain amount of boasting and begging. By contrast, I am absorbed by *serving* in office because in performing creditably you are *giving* your state and its people a thing of value, as contrasted to importuning them to do you a favor at the polls.

This is the system, however, and nowhere is it exemplified with more distinction than in the independent and conscientious response of Oregonians to their obligations as participating citizens. I will always be proud to have received their votes of confidence.

McCall spoke to the Republican Governors' Conference in Washington, D.C., after the 1976 elections. "The Republican Party has made so many fatal mistakes," McCall said, "that it finds itself an endangered species at graveside."

INDEX